Holocaust Trauma and P
Deformation

Written by a survivor of the Bergen-Belsen concentration camp, this moving and important book examines the massive psychic trauma suffered by a generation of Holocaust survivors. It not only provides both an intimate and personal reflection on these harrowing events, but also offers an in-depth, clinical perspective on an often-misunderstood phenomenon.

As a child during this period, the book begins by examining the author's own experience as a refugee in the aftermath of the Holocaust, the psychological impact of displacement after such traumatic events, and his attempt to flee its damage through medical and psychoanalytic training. But the second half of the book broadens the perspective to offer a clinical exploration of the psychic effects of surviving the Holocaust. A range of concepts are addressed and explored, from powerlessness and survivor guilt, to psychic security and recovered memories. The book concludes by examining how psychic trauma is processed, and the clinical implications for when disorders emerge and dysfunction results.

An insightful and honest account of massive psychic trauma, this remarkable book will resonate not only with those affected by or interested in the experiences of Holocaust survivors, but also any clinical practitioner working with clients who have experienced this type of intense trauma.

Alfred Garwood, a survivor of Bergen-Belsen concentration camp, is a retired Honorary Consultant Adult Psychotherapist, a general medical practitioner and Founder of the Child Survivors' Association of Great Britain.

Holocaust Trauma and Psychic Deformation

Psychoanalytic Reflections of a Holocaust Survivor

Alfred Garwood

Routledge
Taylor & Francis Group

LONDON AND NEW YORK

First published 2021
by Routledge
2 Park Square, Milton Park, Abingdon, Oxon OX14 4RN

and by Routledge
52 Vanderbilt Avenue, New York, NY 10017

Routledge is an imprint of the Taylor & Francis Group, an informa business

British Library Cataloguing-in-Publication Data
A catalogue record for this book is available from the British Library

Library of Congress Cataloging-in-Publication Data
A catalog record has been requested for this book

ISBN: 978-0-367-51690-1 (hbk)
ISBN: 978-1-780-49188-2 (pbk)
ISBN: 978-1-003-05483-2 (ebk)

Typeset in Bembo
by Swales & Willis, Exeter, Devon, UK

A photo of my nuclear family a few weeks after our liberation by Russian
cavalry. My legs are less than two fingers in width and my father is only
5 feet tall. My father is wearing the uniform they gave to him and he is
carrying me. My emaciation and rickets-affected legs, as well as the facial
expressions of my parents and sister, speak clearly of our traumatised state.

MIX
Paper from
responsible sources
FSC® C013985

Printed in the United Kingdom
by Henry Ling Limited

This book is dedicated to my parents and sister without whose care and love I would not have survived. It is also dedicated to the approximately 60 members of my family who were murdered in the Holocaust and whose absence has created a psychic space that still generates pain and longing. Last but not least, I dedicate this book to my children who have been my greatest teachers and comfort in my latter years.

Contents

Acknowledgements

The biographical opening of this volume took many years to write due to the emotional pain it retained. Writing and rewriting it reminded me of the unique role my sister, Leonia, played in protecting and supporting me during the worst years of my childhood. By unpredictable twists of fate, we find ourselves sharing these late stages of our lives. Once again, we find ourselves in mutually supportive roles through life's vicissitudes, for which I am immeasurably grateful. Reflecting on my parents' impact on my life, I am less troubled by their destructive interactions and more forgiving and understanding of their inadequacies. Without my father's heroism and resourcefulness and my mother's long-suffering tolerance of powerlessness, we would never have survived. Words cannot describe or adequately convey my gratitude to them all.

I have been blessed with children who have grown into adults that are not troubled by the same issues that I constantly struggle with. They gifted me with grandchildren. Their capacity for playful, creative nurturing fills me with admiration and amazement. I have learned to respect and admire who they are and what they do. They have been my greatest teachers.

The mothers of my children have played unique and differing roles as mothers and as partners. They made sacrifices and endured difficulties that will never be forgotten.

Of the loyal friends that did not abandon us when Diana became ill and died, Frances and Tony Eaton, godparents of my older daughters, have earned my lifelong gratitude.

In the world of Holocaust survival, I must begin with the late child psychoanalyst Judith Kestenberg, who encouraged and supported me in those early days of the emerging understanding of child survivors of the Holocaust. During those heady days of founding the Child Survivors' Association of Great Britain and the London Holocaust Survivors' Centre, Earl Hopper played a unique role in offering guidance and support. He became my group analyst, supporting me in my personal and professional life. Only those that have benefited from his deep core of compassion, as well as the unique intellect and wisdom he brings to his therapy, will understand how much I owe him. The World Federation of Jewish Child Survivors of the

Holocaust & Descendants has grown in importance for me as a community that has made a place for me in which I now belong. In the last 20 years, my co-therapist of the child survivor groups has been Elisheva van de Hal, clinical director of the Jerusalem branch of AMCHA, the organisation for the psychosocial support of Holocaust survivors and their descendants. Clinical work with her has been extraordinary in how she has enhanced the power of our work. She has become a dear friend and an important colleague to whom I can turn. Natan Kellermann, AMCHA's clinical director, has been of great support with my theoretical explorations through his writing and his scholarship. Robert Krell, the outstanding child psychiatrist and Dutch hidden child, as well as Ira Brenner, the child of an Auschwitz survivor and now a leading psychoanalyst in our field of trauma, have been unique colleagues and invaluable sources of friendship and support.

My 30-plus years as a psychotherapist at Claybury Psychiatric Hospital and Forest House Psychotherapy Clinic have been made survivable and fruitful due to Tony Garelick's generous sharing of his clinical understanding in his supervision. Carmen O'Leary, a fellow group analyst and the clinic manager, has become a precious friend. Their support during many difficult years of turbulence in the NHS has been invaluable. Kannan Navaratnem, now a successful psychoanalyst, was an inspiring colleague who encouraged my writing, to whom I am deeply grateful.

Making my clinical experience available to the Baobab Centre for unaccompanied refugee minors has brought me into regular contact with Sheila Melzak, the founder and clinical director. Her support and friendship have made this volume come to fruition through her special understanding of traumatised children.

When trying to complete the biographical opening, I was obstructed by the pain of my continued emotional response to these traumatic events. With the skill of Wayne Milstead and Aaron Tighe, the inspired and gifted founders of Circle of Misse, their writers' retreat, I was able to find the equanimity and support to complete this volume. I am deeply indebted to both of them. During my stay at Misse, I found June Caldwell, a fellow wounded soul, whose prize-winning short story writing and emotional courage inspired me.

Chapter 1

Introduction

This book was written because much of what I had read in the specialist literature, as a Holocaust trauma survivor, felt fundamentally flawed and disappointing. My growing experience of working with Holocaust survivors and trauma victims, amounting to more than 30 years, taught me that my fundamental understanding did not derive from the existing trauma theory; that the insights and the language I used in the work was not found in specialist papers or manuals and textbooks, but had developed from my efforts to understand my survivor community, my survivor family, and my own psychic struggles and processes.

This fundamental misunderstanding led me to begin the book with the statement, "Holocaust survivors were ordinary human beings who were forced to endure extraordinary events. The mental processes available to them to survive these events were the same as those available to all humankind."

The purpose of this book is to attempt to make Holocaust trauma accessible; that is, to make massive psychic trauma accessible. Some of this inaccessibility can be understood to derive from our unconscious defences that are activated in order to protect us from vicarious traumatisation. Due to my own Holocaust trauma, I do not have the ability to avoid painful material with the defensive capacities of non-survivors. This has been a source of understanding as my defences were not adequate to prevent my emotional reaction. I have been unavoidably living with and reliving my trauma history and psychic deformations. When writing, I began to realise that I have been struggling with their effects all my life.

In writing my first papers, I took the unusual step of using material from my family's Holocaust past as well as my own childhood. The response I received led me to believe this had added to the authenticity of the theorisation and brought to life the trauma survivors and their experiences. It became clear to me that in order to make Holocaust trauma, and thus massive psychic trauma, accessible, it would be necessary to offer sufficient biographical and autobiographical details such that readers could consider and understand where my theorisations came from; that it should allow readers to analyse and reflect on these traumata like clinical material they might meet in their clinical work.

The exploration of my family's and my Holocaust experiences involved much material that was a part of my psychoanalysis and my group analysis. Until I had embarked upon writing this book, I was not fully aware of how psychically painful it would be, how long it would take, and how challenging it would become to return to the material and describe these traumata. In order for the biographical writing to have authenticity, these sections needed to be honest, searching and emotionally open. This only came at great emotional cost.

Chapter 2 is entitled "Legacies." This focuses on our pre-Holocaust and Holocaust experiences. I describe my parents' childhoods and a number of events that would have a life-or-death impact on us. This is followed by the brief initial time under the Nazi occupation, followed by the Russian occupation and the effects of the Russian army conscriptions. Next came Operation Barbarossa and the return of the Nazis, the ghetto and Bergen-Belsen concentration camp. I have given careful description to this time and our concentration camp experiences. This chapter ends with our liberation.

Chapter 3, entitled "The war after," describes our return to Poland and our flight as displaced persons. The struggle to gain British nationality follows, and those painful early first years include a period in a children's home. I have focused on our refugee experience and my time at school as these reflect many parallels with current refugee experiences. It proceeds through the next period of becoming assimilated and engaging with English society in order to find a place in English society.

Chapter 4 is entitled "Escape" and describes my medical school training. This is followed by my marriage and a series of disastrous life events and my reparative response to these. This is followed by the war crimes trial and my return to Bergen-Belsen and the struggle to address my Holocaust childhood. Then comes a section on child survivors and my reparative steps and healing, and lastly my psychoanalysis and group analysis as a trauma survivor.

Chapter 5 is in some ways the most important of the biographical chapters. It is entitled "Adaptation and maladaptation." In it, I review the key events and relationships and explore their psychic impact and how they affected our psychic function. A constant focus here is the formative and deformative effects of these events. The last part of this chapter is a candid self-analysis of the psychic function and dysfunction the events of the earlier chapters had on my psyche. My lifelong secrecy made it intensely difficult to be open and revealing in the service of authenticity. This was the most painful and difficult to write.

Chapter 6, entitled "Child survivors of the Holocaust: groups and groupings, healing wounds," begins with a history of child Holocaust survivors as an entity. It describes their efforts to organise psychosocial self-help groups worldwide. International gatherings are described in which I have actively participated as a therapist. These are important sources of healing. In this chapter, I offer a clinical account of my work with child survivors that has taken place in the US, Israel and Europe. It includes working with groups for the abused and homogenous groups for the youngest survivors. Problems of countertransference are examined. This complex work creates many clinical challenges, which are described and explored, including Holocaust imposters.

My psychotherapy training and work led to my writing on the enigmatic subject of survivor guilt, entitled "The Holocaust and the power of powerlessness: survivor guilt an unhealed wound." This paper used my family's Holocaust history to illustrate their survivor guilt symptoms and offered a novel psychic reaction formation as a defence against powerlessness to explain this trauma symptom. This paper was selected by the editors for inclusion in the book *Terrorism and War* (Covington et al., 2002). My next paper was entitled "Psychic security: its origins, development, and disruption." This was awarded the student essay prize of the *British Journal of Psychotherapy*. It arose from observations of my patients in my general practice, many of whom displayed great variation in their security and insecurity. Here, I combined my disciplines, and so it may be regarded as a psychobiological paper.

The third paper, entitled "Life, death and the power of powerlessness," was written and accepted for publication soon after my first paper but was delayed for six years due to administrative problems. It begins with the neonate at birth and presents some recent research that allows a hypothesis regarding our sensitisation to powerlessness, which I suggest is instinctively driven and may have an impact on our development and our lifelong choices. This is extrapolated to its effect on adult life and society. It was included in Earl Hopper's special edition of *Group Analysis on the Social Unconscious* (Garwood, 2001).

My therapeutic work with the youngest child survivors always included the impact of having suffered their traumatisation in their developmental period of infantile amnesia. The inaccessibility of biographical memory and other forms of memory were a frequent focus. For this reason, I address early trauma memory in "Inaccessible memory: recovered traumatic memory, true and false."

Psychologists specialising in trauma theory have for decades described trauma symptoms as being due to a failure of psychic processing. However, normal or successful trauma processing has not been fully described. This lacuna led me to begin observations and hypotheses that resulted in my offering a proposed hypothesis of the initial trauma response being the equivalent to psychic fight/flight, as well as a second set of hypotheses proposing that psychic management of survival is undertaken by the psychic guardian function using established psychic structures and organisations, offered in the paper entitled "Psychic survival management: the psychic guardian and compartmentalisation."

The final chapter is entitled "Functional disorders of the psychic guardian and pathology: clinical implications." It explores some common psychic pathology that appears to be linked to psychic guardian dysfunction. Then some exploration of current treatments are discussed in relation to the psychic organisation and processes postulated.

References

Covington, C., Williams, P., Arundale, J., & Knox, J. (Eds.) (2002) *Terrorism and War: Unconscious Dynamics of Political Violence*. London: Karnac.

Garwood, A. (2001) Life, death and the power of powerlessness. *Group Analysis* 34(1): 153–167.

Chapter 2

Legacies

Introduction

David Faber was sent to Bergen-Belsen concentration camp in his tattered prisoner pyjamas in early April 1945. He recounts the following story:

> I woke on a bunk, dead men on either side of me. The stench of death was everywhere: boach (abdominal) typhus.[1] Delirious and shivering with fever I knew I must get out or die with them. Somehow I dragged myself into the fresh air and sat against the side of the barrack warming my body in the sun (p. 190). Gradually as my vision cleared I saw through the barbed wire a sight beyond belief. Between the piles of bodies a man dressed in normal clothes with a yellow star was looking at me. He was carrying a blonde child in his arms and holding a little girl by the hand. I could not believe my eyes. He called to me in Polish and asked me to look for his "mishpucha," his family. He promised to give me bread. He threw some over the barbed wire and I struggled to reach it in the desperate scramble it created. I clung onto a piece that I ate lovingly.
>
> He returned the next day. I had not been able to find any of his family but he still threw another piece of bread over. That bought me another day's life. The following day, when I looked for him, his part of the camp was deserted. I thought it must have been a delusion caused by delirium. My fever was worse and I soon became too weak to leave the barrack.
>
> Later, I cannot tell how long, I heard the voices of British soldiers. After I had been fed and nursed back into health, a British soldier approached me. Miraculously, it was my brother in law. My sister had gone to England before the War and they had married. He arranged for me to go to London to live with them in Black Lion Yard, just off the Whitechapel Road, the main street of the Jewish East End.
>
> Walking along Black Lion Yard one afternoon I saw a man coming towards me carrying a blonde child. He looked just like the man who had saved my life in Belsen. I hesitated, then approached him cautiously. I asked apologetically so as not to offend him. "Excuse me, but a man

who looked just like you saved my life in Belsen?" The man confirmed that it was he who had thrown the bread. We embraced, wept, then walked arm in arm to the man's tiny flat in Old Montague Mansions, on the corner of Black Lion Yard, amazingly just a few yards from my sister's flat.

(Faber, 1990)

I was that child. The man carrying me was my father. As I write in the relative security of my life today, I am struck by the unreal quality of my experiences. This speaks powerfully of the defensive capacity of my mind. As I continue to remember, that familiar but indescribable awfulness rises to the surface and overwhelms me. It is a reminder that it was all too real and it is still with me. This piece of my history may convey the sense of dreadfulness that has pervaded my life as well as the sense that my existence is miraculous.

Holocaust survivors were ordinary human beings who were forced to endure extraordinary events. The psychic processes available to them to respond were the same as those available to all humankind.

I stress this self-evident truth because it does not seem understood by non-survivors and the psychotherapeutic professions. This has led me to open this volume with a description of the Holocaust experiences of my family and an account of my formative experiences during and after the Holocaust, as a child refugee, a medical practitioner and a psychotherapist. Additionally, I have explored my experiences of many years of psychoanalysis and group analysis as a trauma survivor.

Primarily, my desire is to make Holocaust trauma accessible through a description of my childhood trauma, which was both formative and deformative. My years of therapy have trained me to observe and reflect on my psychic function and responses.

It is now more than 70 years since the beginning of the Holocaust, the Shoah, to give it its Jewish name. In this time, several generations of psychotherapists have trained and have what might be considered to be only a superficial knowledge of this momentous period, which has been called the most tragic event and the most important enigma of modern civilisation.

Child Holocaust survivors will be the last of the living witnesses. From the 1980s, there was a surge of Holocaust testimonies written. Many were remarkable, full of the pain and the miracle of survival. They rarely analyse the post-Holocaust effects of these traumatic events. Few, if any, were written for clinicians working with trauma victims.

The inclusion of this biography may assist in understanding why I have been drawn to certain psychological theories and have rejected others. These have played an important part in the theoretical constructs presented. During the writing and rewriting of the biographical opening, I have included much material that I presented and worked through during my analyses. The main difference during the writing of this book was that I was obliged to re-experience the emotional effects of these traumata in isolation and in a condensed way. This frequently overwhelmed my defences and left me struggling to regain equanimity. My response confirmed that the representations of these traumatic events were still present in my psyche and were capable of being reactivated. Thus, they are still central to my current psychic function and dysfunction.

This volume offers a body of writing, including trauma theories that derive from these reflections. I believe I have had a rare, if not unique, opportunity to examine my family's and my own Holocaust and post-Holocaust traumata.

In most trauma survivors, there is an intense desire to keep their traumatic past in the past. This comes at a high price in psychic energy. There is often a conflicting desire to show the world one's scars, presenting them like war wounds, to shock and shout, "What could you possibly understand if you have not had this experience?" These dynamics may well play a significant role here, but my conscious purpose is to describe enough of our lives to allow readers to understand the impact of massive psychic trauma on my family and of the many post-war generations who suffered their own massive traumata and genocides.

What I present here is part of my fight for my psychic life in which annihilation threat and death were ever-present. When I present some of our history, I can recall how it was told to me, as well as the dreadfulness that permeated the narrative, which gave it the horror and terror that pervaded so many of these moments in my Holocaust past.

Beginnings

My father, Solle Garfinkle (Garfinkel), was born in London in 1917 and was brought back to Poland by his father who failed to make an adequate living in war-torn London. My mother, Mania Garfinkle (Garfinkel),[2] was born in Przemysl in the "Pale of Settlement" in Galicia,[3] from which the phrase "beyond the pale" originates. I was born on 29 October 1942 in the Nazi ghetto of Przemysl. I was 8 months old when we were taken to Bergen-Belsen concentration camp with my 4-year-old sister, Leonia. We arrived with the first transport of Polish Jews on its first day as an exchange concentration camp on 6 July 1943.

The Nazis began with concentration camps that killed by starvation, hard labour and exposure. They then developed extermination camps, industrialised killing factories, such as Auschwitz. Heinrich Himmler, the Nazi head of the "final solution," thought of exchanging Germans in Allied hands with Jewish prisoners, and so he changed Bergen-Belsen labour camp into an exchange camp (Kolb, 1998).

The ghetto

Przemysl station was an important junction in the Austro-Hungarian Empire. Its decor was palatial. To the east was Ukraine and Russia, to the south Czechoslovakia and Austria, to the north Lithuania and White Russia, and to the west Kraków and Germany. My father worked at the station salon. Youthful good looks, multilingual, a sharp wit, and remarkable hair-dressing skills, he was an admired member of the community.

The Nazis established control through terror. Arriving in Przemysl, they immediately went to the station and rounded up 50 Jewish men identified by a Polish collaborator. My father was rounded up in his white coat. A non-Jewish customer told the Nazis that my father was not Jewish, so they released him. They immediately shot the Jewish men as a warning to everyone to instantly obey them (Hartman & Krochmal, 2002).

My mother was pregnant with me when she was forced into the newly formed ghetto.[4] It was surrounded by barbed wire and armed Nazi guards. Rations were 300 calories per day, set to starve to death as many Jews as possible. Any attempt to escape was punished by being shot on the spot. She heard many words of sympathy for being pregnant in such terrible circumstances. She remembered how active in the womb I was, kicking strongly. In the cramped apartment, where two families totalling ten people shared a single room, her friend, who shared her bed, joked that I would become a footballer.[5]

In September 1942, when she was six months pregnant, an *Aktion*, a selection for deportation,[6] was made. All the Jewish prisoners were made to stand on the street. The names of those to be deported were called out. On the list were Chaya Wirtental, Nachum and Lolla Gans,[7] her mother, father, and sister, also six months pregnant. When my mother realised they were being sent to their death, she was overwhelmed. She gave my then 3-year-old sister's hand to my father and began to join them. My father stood helpless. Suddenly, an SS officer ordered her to stay where she was and she was not taken. When the *Aktion* was over, my parents were ordered inside. Later, shots were heard. Many years later, we discovered that my grandfather had been shot in the square and my grandmother and aunt had been transported to Belzec extermination camp, where they would have been gassed and incinerated immediately.

My mother repeated this story many times as an expression of her anguished loss, particularly for her mother, who she constantly described as being so warm and kind that she was universally loved. She seemed uncon-scious of the implication that she had been prepared to die and also would have killed me. Thus, my existence was threatened by my mother as well as the Nazis, even before I was born. Of course, the psychic implications are that my sense of security, what we now describe as attachment, was made even more insecure.

The ghetto was a divided one, and the makeshift hospital was in the second ghetto hundreds of metres away. When her labour began, my mother was forced to walk in severe pain to where Dr Diamont,[8] the Jewish obstetrician, delivered me. It is the Jewish custom to circumcise male babies a few days after birth. This was not done. When I asked why, I was told that they knew they might have to give me away, and this would have helped my chances of survival. When my older daughters were born, I was sent a government pamphlet on how to act in the event of an atomic bomb drop. It reminded me of this decision they took. I was horrified by their situation.

My mother's favourite brother, Mundek, had married a Catholic, Mischka Kusmniek,[9] before the war and had two children. Mundek was caught watching a card game in the ghetto, which was forbidden. He escaped from the ghetto but was hunted down to the Jewish cemetery in Ulica Slowakskiego (Slovakia Street), where he had hidden under a gravestone. The SS dogs found him and he was shot. When the ghetto was formed, Mischka stayed on the Aryan side with her children. When Mundek was shot, she openly brought the children up as Catholics. Why the children were never denounced as having a Jewish father to get the reward of a kilogram of sugar from the Nazis, and thus murdered, is not known. Perhaps having an aunt who was a nun and a senior member of the Church may have protected them.

After many years of avoidant silence, I was told of the murder of Mundek, her older brother. My paternal grandmother was herded into a wooden synagogue in Tarnapol, now in Ukraine, with my aunt, Rusa, and a pregnant stepdaughter-in-law. The synagogue was torched and they were burned alive.

The food rations in the ghetto were set at non-survival levels. People were soon dying from starvation. Outside the ghetto, there was a black market at inflated prices. The currency was jewellery. My father would regularly escape to the Aryan side and hide at Mischka's flat, where he would buy food from Mischka's sister, Bernadetta, who was a nun and ran an orphanage. This justified her need to buy large quantities of food. He escaped by going through the roof spaces of the typical Austro-Hungarian squares of apartment blocks of Przemysl. To do this, he had to pass through the roof of the Gestapo headquarters on the east side of the block facing the railway. The guard dogs would bark ferociously, but the Gestapo never seemed to suspect someone would have the audacity to go through their roof space and he was never caught.

He only used this method of escape after his usual escape route was cut off. This was to walk out of the ghetto in broad daylight with documented justification that he was going to work. In the three weeks of the Nazis' first occupation of Eastern Poland, he had been forced to work in the rail yards. He had retained the authorising document. One day on his way out of the ghetto, an SS officer stopped him. He demanded to know where he was going. My father produced the document, explaining he was going to work at the rail yard. The officer looked at the document, put it in his pocket, and ordered him to proceed. With a calm manner and an ice-cool head, my father proceeded to walk away from the ghetto at a normal pace. He knew that if he had walked back towards the ghetto or had looked back, he would have been shot on the spot. He made his way to Mischka's, where he stayed until nightfall, and then returned through the roof spaces. Some days later, the Jewish ghetto police[10] were sent to arrest him. Although outnumbered, he overcame them and jumped through a toilet window, escaping through the roof space. He was fearless, always taking great risks.

My father never forgot how Mischka risked her life and those of her children every time she sheltered him. Throughout the post-war years, he would send letters to Mischka and large food parcels when she was suffering hardship under the communists. He always hid money, usually dollars, in the walnuts, which he would carefully open, fill and glue back together. He had learned these artful ways of hiding valuables in the Holocaust.

When I was about 11 years old, he told me, in his usual mysterious way, to come with him into his bedroom. Everything was treated as a secret and prior explanation was never given. He took a number of small glass tumblers from a cloth bag with a drawstring. He heated them over a spirit lamp and showed me how to apply them to his back. As they cooled, they drew his flesh into them. This was the medicinal process known as cupping, or *bunkers* in Yiddish.[11] Looking at his back closely for the first time, I noticed a large number of long, horizontal scars.[12] On asking him what they were, he calmly explained that we were freezing in the Polish winter, and on one of the many occasions after he stole coal from the rail yards he was caught by the Nazis. He was sentenced to 25 lashes. When, many years later, I spoke of this to my only surviving Polish uncle, Zigu,[13] he explained that my father could barely walk as he struggled back to our room. The punishment nearly killed him. My uncle always spoke of my father with deep respect and admiration. I am sure that had he not needed me to apply the *bunkers* to his painful shoulders, he would have gone to his grave without ever talking of this trauma. This was part of the mystery of the man. He was admired, and perhaps loved, by those outside his immediate family. At the same time, he ruled us through a reign of violence, cruelty and terror, for which we grew to hate him. Yet he also had great compassion and warmth. Children of camp survivors repeatedly write of the terrible rages their fathers suffered.

When I gained entry to grammar school, he was very proud, and had long, grey flannel trousers made for me at some expense. Like all children, I joined in the playground football games, in which I would invariably fall and tear the trouser knees. After several pairs of trousers were ruined, he exploded with rage and tore the clothes from my body, then beat me black and blue with a leather strop used to sharpen cut-throat razors. He then cut down the legs of an old pair of his corduroy trousers, which I had to wear. They were huge, and they were held up by one of his large belts. The crutch nearly touched the ground and the legs were enormous, covering my shoes. It was deeply humiliating, but in his rage he did not care. When the next day's football game started, I joined in as usual. Kicking the ball, the trousers were so voluminous that the ball instantly disappeared up the trouser leg. This caused confusion among the boys, who had not seen it and set about searching. When the ball was found up my trouser leg, this became one of those legendary stories that schoolchildren retell. However, the humiliation only added to the ridicule and bullying I suffered.

One day in the ghetto, my father saw a boy and girl crying standing by a cart stacked with bodies. He asked what was the matter. They explained that their mother had died and was on the cart. She had hidden her jewellery in her undergarments but they could not bear to search for them. Without the jewellery to buy food, they would soon starve to death. My father found the jewellery for them and refused to take any reward for his help when they offered it. My heart is filled with sadness and loss when I think of this deeply compassionate side of him, which I knew was there, but was rarely shown to us, his children.

Bergen-Belsen concentration camp

In the spring of 1943, a notice was put up in the ghetto instructing those with Allied or neutral nationality to register with the *Judenrat*, the Jewish ghetto administration. Being born in London, my father registered. In early July 1943, we were put on to a train of normal carriages and taken to Montelupich Prison, the Gestapo headquarters in Kraków. My father was interrogated for three days before we were put on a cattle truck transport. The sound of firing squads could be heard all day: the fate of those that did not satisfy the Gestapo interrogators. Our destination was Bergen-Belsen concentration camp in Northern Germany.

Why were we sent to Bergen-Belsen and not straight to the gas chambers of Auschwitz-Birkenau only 200 kilometres away? In 1943, Heinrich Himmler, the head of the Gestapo, decided to build a detention and exchange camp, an *Aufenthaltslager* (Kolb, 1988), for the holding of Jews with Allied or neutral nationality or connections for exchange with German nationals in the hands of the Allies. An exchange took place with German Templers captured in Jerusalem (Fransman, 2005; Pazner, 1986).

My father had been born in London on 16 December 1917. My Polish grandfather, Abraham Garfinkel, with my Hungarian grandmother, Gisa, née Herz, had come to the Jewish East End in search of opportunities to better themselves. My grandfather was described by my father as a talented cabinet-maker, a now obsolete term for the trade of master furniture-maker. However, he is described as a French-polisher on my father's birth certificate, a much humbler profession. My grandfather probably arrived some time before the outbreak of the First World War as my father's two older sisters and a brother were with him in London. My grandfather eventually returned to Poland with his family. He had found life and supporting his family too difficult in London.

We arrived in Bergen-Belsen on 6 July 1943 on a transport carrying 2,500 Jewish prisoners on its first day as an exchange camp. Within a few weeks, all but 300 had been sent to their deaths in Auschwitz. Ariella Low-enthal Meyer, also born in Przemysl, was 8 years old when she shared the carriage with us to the Gestapo headquarters in Kraków. She travelled with her uncle and aunt who took her under their care after her parents had been murdered. There was another barber who accompanied us with his wife and child. My father reported that the barber, still wearing his barber's white coat, was so distressed and terrified that he was unable to eat, and chain-smoked constantly until he died a few weeks later. Ariella, who survived and now lives in Toronto, told me how some weeks after their arrival in Belsen, my father appeared in their barrack. Being a *Lager Friseur* (barber) for the children, he could move freely around the camp. He surreptitiously dropped some bread on to her bunk and left without saying a word. He was risking his life with this act of kindness.

As I write this, my frail and dementing mother is still alive at 91 years of age. It is hard to face the fact of her increasing frailty, and thus her demise in the foreseeable future. Of course, her dementia means the person who was my mother has long since gone, but her physical presence still has an impact. My mother breastfed me in Belsen and was able to produce milk from one breast throughout the nearly two years of our incarceration. This adds to the sense of our miraculous survival. My mother was obliged to stay in the barrack with us children. She was not required to work except on one occasion. My father was billeted in the men's camp but could visit using his pass as a *Lager Friseur*. My mother must have developed an extraordinary alertness to danger and a capacity for calm self-containment to protect and provide for my sister and me during this time while being forced to be passive.

Like all children, my sister and I played in Bergen-Belsen. We now understand more clearly how children recreate their predicament in play and take a role that may evoke, in fantasy, mastery rather than helplessness. Death was an everyday event, and thus the subject of play. My sister relates how in play, I passively submitted to being completely buried in a mound of sand by the children of our barrack led by Micha Gelber, a Dutch boy, and his brother, Yehudi. My sister ran to fetch my mother just in time to prevent my suffocation. When they buried me, they were, in fantasy, empowered with the power of life and death over me, and in play they were no longer the potential victims. Micha (Michael) and Yehudi (Edward) survived, and we met again 50 years after the liberation.

The Holocaust

The dreadfulness of what was done by the Nazis to men, women, and chil-dren defies description. I struggle with my distress when I attempt to describe it. Our conscious and unconscious defences protect us from the threat, pain, and horror to which I am less able to defend because they are an ever-present part of my psyche.

My paternal grandmother, Gisa, was herded into a wooden synagogue in Tarnopol, now in Ukraine, with my aunt, Rusa, and a pregnant stepdaughter-in-law. The synagogue was set alight and they were burned alive.

In Belsen, we played among the dead bodies. There was chaos towards the end, and the dead lay where they died and rotted. Irma Grese, the notorious head of the female guards, formerly from Auschwitz, had black Dobermann hounds that she deliberately starved. For her amusement, she would let them loose to tear prisoners to pieces. She was so sadistic and voracious in her murderousness that the Jewish administration decided something must be done. Albala, the *Juden Altester* (Senior Jew), sent my father to the French women's section to buy costume jewellery from them for bread. They took these to the jeweller to put real gems in the centre of the jewels to give to Grese, to make her think she was getting valuable jewellery. This was meant to make her less vicious and, to quote my father, "to keep her sweet". She never discovered the deception, and she was hung for her crimes after the liberation at the Nuremberg trials.

Prisoners were hung as punishment and their bodies were left as a warning against disobedience. The stench of the open toilets and the rotting corpses is indescribable and was inescapable. Those weak with typhus and diarrhoea often collapsed on the toilet. Some drowned in excrement. Being shot on the spot by the guards or beaten to death by *Kapos*[14] was a daily event. I shut out the screams of agony and terror, theirs and my own silent cries of anguish, as I write.

The barracks were converted stables and had no glass in the windows. The rain and wind sent blasts of bitterly cold air through them. Our hunger constantly ate away at our guts and the constant biting of the lice in our unwashed clothes added to the overwhelming misery. How do I find words to describe the constant fear? How does one describe the fear of dying, the intense battle with exhaustion not to succumb and die? Children did not survive without adults. Watching the adults become weaker, approaching death, and being helpless to prevent this, never knowing from moment to moment if we would live or die, how does one capture and convey this?

How did we survive?

"How did we survive?" you may well ask. There is no simple answer. All Holocaust survivors will tell you it was a mixture of determination, resourcefulness and a great deal of luck. A primary factor was my father's resourcefulness and skills. He was a *Lager Friseur*, a barber, one of the very few needed camp professions. Prisoners arriving in a camp were shorn of all scalp and body hair. From then on, their heads were regularly shaved. When he was 10 years old, his father had died in a typhoid epidemic, leaving his mother widowed and penniless. Of necessity, his mother remarried quickly as she had no trade to fall back on. She married Moishe Klein, a widower with three children. Sadly, their home was too small to take both sets of children. He was sent to live with his grandmother, but he missed his family deeply. To save the cost of his keep, his grandmother found him an apprenticeship with a barber. In the 1920s, this meant you were sent to live with your master. His new home was many miles from his home in Tarnopol. He hated being away from home. He often described how he repeatedly ran away and made his way home barefoot. His determination and fearlessness were strong parts of his character. His defiance and boundary-breaking would now be described as an emerging borderline personality disorder. He completed his apprenticeship, learning his trade, which then included medieval remedies such as bloodletting using leeches. He was blessed with having a sharp, analytic mind, a quick memory, and extraordinary manual dexterity. He was described as having "golden hands." He also had a remarkable ear for languages. Przemysl was at the crossroads of many Slavic countries. He was fluent in at least six languages before the Holocaust and learned a further three by the war's end.

The River San, which cuts my birthplace into two halves, was the frontier when Poland was divided by the Molotov–Ribbentrop Pact of 1939. This meant my parents were initially only in Nazi hands for three weeks. Due to its important rail connections with all of Central Europe and Russia, Przemysl had been a major garrison town of the Austro-Hungarian Empire. After the pact, the Russians occupied the town with a substantial military contingent and began to conscript young Poles into the Soviet Army.

Outside of his home, my father was known as a lovable rogue. He had great wit and charm. He related the following story. A Russian general came into the barbershop and demanded to be shaved. This was in the days of cut-throat razors. He warned my father that if he cut him, even the smallest nick, he would have him shot. My father calmly proceeded to shave him and finished without even the slightest nick. The general, noticing my father's coolness, asked him why he was not nervous. My father replied, in fluent Russian, with his usual candour and a twinkle in his eye, that he was not nervous because had he cut him, he would have then cut his throat. The general laughed heartily and left. This was typical of his wit and risk-taking. Others with less charm would have been arrested and shot. This may have had some influence on my father being conscripted into the Russian Army (21st Rifle Brigade). More importantly, my father was a fast learner and a perfectionist, and with his linguistic skills was soon promoted to lance corporal and put to work training the Polish conscripts.

In Belsen, my father would rise at 3 a.m. to shave the *Kapos*, for which he would receive a little butter or extra bread. This marginally delayed our starvation. He would give the extra food to my mother to hide and share. When my father began to develop oedema, a sign of protein deficiency, my mother insisted he have more of the extra food. Reciprocity was essential to survival (Davidson, 1992).

They developed a close friendship with Bruno Schlachet, a skilled Dutch bootmaker. He was in great demand by the SS, making and repairing their boots. For this, he was given a special place to work that was heated by a small stove. This was usually reserved for *Kapos*. In the latter chaotic days of the camp, he allowed us all to share the warm space with him. In these last weeks of the camp, no food or water was brought into the camp. Thousands of Jewish prisoners were arriving from the death marches from the closing camps in the east. Jews were dying so fast from the typhus epidemic and other diseases that they overwhelmed the organisation of the camp, and large mounds of corpses were found everywhere. The starvation was so complete that people were forced to survive by cannibalism. The survivors from Auschwitz thought Auschwitz was hell on earth until they arrived in Belsen. It is not possible to offer a simple coherent answer to how we survived. Despite my father earning extra bread and my mother being able to breastfeed me, the conditions were so terrible that it is miraculous anyone survived.

The lost train of Troibitz

The Nazis, in their habitual rigid way, hung on to us, the exchange Jewish prisoners of the *Stern Lager*, as our special section was known. One week before Belsen was liberated, all 7,500 *Stern Lager* prisoners were put on three trains consisting of cattle trucks. Historians are undecided regarding our intended destination. Most believe we were to be murdered in newly completed gas chambers in Terezin (Theresinstat), the model concentration camp near Prague. One train reached Terezin.

Ten miles from Belsen is the pleasant town of Saltau. Our convoy stopped at the station. At this time, the Allies had gained air supremacy and air raids were a constant danger. Thus, our convoy was slowly moved just beyond the station. Within minutes, Allied bombers attacked the station, destroying it. The train spent two weeks wandering around Germany trying to find an intact bridge to cross to Eastern Germany.

When the northern Greek city of Salonika was emptied of its large Jewish community, a number of prominent community members arrived in Belsen. Among these were the chief rabbi, Dr Joseph Koretz, and Jaque Albala, a wealthy individual. Albala was reputed to be a successful and educated entrepreneur. Albala arrived in Belsen with his wife, their nanny, and his son, Sigurd. Sigurd and I were born on the same day, and Albala took a special interest in my welfare. I was reportedly a very blonde, blue-eyed, pretty child. On one visit to the camp by a senior Nazi, I immediately gained his attention and my cheek was tweaked. My father's usefulness to Albala, as well as my sharing his son's birthday, had many repercussions. Albala was made the *Juden Altester*, the Jewish camp administrator. My father had access to him and performed many services that were appreciated and remembered. On the transport, my mother, father, sister, and I were put into the same carriage as Albala and his family, as well as Dr Koretz and his wife and son. A measure of the relationship my father had with Albala was shown on the day before the train was liberated. Albala's son, Sigurd, finally succumbed to starvation and disease. The train frequently stopped between stations and the prisoners were allowed off the train to scavenge for food. When Sigurd died, Albala asked my father to bury him. It is hard to imagine what my father must have been feeling when burying this child who was born on the same day as me. When quietly describing this event, my father's gaze seemed to turn inwards and his voice softened, as though he was reliving the experience. There are so many experiences like this in our story.

On the final train journey, my mother and I were so sick with typhus that we were close to death. The train was so packed that we barely had space to lie down. Suddenly, the train stopped. We were being bombarded by artillery. My sister remembers looking out and seeing the SS guards running away. She shouted to my parents frantically. They jumped off the train. Artillery was exploding all around us. I was too sick to be aware of this danger. Leonia remembers my mother and father carrying us and jumping into a shell crater. They laid us down and flung their bodies over us to protect us from the explosions and shrapnel. We had wandered into the front line of the advancing Russian Army. When the explosions passed beyond us, my father saw Russian cavalry charging at the fleeing SS guards. These were General Zukov's legendary cavalry, the Cossacks, surrounding the train. When it seemed safe enough, my father approached them with hands held high, calling out "*tovarish*" (comrade). He was soon speaking to them in his fluent Russian, explaining we were Jewish prisoners and he was a former Russian soldier. He was given a uniform, a rifle, and a large bottle of vodka. Leonia remembers looking around the battlefield. The fields were full of scattered body parts and dead soldiers. When he found an abandoned house, we took shelter. By evening, the Cossacks made camp and were eating around the campfires. My father went out and brought back some food for us. Leonia remembers finding a doll in the house. This was a luxury she had longed for throughout her time in Belsen. When my father came back with a Russian officer, the officer saw Leonia's doll and took it, saying she did not want a dirty German doll. She was devastated and still remembers it to this day.

My father often reminded us of how he and my mother lay with their bodies over us, particularly when we were teenagers and trying to defy or challenge him. When writing this, I find myself unable to stand outside myself and read this as an observer. I am swept along and overwhelmed by emotion. I find myself hanging on and fighting back my tears.

The Russians liberated us just outside the village of Troibitz near Leipzig in Eastern Germany on 23 April 1945. My mother and I were too weak to walk. What remained of the 2,500 prisoners were suffering the full range and severity of diseases discovered by the liberating British Army in Belsen eight days earlier, captured on the infamous films made by Alfred Hitchcock's cameraman and narrated by Richard Dimbleby, the famous BBC news reporter. Due to the typhus we all had, the Russians quarantined the village and conscripted the German inhabitants into caring for the sick. They had no drugs and minimal medical personnel. One in five of the prisoners died, including Dr Koretz. This was the same proportion as those liberated by the British in Belsen. His son, Aria, led a movement to erect a memorial in the village, which took place 50 years after our liberation.

My father had seen some retribution taken on the *Kapos*, the brutal collaborators who acted as guards. In order to survive, my father had risen at 3 a.m. every day to shave the *Kapos*, and thus earn a little extra food. However, there was such bitterness in the survivors; anyone who had the means to obtain extra food was deeply envied. My father was not prepared to risk our fate to uncertain justice. He feared that he, Albala, and others would be strung up. Using his newly acquired Russian rifle, he "liberated" a dog cart. This was a commonly used smaller version of the familiar cart pulled by horses. Laying my mother, sister, and me in it, he left, pulling it by hand, walking away to find shelter. It is amazing that he had the strength. He was driven to return to find anyone who had survived. He often said that he had been prepared in survival by the hardships of his childhood and his demanding working life. Unlike today, hairdressers were regarded as little better than road sweepers in the class-ridden societies of the pre- and post-war periods. This contrasted painfully with his bravery in the Holocaust and the respect he had gained from the Russians. He pulled us until he was able to "liberate" a bicycle with which to pull the cart.

We were liberated, but we were far from freedom.

Notes

1 *Abdominal typhus.* For centuries, epidemics of louse-borne typhus have occurred when people are crowded together under poor hygienic conditions and become infected by lice. In the unsanitary conditions deliberately created in the ghettos and the concentration camps, these were perfect conditions for lice and the development of typhus epidemics. Abdominal typhus was characterised by torrential diarrhoea, rapid dehydration, and death. Anne Frank is reported to have died from abdominal typhus in Bergen-Belsen.

2 *Names.* My parents' names are not a simple matter. My father was called Sulek by his Polish friends or family, or Solle by his English Jewish friends, which is perhaps the diminutive of Solomon. When I was bar mitzvahed, my name in

Hebrew was Avraham ben Shulem, Abraham son of Shulem. On the official records of Bergen-Belsen, my father is named as Salo Garfunkel. I assume this is consistent with his official Polish recorded name. My mother is named Mania Garfunkel-Wirtenthal in the official records of Bergen-Belsen. My parents were married by a rabbi in their home but they could not afford a Polish marriage license, and thus were classed as unmarried. This was a common situation in the Polish Jewish community. I assume this may make me illegitimate.

3 *The Pale of Settlement.* This was a collection of 25 provinces of czarist Russia in Poland, Lithuania, Ukraine, Bessarabia, and Crimea where Jews were permitted permanent residence. Only certain groups of Jews were permitted to live outside it. The fate of Jews found outside its confines without permits was at the arbitrary whim of the local governor.

4 *The ghetto.* 29 September 1939 was the date set at a secret conference for the reintroduction and construction of ghettos in Poland. Ghettos such as these had not existed since the Middle Ages. The "ultimate aim" was that the Jews should be confined to as few concentration camps as possible. This was kept secret and was a disguised call for the preliminary steps to the elimination of all Jews under the control of the Nazis. Ghettos were usually constructed in cities near the railway station to facilitate deportation to the extermination camps. Austro-Hungarian city organisation, with its apartment blocks built in squares around a central courtyard, lent itself to the formation of ghettos and gave privacy to the murder of those herded into the central squares. Przemyls's rail yards were important junctions for railways in all directions.

5 This friend did not survive, but my parents found her sister, Heika Genat, in Israel.

6 *Aktion.* An *Aktion* was a roll call of all the ghetto prisoners and a selection for deportation to the extermination or forced labour camps. Often there were executions by firing squads of the elderly, the frail, and children.

7 Chaya and Nachum only married by a religious ceremony, and thus kept their maiden names.

8 Dr Diamont was a Jewish obstetrician who set up a ghetto hospital. He survived and emigrated to Israel. He also delivered Dr Maria Orvid, the Polish child psychiatrist and founder member of the Polish Child Survivors organisation.

9 *Mischka Kusmniek.* My mother's older brother, Mundek, who was well known for his distinctive red hair, married Mischka, a Polish Catholic, and had two children, Janusch and Ruta. Mundek and was murdered by the Gestapo. Mischka showed extraordinary loyalty and put herself and her children at risk by sheltering and helping my father during the Holocaust and our entire family after the liberation. She nursed us back to some degree of health after our return to Przemysl despite the risk of typhus. After Mundek died, she brought up her children as Catholics and changed her name back to her maiden name. If her children's Jewish father had been denounced, they would have been sent to the gas chambers. My father never forgot her kindness, and throughout the difficult years of austerity after the Second World War, he regularly sent large parcels of food and scarce goods to Mischka. He also brought Janusch and Ruta over for visits to England despite the communist regime making this very difficult. My mother was too anxious to invite Janusch to emigrate, fearing the responsibility and difficulties. They did not respond to my strong pleading on Janusch's behalf. My complex mixture of fear and need, as well as the language barrier, has always obstructed my making regular contact with my Polish family.

10 The Nazis appointed a Jewish ghetto administration, the *Judenrat,* and police. I describe in Chapter 7 a meeting with Mier Dormbusch in Paris, who was one of the ghetto policemen who came to arrest my father.

11 *Cupping*, or *bunkers* in Yiddish, was one of the surgical skills my father was taught in his apprenticeship as a barber. The heated glass cups are applied to an area of skin over a painful muscle or joint. As they cool, they suck the skin and flesh up into them, causing an increase in circulation and a counterirritation. They were also used for bloodletting.

12 The horizontal linear scars show by their pattern and shape what was most likely to have caused them. Many years later, I examined a man from Iran who had been whipped because of some political offence – the scars were identical.

13 Zigu described this punishment on our journey back to Przemysl.

14 *Kapos* were Jewish prisoners who were given privileges for acting as guards. They were notoriously more savage and cruel than the many of the Nazi guards in order to save their own skin.

References

Davidson, S. (1992) *Holding on to Humanity: The Message of Holocaust Survivors – The Shamai Davidson Papers*. Ed. I. Charney. New York: New York University Press.

Faber, D. (1990) *Because of Romek*. San Diego, CA: Los Hombres Press.

Fransman, J. (2005) *Zachor: Child Survivors Speak*. London: Elliott & Thompson.

Hartman, J. & Krochmal, J. (2002) *I Remember Every Day: The Fates of the Jews of Przemyśl During World War II*.

Kolb, E. (1998) *Bergen-Belsen: From 1943–1945*. Gottingen: Vandenhoeck & Ruprecht.

Pazner, H. (1986) *From Bergen-Belsen to Freedom: The Story of the Exchange of Jewish Inmates of Bergen-Belsen with German Templars from Palestine – A Symposium in Memory of Dr Haim Pazner*. Jerusalem: Yad Vashem.

Chapter 3

The war after

Introduction

The title of this chapter has been borrowed from the book *The War After*, authored by my friend Ann Karpf (1997). Ann is the daughter of the Plashov and Auschwitz concentration camp survivor and renowned concert pianist, the late Natalia Karpf.

Przemysl, Poland

My father said little of this part of our survival. He had "liberated" a bicycle and had a Russian uniform and rifle, which gave him power and authority. He remembered the first time he used the rifle. He saw a chicken within range and, being the trained soldier he was, he aimed and shot. He then discovered his rifle was loaded with dum-dum explosive bullets, which, when the bullet exploded, made the chicken disappear before his eyes. In his weakened state, he could not keep track of the events, but he believed we arrived in Przemysl around 3 May 1945. He went straight to Mischka's home, where he always hid when he had escaped from the ghetto. As always, she came to our rescue. Taking us in, she began to nurse us back to health. This was no simple task as we had abdominal typhus and life-threatening malnutrition. Too much or overly rich food would have been fatal. Both she and her children were at risk from the typhus and any other disease we may have carried. My sister, Leonia, had double pneumonia, which some 40 years later was discovered never to have left her. I had rickets, a calcium deficiency of the bones, particularly of the legs, preventing them from hardening. This made standing and walking very painful. Despite my parents' emaciation and psychological trauma, they were able to enjoy being free. My mother recalled with laughter, and a measure of revenge, that once when she took off my nappy, I pissed a fountain of urine straight into my father's soup. Apart from our recovery, my father's greatest concern was to see if any family had survived. Of our approximately 70 family members, he found two: my mother's second cousin, Dorcha Kellermann (née

Rupp), and her husband, Zigmund Kellermann. For 11 months, they had been in hiding in a cellar after the ghetto liquidation. Their son died in a fire and they had recently had another son who they named Alfred.

The Army of Krajova were Polish nationalists and some were racist extremists. They were murdering Jews who had survived when they returned. A midnight knock on the door, we understood, was an attempt by the Army of Krajova to murder us. This was all the warning we needed. Also, we did not want to put Mischka and her children at further risk. We immediately left Poland and sought a displaced persons (DP) camp outside of Prague. My uncle, Zigu, also left with his family, heeding this warning. They went to Germany. The stay at the DP camp was brief. The vodka given from our Russian liberators was traded for visas to Lyon, the site of the nearest British consulate in France, where we sought British papers.

My mother described our lodgings on the top floor of a dilapidated tenement as filthy and infested with rats. She particularly feared rats despite having survived the horrors of Belsen. My rickets made walking very restricted. My mother feared I would be disabled. The available treatment was ultraviolet light, with sunlamps used as a sunlight substitute. I was treated for months but I still found walking painful for years. This reduced my height and strength. I was half the expected height and weight for my age.

My father soon found paid work as barbers were needed for shaves and haircuts the world over. Among his customers were some educated Polish Army officers who often gave advice and guidance. They suggested he take his history of being born in London to the British consulate. There, he gave the details and waited. Some months later, he was summoned to the consulate. They had obtained his birth certificate. He thought he was home and dry. However, the official said, "How do we know that a dying friend did not give you all these details as a last gift? How do we know you are the person on the birth certificate? Can you find someone who could certify you are Solle Garfinkle?" To ask this of a Holocaust survivor was almost asking the impossible. His two surviving family members from Przemysl were somewhere in Germany. Despite the liberation of the concentration camps and the terrible photos in all the newspapers, the British establishment were still fundamentally anti-Semitic and were not keen to let Jews in. Fortunately, my father's maternal family had settled in France. Using his resourcefulness, he somehow found them in Périgueux, where they had been in hiding in Vichy, the unoccupied southern part of France that the Nazis allowed to be largely controlled by a French puppet government.

Remarkably, his maternal grandfather was still alive. My father recounted that his grandfather had come to London in 1917 for his birth. Several members of his mother's family were living in Périgueux. When he explained that we had survived Bergen-Belsen, his great-uncle mentioned there was a woman living nearby who had also survived Belsen. They called her to their home, perhaps to authenticate his story. He implied he had not been welcomed or trusted. Perhaps they were concerned he would want money from them. When the woman arrived, she confirmed she knew my father and that "he had had it good." In his Holocaust survivor guilt, hypersensitive way, he took this as an accusation that he had collaborated with the Nazis in order to survive. This was never forgotten and caused a rift for more than 40 years. However, he was able to obtain a sworn statement witnessed by a notary to give to the British authorities. In contrast, he described meeting his great-uncle, André, and the generous way he treated him and Leonia, who accompanied him. André took them both to a restaurant for a good meal, the sole act of generosity he recalls from this journey. Back in Lyon, he presented the document and waited. Eventually, the consulate called him and confirmed they had given him British nationality by birth, nationality by marriage to my mother, and nationality by descent to Leonia and me. We were directed to Paris to eventually be sent by ship to England.

We arrived in the Jewish East End of London in January 1946 with only the clothes we stood in. It was one of the coldest winters for decades. Cold, damp, and alone, we knew no one. My father still wore his Russian Army uniform and my mother wore the only dress she possessed. Although my father worked as a hairdresser in Lyon, he earned barely enough to feed us. We were almost penniless. We found our way to a Jewish café to decide what to do next. Jewish cafés were easily identified by the kosher food sign in the window. My parents' conversation in Polish and Yiddish was overheard and we were approached by other Jewish customers. We had nowhere to stay. They directed us to the Millen family, a London Jewish family who were helping Jewish Holocaust survivors. I believe they had also come from Przemysl. They lived in the then wealthy suburb of Upper Clapton. I do not remember the journey, but I remember the house with tall Victorian ceilings and carpets on the floor. The room was spacious and warm, with two beds and some armchairs in it. We were clothed and fed. Leonia and I were put together in the same bed, as usual, and I was soon asleep. My parents were given the contact details of the Goldsteins, a prominent Jewish clothes-manufacturing family of Polish origin. The Goldsteins, together with the Ellis family, manufactured the famous Eastex brand of clothing, which is still in existence. When they heard we were survivors of Belsen, we were assisted without question. My parents never forgot their kindness. My mother remained friends with Mrs Goldstein until her death in her nineties only a few years ago. We were helped to find lodgings in a tiny top-floor flat in Old Montague House in Old Montague Street.

Having no money and no employment, and speaking no English, my parents took us to the nearby office of the Board of Guardians in Mansell Street, the main Jewish charity of the day, the bright front door with its brass knocker sounding loudly. We went up the carpeted stairs to the clean, warm office in which we were examined. The room was well lit by a large window. The doctor wore a white coat and the nurse a crisp uniform.

While my parents were being questioned, tea and cakes were brought in on a tray of bone china crockery, for the doctor. We were emaciated and hungry. Leonia and I were half the height and weight we should have been. I watched while the doctor drank his tea and ate his biscuits. We were not even offered a glass of water. I could not speak English, and so I watched Leonia and followed her lead. The doctor examined us. The effects of rickets causing the bowing of my legs could be clearly seen.[1] I watched the doctor talking to my parents. I felt anxious when their facial expressions showed concern. The doctor had reached his decision. He informed my parents that what my sister and I needed was country air and good food. He told, not asked, my parents that he was going to send us to a children's home in the country, to Broadstairs in the county of Kent. I believe my parents, having only just received British passports, were too frightened to challenge this representative of the "authorities."

The children's home, typical of its time, segregated the boys from the girls. I was immediately separated from my sister. I was 3 years and 6 months old, frightened, and silent. I do not remember the journey, but recall that soon after our arrival, I was made to strip naked and join a queue of other naked boys and sent into a large, echoing shower room. The link with the gas chambers was clearly on my mind. As I write, I remember it with a vividness suffused with terror. We were lined up in readiness to be showered. We were washed by women with rough hands. The women laughed and joked with each other but ignored us. I was not spoken to. I was pulled and pushed under the shower and then passed to the women who rubbed me down with a rough, damp towel. I remember the cold, large dormitory. The strange bed was in the centre of a huge, cold room. It had a metal frame and cotton sheets that were cold. The rough blankets scratched my skin. I had learned to be silent and uncomplaining. I had learned that children who cried died (Kellermann, 2009).

Predictably, my reaction to what was my first maternal separation was regression. I woke the next morning having wet the bed, enuresis. This was a grave offence. The matron then carried out the required punishment. I was made to stand on a chair in front of all the children at breakfast while they ate. I was denied food or drink. I was to be shamed and isolated. I could see my sister sitting at the girl's table looking troubled. I still see it as I write. Leonia told me she tried to protect me and saved some food for me.

The matron was threatening and cruel. Visiting was allowed on one Sunday per month. We were threatened with dire consequences if we said anything of my punishment or complained to our parents. We were helpless and terrified.

Today we understand the traumatic effects of separation and would not be surprised by my regression into silence, enuresis, and eventual encopresis (Robertson, 1952). My daily humiliation and food deprivation continued. Eventually, my bed was taken out of the heated dormitory and put into the unheated corridor. This was the coldest winter in Britain for decades. After nine months, I had lost more weight and developed such severe chilblains, a form of frostbite, that I could only walk with a limp. After nine months, my father, on his monthly visit, noticed me limping in pain. He took of my shoe. He was appalled by the sores on my feet. Leonia and I then broke down, relieved we could tell him about our ill treatment, our distress overcoming our terror of the matron. We told him everything. He demanded to see her and told her he was taking us home immediately. My mother was so afraid of challenging the authorities that she dissuaded him from taking us immediately without permission. He promised to return on Thursday to take us home. I can see it as clearly as if it was yesterday.

I cannot remember him coming to take us. Perhaps I slept in his arms. I can remember seeing our living room filled with Polish Holocaust survivors at the table, with my mother serving food. I can still remember being carried over to our bedroom and kissing the Jewish traditional mezuza that contained the prayer to bless the doorway. This brought praise and delight from our guests. I can still see Leonia getting into the foot end of our shared bed covered with a blanket of hand-knitted squares and an old overcoat in the minute box room we shared, only wide enough for a tiny bed.

The only entire Jewish nuclear family of Polish Holocaust survivors in the East End, we were a magnet to the trickle of newly arrived Polish Holocaust survivors. Our tiny home was full of survivors every evening sitting round the small table, eating the simple Polish food my mother cooked. It always smelled so Polish, perhaps because of the generous amount of garlic. There was always heated conversation in Polish and Yiddish about their Holocaust experiences and their murdered families. The talk was always about being stateless and where they could go. Many hastily married British women to obtain citizenship and suffered long years of unhappiness.

For a period, life seemed happy. However, one of the lessons of the Holocaust was that joy always came at a price to pay in pain. I made friends with a few boys and we regularly played in the ruins from the Blitz. One warm summer evening, we were playing while our parents chatted on the steps where Black Lion Yard joined Old Montague Street. Perhaps my rickety legs could not support me. Suddenly, I fell against the wall. Putting my right hand out to protect me, a searing pain passed along it. Fun turned to agony. I had broken a finger.

Gardner's Corner was a famous Whitechapel landmark. It was a wedge-shaped department store. The large windows were full of tailored clothes and leather shoes. We often walked past it to window-shop and dream of the unattainable luxuries before crossing over to the bustling Jewish market, with the sound of bagel sellers and the smell of herrings, Jewish traditional life. Gardner's seemed so smart and expensive. When I was about 4 years old, to my amazement, my parents went into the store rather than just looking in the windows. I was taken to the shoe department and fitted with a beautiful pair of shiny, light brown, leather shoes with a gold buckle. Wearing them in the street outside the store, I was so proud and happy skipping along. I had never owned anything so smart. Suddenly, I stumbled and scuffed the perfect shiny uppers. This provoked my father's explosive rage, and he beat me around the legs and backside cruelly. Instantly, my moment of happiness had turned to abject misery. Joy never seemed to come without a price in pain.

Old Montague Street was close to the centre of the East End, with its two markets and the famous Blooms kosher sausage factory, where Shepsel, one of my favourite survivor proxy uncles, worked. He used a butcher's bicycle with a basket on the front. He would lift me up carefully and place me in the basket for an exciting ride. He was always kind and happy to see me. Some mornings, I would walk with my mother and Leonia to the factory and then turn down a narrow alleyway opposite where Leonia, now anglicised to Leonie, would enter the gate of the school she had started attending. I do not recall ever questioning why she entered the gates or even knowing what it was she was doing. I was 4 years old. My hand was always carefully held while I was being taken to another experience by my mother. There were always smells and noises. The greengrocer with its discarded rotting vegetables. The smell of blood from the slaughterhouse. The pungent smell of pickled cucumbers from the Polish deli. But most special was the wonderful smell of vanilla from the sweet shop opposite the deli. It sold ice cream and sweet vanilla-smelling cream soda. This was sold in heavy glasses filled by pulling on a handle like pulling pints. We never had enough money for such luxuries. I could only dream of such things. Crossing Brick Lane, we approached the Blooms factory and came to the narrow alley way Leonie would walk down. There was a tiny kiosk with wooden shutters barely wider than a door. The young woman who sat there from morning to night was always wrapped up in lots of scarves, coats, and hats. There was no heating, and she always wore several pairs of woollen gloves, which were noticeably fraying, when she served the customers with cigarettes or sweets and handed them their change. She sold solitary sweets for half an old penny. Even now, I think of her lonely, miserable existence in that tiny prison of a kiosk for all those long years. One morning, which did not seem different from all the rest, my mother and my sister walked to the kiosk and unusually we turned left into the alley. I was happily skipping along the cobbled street, oblivious to where we were going. When we stopped, to my surprise, we went through a wrought-iron door. Nothing was said, and I just followed my mother, who was holding my hand. We entered through some double swing doors and along a brown-tiled hallway and up some stone stairs. I was surprised but followed my mother without question. She took me through a green door with four square glass panes and approached a middle-aged lady dressed in a pinafore. I was now wary and watchful. I began to cling to my mother's leg through her dress. She tried to hand me over to the woman, who I soon realised was a teacher when I saw the children sitting at the desks. I started to cry bitterly and increasingly desperately. I clung in terror to my mother when she tried to leave. I feared this was another children's home. I had not been forewarned. Eventually, we were prised apart and my mother left. I did not speak English and could not understand what the teacher was saying. No one spoke to me. I sat all day high up the sloped classroom by a window with a hardback textbook in front of me, not understanding a single word spoken. This was Commercial Street Primary School. The next day, my sister took me with her, and my mother stayed at home. As soon as my sister let go of my hand, joining her friends, I crept out of the gate and walked back to our block of flats. The block had a flat roof and a small walled parapet behind which I hid. I stayed there all day, only descending to our front door when I saw my sister returning. I continued to play truant for five days before my absence was discovered. The following day, I was taken by my mother to the headmaster's office. I was dreading the inevitable beating I expected. The headmaster, who spoke in a gentle way, gave me a wad of white paper and coloured pencils, an unaffordable luxury, and invited me to sit on his warm, carpeted office floor. The model of the Lord Mayor's gilded, ceremonial coach and horses immediately caught my eye and mesmerised me. I began to draw. I was fascinated by the horses and drew them over and over until I had managed a likeness. I spent three days in his office, drawing all day. I do not recall being sent to the classroom, or dinners, or being taken home. What I do recall is my mother coming to the school hall to see me doing a gymnastic demonstration with other children. We were doing forward rolls, head over heels at great speed. I was the fastest. I really enjoyed it and smiled broadly to my mother. I do not remember the process, but it seemed only a short time later that I was speaking English and had happily adjusted to school.

With today's understanding of attachment disorders and separation trauma, readers would correctly predict the insecurity and separation anxiety my childhood had generated. From then on, and for many years, I was terrified of being returned to the children's home. My mother needed surgery in our first years in Britain. This meant I was sent to a children's home twice more for the several weeks' convalescence for which she was sent. My father would deliver me and always take fresh eggs for me as this was my favourite food. When he left, I became withdrawn and anorexic. I would sit forlorn and silent. I did not play or speak. I recall the anger of the lady who served the warm boiled egg for breakfast, a luxury in these times of rationing. I was so distressed that I was unable to eat, and the eggs were untouched. I believed my refusal to eat, and thus my starvation and weight loss, would magically be communicated to my mother, who would come and rescue me and take me home to ensure I did not starve. Leonie was old enough to be kept at home, so these separations were endured alone.

I believe that psychically, I blamed myself and promised to be good if I could be spared this separation. I was always terrified and deeply disturbed during these two further separations. As I recall them, the sadness floods through me and I turn to the comfort of milky coffee and croissant.

My attachment insecurity increased in the summer time. Every year, I was sent to Seaford in Sussex by the Country Holiday Fund charity on a holiday for the poorest children. I would always be given a few old shillings as pocket money. I only allowed myself 3 old pence per day (approximately 3 cents) for sweets and saved the rest. On the penultimate day, we were always taken to the Woolworths store to buy presents for our family. I had saved 90 per cent of the money and would spend virtually all of it for presents for my mother. They always had moulded glass fruit bowls that I would purchase. I would return laden with gifts for her and none for my father or sister. I do not recall ever being chastised for this behaviour by my sister or father. I do not know how they understood this. I now see this as an expression of my extreme separation anxiety and attachment insecurity. I was pleading with my mother, showering her with gifts, begging her not to send me away again.

My London childhood was dominated by health problems. I suffered recurrent otitis media, painful earaches. I was taken to numerous doctors. When the National Health Service began, I was treated at the London Hospital. They were planning to perform a mastoidectomy. This was a hazardous procedure with a high risk of serious complications such as deafness and lifelong infection. Fortunately, penicillin was just becoming available. I was prescribed injections of half a million units daily instead of surgery. These were painful. I was condemned to repeated courses for many years. From the age of approximately 8 years, I would walk alone to our doctor and have these daily injections several times each winter until I outgrew the condition. I had learned to suffer pain without complaint.

Throughout this time, my father's explosive rages became more frequent and unpredictable. They usually ended in violent beatings. My mother was deeply depressed and used me for solace and her ally in her misery. She sank into ill health. After an outburst from my father, she would complain of chest pain, suspected to be angina. The doctors would panic and admit her for several weeks. However, at the time of writing, she is 90 years old, and I can say with the authority of full investigations that her heart pain was not angina, but emotional heartache. She did not have angina.

Her depression, generated by her losses, her trauma, and her miserable life with my father, was intense and authentic. I recall, soon after returning from the children's home, seeing her sitting in the kitchen area, silently staring into space with a look of desolation on her face. It was as though having arrived in the safety of London, she was faced with all her losses. She rarely talked about being admitted to hospital while we were in the children's home and being subjected to electric convulsion therapy. She later complained that it destroyed her memory. During her middle age, she developed psychotic depression with paranoia.

In 1949, we moved to one of the first new blocks of municipal flats in the East End. It seemed luxurious. It consisted of a purpose-built kitchen, a bathroom and separate toilet, a lounge, and a bedroom for each of us. The new Jewish primary school I then attended was a good experience for a few years. While at this school, I cured my rickety legs. I always ran a lot, playing football, quickly ruining any shoes my father bought me. He became so fed up that he bought me a pair of builder's boots with steel toecaps. He had a cobbler put as many nails into the soles that could be squeezed in. When I first put them on, they were so heavy that when crossing the road, my feet were too heavy to lift out of the gutter. I had to walk until I could find a low pavement and lift my leg with my hands. When I got to school, I discovered that the nails in the soles caused a spark on the stones in the tarmac. It was a great new game. A few short steps and I slid down the playground's slope, sending sparks in all directions. The shoes lasted a week while my legs quickly became stronger. My father could not believe it. I pled ignorance when I was interrogated about how I wore them out so quickly.

When I passed my eleven-plus examination, this won me entry to a grammar school, reserved for brighter students. My parents were immensely proud. They arranged an evening with close friends, all survivors. They filled our rarely used sitting room, with its plastic covered furniture and untrodden carpet. There was an emotional discussion in Yiddish and English, with the adults talking over each other. No one listened to anybody else. I was the subject but I was not permitted to say a word. I sat silently through the heated debate. My usually oppressed mother came alive and my usually brutal father was being polite. What career would I follow? A profession was imperative. Medicine, dentistry, or accountancy? It was a rare evening of celebration and hope. It was a sham. It had no relationship to the misery of my everyday life. It was Kafkaesque.

The move to a grammar school proved devastating. I was the smallest boy even in the third form at 13 years. Having successfully stood up to bullies in the primary school, I found this impossible against 6-foot teenagers. Also, my parents constantly feared that I would be taken by some mishap, like their loved ones, and were immensely overprotective. In the cold weather, I was wrapped up in multiple and visible layers. The Polish traditional use of garlic as protection against illness was a huge unintended embarrassment. It remained strongly on my breath and came through my pores. I reeked. At assembly, when I opened my mouth to sing, the form in front ducked. I was soon nicknamed "Garlicfinkle." The constant bullying at home and ridicule at school made me overreact. Instead of learning not to draw attention to myself, I became attention-seeking, thus inviting the attention of the bullies. Life became filled by bullying at school and beatings at home.

My bar mitzvah, the Jewish coming of age, was a turning point in my life. At the celebration, all the guests were Holocaust survivors. We were a traumatised family within a traumatised community. By this time, I had virtually no friends and was socially dysfunctional. I did not know how to make small talk or how to just join in with others of my age. The burdens of my father's abuse and my mother's use of me for solace were overwhelming. I was so miserable that I asked to leave the school, which was refused. My father was immensely envious of my education, which constantly reminded him of his own lack of status or recognition of his intelligence and his Holocaust heroism. He would remind me that he left school at age 10 to become apprenticed, as well as how he spoke and read several languages. If I was defiant, he would remind me that he had covered me with his body to protect me from the Royal Air Force's bullets.

My response to these painful circumstances began by rejecting Judaism. So many of my Hebrew teachers who could have been role models were cold and authoritarian. They obeyed the religion rather than celebrating it. They lacked any understanding of the need of a young man for male role models. I rejected Judaism and God with an act of defiance. I threw a stone through their window. I was angry and disappointed.

At that time, the second important influence on my psyche was my sister's engagement. Her fiancé came from a relatively normal Jewish family. They were far less dysfunctional than my family. They were open and welcoming, and thus I had my first prolonged contact with a non-survivor family. Their ways and values were so different to ours that it was almost surreal. They were sociable, calm, and frequently playful. This could not have been more unlike our household. We were constantly engaged in heated arguments and emotional crises that often ended in beatings or my mother being admitted to hospital with chest pain. They were reasonably consistent and predictable, in contrast to my family interactions, which constantly involved conflict, threats, and guilt. I spent as much time with them as possible and realised that "normal" people did not behave and function like us. This was a revelation. Until this time, I was, of necessity, deeply introspective. My continuing internal struggle forced me to focus on my inner world. After they married, my brother-in-law became like an older brother. His friendship and loyalty to family, which then included me, was one of his most admirable qualities. His friendship was a vital attachment relationship. He became a role model. Sadly, he died prematurely at 53.

This helped me to begin to realise that my upbringing had been a training to survive the next Nazi Holocaust, not post-war English society. In order to escape this predicament, I realised I must psychically separate myself from my parents by emotionally disentangling myself. I then developed a strategy to achieve this. I spent most evenings walking the nearby streets, examining my life, starting with the day's events and what had gone wrong. I struggled to understand how I might avoid the painful interactions with my peers.

I was attempting to bring myself up, to become my own parent. This regular self-examination was born of my need to understand my psyche and those around me. I had begun what became my preparation for working with the psyche and my own psychic healing. In a sense, I began my first tentative self-analysis. In some ways, it was successful. I refined my convincing English middle-class veneer. Not sounding Polish, and looking more English than Jewish, with English politeness, eased my progress. However, this was at great emotional cost. Psychically separating myself from my only attachments created a deep inner loneliness. I also developed, for most of my adulthood, a protective introspection that inhibited my socialisation.

One Sunday morning, when I was about 17 years old and my father was then in his early forties, he suggested we go shopping in Brick Lane Market, a favourite Sunday activity. We walked from our latest council flat behind Stepney Green Station the few miles to Commercial Road. Out of the blue, my father announced that he had been born in Christian Street, the turning we were approaching, and wanted to see if the building was still there after the devastation of the Blitz. After a short walk, we found the dingy Peabody Trust's Victorian mansions. My father then suggested we try to find someone who may have remembered his family. Being a self-conscious teenager and knowing this would involve knocking on doors disturbing people's Sunday morning, I tried to dissuade him. I also thought it would be a pointless, self-defeating quest, but he was determined. I followed him into the dingy, brown-tiled communal stairwell and knocked on the first door. A young woman appeared. To my surprise, she was not irritated by being disturbed. Perhaps it was because of my father's good looks and charm, obvious to most but to which I was blind. My father explained that he had been born in the block and was looking for someone who may have remembered his family. She explained that she had only been there five years, but the lady on the floor above had lived there before her. We mounted the stairs, knocked on the door, and repeated the explanation. She had lived there only ten years, but the lady on the floor above had been here much longer. Up one more floor and we repeated the process. She had been there only 20 years, but there was an old lady on the top floor who had been there much longer. We mounted the last flight of stairs and knocked on the door. The door was opened by a frail-looking old Jewish lady. My father explained. "What was your name?" "Garfinkle," he replied. The lady, showing no emotion, nodded and quietly directed us to the two brown leatherette armchairs in her tiny, 6- by 8-foot sitting room. It was filled with heavy, dark furniture with family photos on the mantelpiece and sideboard. She offered us tea, taking an age to make it, all in silence. She moved silently and slowly brought the tea she had made. We drank it in silence. Quietly, she asked my father once again what his name was. "Garfinkle, Solle Garfinkle," he repeated. She nodded and slowly stood, went to a sideboard, and took out a small cardboard box that she presented to my father. It was full of pictures of his mother and of him as a baby with his older sisters and brother. I have difficulty describing the emotions of that moment because my eyes fill with tears as I recall this. They embraced and cried for a long time. When she was able to speak, which was all in Yiddish, she explained that my father had been born in the flat next door and she had delivered him. She had been his mother's close friend. After they had returned to Poland more than 40 years earlier, she had kept the photos. Even after the Holocaust, she had kept them in the hope that someone may have survived. They talked for a long time about how hard life was and how unhappy his mother had been. His father had been a stern and cruel man. She asked after his brother and sisters. His brother, Joseph, had died from tetanus in Budapest, and his mother and sisters had been murdered in the Holocaust. My father had lost all the photos of his family in the Holocaust. Later I discovered he often visited the lady alone. He never mentioned her name again, in his usual secretive possessive way. On reflection, I marvel at the lady's loyalty and hope, as well as his tenacity.

My painful history at grammar school included many academic failures and a few successes. In my first years, I had come bottom of the bottom class. I stayed there for several years. The school decided that chemistry as well as physics would be too much for my feeble brain, and they forced me to drop chemistry. Resenting this, I decided I would retaliate. Before the next term's physics exam, I did some revision and came top of the class by a wide margin. The physics teacher was convinced I had cheated and reported me to the headmaster. The head knew of my concentration camp experience. I was summoned to his office and made to sit another physics exam. I obtained a similar mark. When he had marked my paper, he became momentarily silent and then said, "Change your friends," and dismissed me. I had no friends, and he clearly did not understand that this advice was of no help.

After being the smallest boy in the school even in the third year, I began to grow. When I left at 16, I had reached 5 feet. With my starvation-delayed development, I was slight but quick on my feet. Our physical exercise (PE) master, Norman Page, had represented Great Britain in the 1948 Olympics in gymnastics. He encouraged us all to do vaults in our classes. Being light and relatively fearless, I was always the first to vault, always succeeding with his helping hand while in mid-air. Being the smallest, I was always chosen as goalkeeper when we played football. By now, I was very short-sighted and wore thick, black "Buddy Holly" glasses. Deciding that if I was always to be in goal I would learn to do it properly, I went with my only friend from the council flats to the local park. There, I asked him to throw the football to me but to the side. I soon learned to dive and land without injury. I bought some thick elastic bands to hold on my glasses. My parents had bought me a fisherman's heavy, roll-neck jumper, which goalkeepers then wore. I was soon spotted by Norman Page and given a trial on the concrete school playground, leaping and reaching the 8-foot crossbar and diving fast and low. I gained the first team place, which I kept for several years.

One memorable game, we played West Ham County High. They were affiliated to the famous professional West Ham First Division team (now the Premier League), playing in their youth academy. They were all 6 feet-plus. We were a team of mainly Jewish boys a little taller than 5 feet, on average. When they saw all 5 feet of me, with "Buddy Holly" glasses and the long jumper down to my knees, they thought I was the mascot. In the first few minutes, the ball came to me and I collected it. Their enormous centre forward came thundering towards me; as shoulder-to-shoulder barging was legal, our captain, who had sheltered the ball for me to collect, said, "Go easy on him, he is only little." The forward took pity and walked away. By the end of the first half, we only trailed by one goal. I had been kept busy, goalkeeping tolerably competently.

At the beginning of the second half, they attacked and their centre forward hit a fierce shot straight at me. It went straight through my hands, hitting me between the eyes. The world became a blur. My spectacles split and the elastic catapulted them to the back of the net with the ball. Being half blinded by my myopia, I was sent to play in a quiet corner of the field. I found I could not see the ball until it was passed to me or hit me in the face, so I was put back in goal. My short sight blurred the ball, making it appear larger. I constantly misjudged its size, causing it to hit me between the eyes. We lost thirteen nil. Despite this, we jointly won the regional five-a-side competition.

I left school still opening the first cricket team batting and bowling, and was still the first team goalkeeper. Perhaps I had inherited my father's golden hands and a small amount of his fearlessness. Perhaps my father's cruelty taught me to tackle obstacles and persist until they were overcome. How much of this was due to my desperate attempts to have a more normal life or inherited resilience is uncertain.

I left school with a few O Levels (GCEs). I continued to struggled with concentration. I was still trying to develop my values. I considered the ethics underlying Judaeo-Christian beliefs, the Ten Commandments, Christian charity, pacifism, and humanism. Although, having made the leap from non-faith into atheism, I retained a set of ethics to live by. Given this existence I had been miraculously gifted, I spent much time on how I should behave. I had been introduced to the ideas of Marx, and most seemed just. My pacifism precluded revolution. I finally rejected active politics and politicians. I hated their hypocrisy and sophistry. I avoided the risks of doing harm to others by setting my life's direction towards reducing suffering by healing. This was clearly related to my parentification. I had become a dedicated carer of my mother. I eventually came to the belief that no other life than that of a doctor allowed me to live by my principals. I became determined to prevent physical and psychic pain.

I had by then learned to use the quiet space of reference libraries as a sanctuary. I also discovered that to enter the paramedical professions, you needed the same exam results as medicine but at lower grades. This gave me an objective and the hope that I might reach it.

Working for and obtaining the requisite results by part-time evening study while washing up in a coffee bar, one of many jobs, I applied to the prestigious London medical schools. Not surprisingly, this was without success. Medical school entry in the early 1960s was like passing through the proverbial "eye of a needle." They were suffused with class prejudice and a large and undisguised measure of anti-Semitism.

The wise elders of our Jewish communities had for many generations understood that if you provided spaces and opportunities for young people to enjoy youthful occupations such as pop music, dancing, and table tennis, they would meet and make friendships with members of the opposite sex and of the chosen religion. These were youth clubs. Fortunately, for my further adjustment, there were several local Jewish youth clubs that I attended, Stepney Club being the nearest. In this community, which was skilfully managed, so relatively accepting and predictable as compared to the chaos of my home life, I began to blossom, cherishing this place where I gained the friendship and the respect of my peers.

I met Leah at the youth club. She looked older than her 15 years old. She was a pretty, natural blonde. She had set her sights on becoming a hairdresser and left school to start an apprenticeship at 16. She was my first girlfriend. She had a natural intelligence and a happy disposition. She laughed spontaneously and easily. We got on well. I was welcomed by her family. I was Jewish and I suppose I had good prospects. The chance of being accepted into what I hoped was a more normal family and an alternative to my dysfunctional home was a strong but unconscious factor. Her mother was a matriarch. She ruled the home with an iron will. Her warm and gentle father was kept under the thumb in all matters, except for an extravagant flyer's moustache that he defiantly wore. We got on well, and I spent as much time at the youth club and Leah's home as I could. They were havens of sanity from my family. They were at that time one of my few salvations. After being appointed club captain, I had regular contact with the management. A new club manager was appointed, who I immediately got on with. He was Peter Janusch Pallai. He was a Hungarian student who had escaped from the Russian forces during the armed repression of the student uprising in 1958. He was also an Olympic athlete in two disciplines, kayaking and swimming – a remarkable achievement. The English universities had set up English courses for escaped students and they were enabled to finish their degrees. He completed his degree in sociology at the London School of Economics. He won the annual kayaking competition on the Serpentine lake in Hyde Park every year for a decade. He loved jazz and found employment with the BBC World Service Hungarian section with a regular music programme. He also became a BBC political correspondent. He encouraged me to swim competitively and included me in some of his social life. By this time, I had developed my intellectual skills. He always showed respect for my opinions. He knew of my childhood in Bergen-Belsen concentration camp and he regarded me as a Holocaust survivor. He was Jewish and a few years older than me, and he had survived the Nazi Holocaust in Hungary. When I asked him about how he survived and avoided being sent to Auschwitz, the fate of most of Hungary's Jewish children, he dismissed his time as a Jewish hidden child as insignificant compared to my survival in Belsen. Yet he was undoubtably a child survivor of the Holocaust. The Jewish youth clubs had residential hostels attached to them in which a number of child survivors were living. There, I met two of the famous orphaned children that were found in camps when toddlers. They were sent to special Jewish orphanages, Brocklebank and Lingfield, and their care was guided by Anna Freud. Dennis was a distinctive teenager with a shock of red, curly hair. He rarely spoke. Hunka was pretty and had striking black hair. She was so young during the Holocaust that she knew next to nothing of her family or her identity. I met her in Jerusalem 40 years later after she had found her twin in Israel. They had been the subject of experiments by Dr Mengele, the "Angel of Death," in Auschwitz.

I went out with Leah for a relatively short time before our parents were pushing us into getting engaged. We were young and immature and were not able to resist our parents' pressure, nor could we judge whether we would be happy. Our Jewish wedding cost Leah's parents their life savings. My behaviour was more sociable but suffused with overcompensation for my past humiliations, making me attention-seeking and distinctly unlikeable. I had by this time met several women whose company I enjoyed more than Leah's and with whom I would have had a far better marriage. But I did not have the strength to oppose my parents and call off the wedding, even though I had such strong doubts. Perhaps predictably, but still to my surprise, our marriage developed into a version of that of my parents'. I became intensely controlling and possessive. Leah put up with me for only 11 months before she left. I have no doubt it was the right thing for her to do. On reflection now, I hope I did not ruin her life. I never heard from her nor found out what she did with her life. She understandably avoided her painfully controlling mother and had no contact with her family after she left. No one heard anything of her for several years and I obtained a divorce as soon as I could.

After several years, my father had his first heart attack at age 47. He had recently moved from his first tiny back-room barbershop, adjacent to the London Hospital, to much larger premises nearby. Although it was initially successful, it was not financially viable if he could not work. Heart attacks in the 1960s were often fatal or meant severe disablement and restriction. The uncertainty of his future obliged me to leave my scientific work to learn how to cut hair to support my parents and save him from bankruptcy. I had been sent to life-drawing classes at art school at 15 and had been accepted for art school training. Perhaps this enabled me to learn and become competent in cutting hair in six weeks. When he recovered, my father continued to live in his headstrong way, only heeding the warning regarding ceasing smoking. He worked when he was told to take strict bed rest and he soon recovered. We now know activity was far more rehabilitative than inactivity.

Ironically, many of my father's customers were London Hospital medical staff and students, including a number of the professors. Professor White was a tall, slim man with a gentle English manner. I believe he was a professor of anatomy. He had heard of my ambition to train for medicine. One day, he arrived with some questions from an IQ test. He handed them to me and asked me to try them. I seemed to manage them successfully. We often had interesting conversations when I was cutting his hair, and perhaps he had compared me to the medical students he taught. After the test, he encouraged me to apply for entry to the London Hospital. He knew of our survival from Bergen-Belsen. He was a very decent man and perhaps he had been moved by my Holocaust past. He indicated that he would make efforts on my behalf, and somehow he arranged for me to be interviewed by the dean, the late Professor John Ellis, later elevated to a knighthood. The medical school application forms contained the question, "Where was your father medically educated?" My name was still Garfinkle.

The interview was with three interviewers. We were placed in a circle of low armchairs such that when I answered one interviewer, I could not see the others.

They began by asking "'Garfinkle', that's not an English name?"

To which I responded, "No, it is Polish." I was becoming increasingly uncomfortable.

"I see you were born in 1942." A pause. "That must have been difficult?"

To which I replied that I had been in Bergen-Belsen but was too young to remember it. They wanted to know about my rickets. The interviewers continued to question me about the camp. They seemed much more interested in my Belsen experience than in offering me a place in their prestigious medical school. Eventually, they asked about hobbies and tested my knowledge of the golden age of bel canto, opera singers such as Caruso, Gigli, and Galli-Curci. I felt encouraged by these interest questions. I was on sure ground and knew my subject. I tried to read their faces. They were immaculately polite but inscrutable, like I imagine Foreign Office diplomats would be. It is hard to know if my judgement was correct, but I sensed underneath the politeness no intention of offering me a medical school place. In retrospect, I can now see their logic. I was a known, skilled hairdresser and good with my hands. Dentistry needs surgical dexterity and accuracy. I suppose I acquitted myself adequately or they would not have offered me a place at the dental school. By now, my desire for medical training had intensified, so this offer, which some would have jumped at, was a deep disappointment. The mere fact that I had obtained an interview and been offered a dental place made me feel that I was nearer and had some chance if I kept trying. It was a memorable experience, albeit an unpleasant one.

Note

1 *Rickets.* A disease of malnutrition preventing bones from hardening, which causes bowing of the legs due to the softness of the bones.

References

Karpf, A. (1997) *The War After: Living with the Holocaust.* London: Faber & Faber.

Kellermann, N.P.F. (2009) *Holocaust Trauma: Psychological Effects and Treatment.* New York: iUniverse.

Robertson, J. (1952) Some responses of young children to loss of maternal care. *Nursing Times* 49: 382–386.

Chapter 4

Escape

Introduction

I met my future wife, Diana, at a dinner party. She had been invited by the married medical student living in the attic flat above my father's shop. They politely asked me to join them to make up the foursome. Surprisingly, Diana and I got on. She was an only child and not the most confident of persons. She was training to become a social worker. As we talked, I quickly learned she had a strong sense of public service and was deeply compassionate. This we shared, as well as our ethical and social values, which created a strong bond. Her father was a policeman and her mother a retired nursery nurse. They had clear moral values that they lived by, for which I deeply respected them. Her parents had a love of culture, classical music, literature, art, and current affairs. They were members of the Workers' Educational Association (WEA). This was a noble adult educational institution founded by the trade unions for working folk who wished to better themselves. They had meetings every weekend to listen to music or discuss the politics of the day. Although I did not take up the art school training, my passion for fine art continued to grow. I regularly walked to the National Gallery to enjoy the masterpieces. At the youth club, I had attended opera appreciation classes. My father had introduced me to the singing of Gigli when I was 7 and I developed a great love of his beautiful voice. Listening to classical music and beautiful singing was like an opiate drug. It took me away from my constant tensions to an inner place of peace and sanctuary. At the library, I was avidly reading the works of important writers and philosophers. They also lent out classical music records.

Diana was a talented amateur pianist and cellist. Our shared love of classical music as well as ethical values created a strong bond as the basis for our relationship. After some years working in the Tower Hamlets children's social work department, the stress forced her to seek less stressful work. I persuaded her to train as a teacher specialising in music. This was an inspired choice, and her life and our relationship improved immeasurably. We soon had our home filled with live music, piano, chamber music, and singing. We also made some important lifelong friends who shared our musical life. Most importantly, Diana, not being Jewish, did not evoke my dysfunctional behaviour. This had been my response in my first marriage, in which I re-enacted my father's controlling dysfunctional behaviour of our survivor family. My behaviour was more thoughtful and reasonable. I respected Diana for her devotion to disadvantaged children of the East End. She had trained as a social worker with the specific goal of becoming a childcare specialist in Tower Hamlets. She knew of the poverty and deprivation of the East End. Nor was she religious. Perhaps conversations with her mother, who had run a children's nursery, had shaped her values. Diana knew from our conversations that I was not interested in just making money, but was determined to become a doctor, to become a healer. It would, if given the chance, become my vocation. She shared these values and beliefs and supported my hope to study medicine. She encouraged my ambition. I was still running my father's hairdressing salon. A surprising number of customers had missed out on their education due to poverty. A number were black cab drivers who joined the new Open University, which allowed older adults with families to study part-time and obtain degrees. They aimed to become lecturers and encouraged me in my ambitions and followed my progress. My efforts to gain a place were followed by two old friends who had succeeded in joining professions. They encouraged and advised me. I left full-time hairdressing, choosing computer programming and systems analysis for the Post Office. I became a civil servant. I continued to work as a hairdresser on weekends to allow my parents to have holidays. The money helped us to obtain and furnish a home.

After almost ten years, I began fresh efforts to gain entry to medical school. After several years of applications, I was offered a place at Sheffield University Medical School, on the condition that I had to retake a key A-level exam to achieve a top grade. I was elated. This was a once in a lifetime opportunity to devote my life to a noble and learned profession. On starting, and despite being ten years older than my peers, I was 29 years old. I shared and, in many cases, exceeded their idealism. I now understand that one of my unconscious motives for becoming a healer was in order to heal my own wounds and especially my family's Holocaust wounds. My friends were progressing in their careers and my East End peers were entering the Open University. It was unusual for a hairdresser to go to medical school. Apart from becoming part of the East End gossip, it gave encouragement to the cab drivers, all of whom made careers in the Open University.

In my pre-clinical years, I wrote a dissertation on maternal deprivation.[1] This, I believe, was unconsciously motivated by my maternal deprivation when sent to the children's home. During my medical school psychiatric attachment, I met and began training in psychotherapy with Dr Colin Woodmansey. He was a famous senior child psychoanalyst and child psychiatrist at the prestigious Sheffield Children's Hospital. Our first child, Anna, was born the day before Woodmansey's first tutorial, in which he gave all his students his paper entitled "The transmission of problems from parents to children." Another seeming miracle: to find a role model who also shared my desire to heal psychic wounds and shared my perspective. Woodmansey had acquired a notorious reputation and was greatly feared by the students and his less psychologically minded colleagues because he maintained a constant psychoanalytic, reflective stance. This meant when spoken to, he did not immediately respond. He would be silent and show no emotion while he considered a response, if any. He often simply received a communication with silence or reflected back what the communication was. That is, he acknowledged he had received the communication and he would think about it, but rarely responded immediately. This was found immensely intimidating by most of his colleagues and students. This, I suspect, was needed as a defence to survive the continual envious attacks he suffered from his colleagues. They seem to have felt threatened by his capacity to maintain his ability to reflect, think analytically, and not retaliate despite their envious attacks. His supervision was, of necessity, a mixture of personal therapeutic interpretations as well as instruction regarding the work. The Midlands and the North of England at that time were a psychoanalytic desert, with the oases of only three psychoanalysts working there. Thus, a personal analysis or therapy while training was unavailable. Towards the end of my medical training and just after the birth of our second daughter, Diana suffered a loss of vision in one part of her eye. This was the first possible sign of my wife's multiple sclerosis (MS). This seemed another example in my life in which success was always followed by a disaster around the next corner. This was the price for getting into medical school. I studied the textbooks. They suggested there was a 60 per cent chance this could be a solitary attack, so I decided that I would keep the possible diagnosis a secret. At that time, the diagnosis of MS, like cancer, could be more terrifying than the illness. In discussion with the dean, who was also my social tutor, it emerged that I was now obliged to abandon all hopes of a specialist psychotherapy career, which would need the support of a stable home life for ten years to facilitate my studies. The dean advised me to become a general practitioner in London and live near to my mother-in-law, who could act as a safety net to look after the children should Diana become ill. This decision to keep the diagnosis secret seemed rational and may have related to my mother's example of how to deal with bad news: secrecy and overprotectiveness. It resulted in becoming an overwhelming psychic burden and made me constantly anxious and stressed. This led me to fail my final examinations despite my success in all exams so far. I was obliged to resit them, fortunately passing at the second attempt. I had been advised by one of the two friends I had made at school, who was a doctor, to take an independent qualifying medical exam run by the Royal Colleges of Medicine and Surgery as a plan B. This took place at the Royal College of Surgery in London. By another coincidence, the visiting and head examiner was my college dean and social tutor who had been advising me. I had underestimated the impact of knowing many of the senior professors in my medical school from my medical ethics activities. I had become president of the student body, the Sheffield Medical Group, and had organised debates and conferences on the subject of ethical controversies such as abortion, which was not legal, and treating dying patients. Knowing my senior examiners and failing had been a traumatic and shaming process.

Being in London, with all the examiners and candidates being strangers, I felt under less pressure and passed sufficiently well to merit a distinction oral exam known as a viva voce. I did not think beyond the week of constant exams to find out about the passing out ceremony. All the successful candidates, myself included, were marched single file into one side of the long room of the Royal College of Surgeons. Then, from another door, the examiners, led by my dean, Professor Duthie, as the head examiner, filed in opposite us. I was the only candidate from Sheffield. Our eyes met and a smile crossed his lips when he gave me a long knowing look from across the hall when all the examiners bowed to us, as we were now doctors and fellow members of the Royal College. I felt a special sense of satisfaction that after all the help Professor Duthie had given me, I had represented our medical school, mine and his, and had not let the honour of the school down. I also felt a belated sense of relief. This ceremony coincided with my nephew's bar mitzvah that evening, and my medical school friend, who had guided me and advised me to take the exam, was a guest and could share the joy of Diana, my family, and my friends in my finally qualifying. Diana wore a beautiful silk suit and looked radiant. A rare, truly happy day. I was 35 years old.

I entered general practice training with idealism as well as a determination to continue learning and practising psychotherapy. In 1979, at Claybury Psychiatric Hospital, I was appointed to the post of honorary psychotherapist. After a few years, I asked the consultant to suggest a psychoanalyst as I felt a strong need for psychotherapeutic help. Perhaps it was the impending sense of doom regarding Diana's illness. I took the three potential psychoanalysts to Woodmansey, who selected Ann Hayman, who had recently become a training psychoanalyst. I was so needy that there was no question of my interviewing her to see if I felt comfortable with her. It was like the opening of the floodgates of my psyche. I went straight into four-times-a-week analysis. As I was approaching the age of 40, the issue of applying to the Institute of Psychoanalysis became a matter of urgency. I had not had much psychoanalysis and was far from ready, but the application was necessary or I could not have applied later. Of course, I was rejected by the Institute.

Something that, in retrospect, became increasingly clear to me was how much I needed the quality of warmth in my psychoanalyst. If Dr Hayman had it, I never felt it. I am also aware that when reflecting on this, I find myself struggling with my maternal transference and parentification, which produces a tendency to overprotect the women with whom I have a caring relationship. I experienced Dr Hayman as cold. Suffering severe early trauma, causing the borderline personality disorders of insecure attachment and intense separation anxiety, I now realise this sensitivity to warmth, its presence or absence, is part of what the abused, the silent watchful child, watches for. This need is transformed into hope and yearning that safe warmth will be available. Its presence may act as a magnet. It may also be misused. When I reflected on warmth and its psychic derivation, I concluded it related to an unconscious aspect of the psyche that tolerated and did not regard neediness in another as a potentially dangerous quality that needed defending against. Coldness might be thought to be the psychic maintaining of distance when in the presence of neediness and a yearning for proximity. I had noticed in my early psychotherapy work a great need to understand the patient's communications and the finding of the optimal intervention. As I developed in experience and security, I tolerated uncertainty more and seemed to become more readily available to be used as a containing object. This felt as though my inner warmth seemed to become more accessible to me and my patients. It might be considered to be a maternal, but genderless, containing capacity.

It is very difficult making a judgement on one's own psychoanalysis. There is no doubt I learned a great deal about my unconscious. My impression was that her technique seemed impeccable and flawless. Did we address my Holocaust childhood? On one occasion, when I began talking about it, she commented that I kept going back to it, as though this was reprehensible. I felt this was an admonishment. Whether this was so or just my hypersensitivity, I cannot be sure. Perhaps, like the admonishment of my mother, I felt this was now forbidden. We were in the middle and late 1980s. Some years later, when I was more familiar with the literature, I realised that psychoanalytic theory had not successfully met the challenge of understanding and treating Holocaust trauma. Of the many Holocaust survivors I knew that had undergone psychoanalysis, virtually all were hostile to it. I still defended it as it seemed to me that psychoanalysis, with its constantly developing and self-critical body of theory, was the only discipline that tried to understand the psyche of trauma victims. However, I found the psychoanalytic literature unhelpful. At that time, the prevailing view based on classical theory suggested that survivor guilt was due to unconscious destructive, possibly murderous, fantasies regarding lost loved ones and the process of identification with the aggressor, and that survivors' symptoms were due to unresolved grief obstructed by these psychic processes. This seems a shallow and inadequate theoretical explanation. It does not provide insight into my community of survivors or my survivor family.

My life as a doctor was rapidly developing. General practice was not the second-class and second-rate sub-speciality suggested by the prejudices prevailing at medical school. Gaining competence and adequate knowledge in most fields of medicine required for the care of my patients was a demanding challenge. One of the greatest intellectual challenges came from confronting the many medical conditions that were neither well understood nor their treatment established. In order to make sound judgements regarding the best way to help patients, examination of the prevailing explanatory hypotheses, the aetiology, was required, and when found wanting necessitated the construction of new working hypotheses. These were constantly empirically tested and amended according to the available evidence and clinical experience. Patients suffer many common, chronic conditions that are treatable but incurable. Thus, finding accessible ways of understanding disease processes to offer to the sufferer was needed to assist them to live with their condition. Developing this skill had a great impact on my work and thinking. This constant examination of hypotheses and the selection or construction of alternatives became invaluable when studying the developing body of psychic trauma theory.

By the 1980s, I had rebuilt my life through my happy marriage, two lovely daughters, and a fulfilling professional life. Diana had shown no signs of MS for seven years. Our social life was full of interesting friends. Our home echoed to the sound of the piano, cello, chamber music, and singing. Our leisure time was filled with the enjoyment of art and culture. I felt I had managed to put my survivor past behind me and escaped into the pleasures of middle-class English life. Sadly, the MS returned. By 1988, my wife was dying from brainstem MS, its cruellest form. Despite my medical skills, I was helpless to prevent its painful progress or protect my daughters from the sight of their mother suffering and slowly dying. Watching her wasting away, paralysed, mute, and blind was like watching the *Muselmänner*,[2] the living dead in Bergen-Belsen. My Holocaust past had returned. Our friends were horrified by Diana's illness and most abandoned us. Perhaps they were terrified by the disease? Perhaps they felt helpless? Whatever their reasons, it meant I found myself alone, caring for my daughters, running my practice, and constantly watching over her care. I would not, could not, abandon her to impersonal hospital care. I knew that even in a coma, she could hear music, and ensured she had her beloved music to listen to. Whenever I visited her, I would check her notes and also that she was properly cared for. This always left me tortured by her suffering and my helplessness. My daughters could only rarely face seeing her suffering. There was no treatment and she was not of interest on the acute neurology ward. Her treatment would now be understood as palliative, compassionate care for the dying. Medical practice had not caught up with this medical need. Hospices for cancer sufferers were just being opened. Having developed a working relationship with the director of St Joseph's, the local Catholic hospice, I decided to ask if they could accept Diana. Fortunately, the new director could see how appropriate this was and she was admitted. Thankfully, this transformed her last few months. When she entered her final days, I wanted to ensure she did not feel abandoned. That she heard a familiar voice. Felt a loving touch. Sadly, her young body fought on. It took three days and nights for her to end her struggle. I arranged a funeral full of her beloved Schubert and Mozart. Her funeral was filled with love and sublime music.

Having now become severely isolated, I feared that when my parents, whose health was always a preoccupation, had died, I would be condemned to a lonely life of work and social isolation. I feared that my children would be burdened by the problems I had suffered in my childhood, that of an isolated nuclear family. I now realise I falsely projected this on to them as they did have an extended family on their mother's side.

A small consolation for my children and for me were the annual French rural holidays we took. I loved France and was happiest when in the tranquillity of the French countryside, enjoying the French love of good food and wine. Throughout their childhood, we holidayed there. I had not consciously associated it as the first country I lived in where I was not persecuted or in danger. We take for granted the wonderful aroma of fresh coffee and baked bread. We forget that the French bake fresh bread twice a day and fill the streets with these wonderful scents. The French insist that even simple food is cooked as skilfully as possible, and ordinary food from a café, such as a ham or a cheese baguette, is delicious. Fresh bread and butter for breakfast was a delicacy I only found in France, making the journey worthwhile. Perhaps the experience of living in France after our liberation has left an indelible mark on my memory. At school, I was always asked to read aloud in the French class. Perhaps the sound of French is deep in my heart and associated with freedom.

Due to the perceived insult described earlier, my father had avoided contact with most of his surviving French family for 45 years. After several years of attempts, I managed to persuade my father to give me a contact address in Strasbourg he had kept secretly. I knew he had it because we received Jewish New Year cards from André. I immediately made contact and arranged to visit them with my parents. This was a revelatory experience. I arranged to meet Marcel, my cousin, first. When we met, I was astonished by something that for most would not be surprising or exceptional. Marcel and I shared a strong facial resemblance and body proportions. I shared some of my parents' facial features, but until now had never met anyone who shared our distinctive appearance. I resembled Marcel even more closely than my father. We could have been twin brothers.

My father was self-conscious and ill at ease in these middle-class French social situations. He said little and was very watchful. When we got back to our hotel after our first contact, my father began to comment on the qualities of *his* family. He continued to talk about *his* family. When eventually I realised this, I corrected him, but he was unwilling to accept they were also *our* family. In his mind, they were solely *his* family, not his wife's or his children's. The murder of almost all his family had not, could not have been fully mourned, and made him pathologically possessive of them. They were like a psychic stockpile of food or jewels to be turned to in case of special need. Perhaps the annihilation threats of the Holocaust created a deep need for psychic objects to be turned to in times of need that were more likely to be trusted. He seemed to be psychically storing them in a secret place so no one could steal them. He had no insight into what he was doing or the impact it might have on the rest of his immediate family.

This contact with family with which shared genes had created a deep biological connection is taken for granted by non-survivors. Its impact reduced the intensity of the isolation I found myself in. This was further helped by André Rottler. He was my great-uncle (i.e. my father's uncle), even though he was younger than my father. This relationship was created by my great-grandfather remarrying after his first wife died. He had nine children from his first marriage.

He had a further seven children with his second wife. My father was born to the eldest child and André was approximately fourteenth. André was very kind and helpful. He took us to the local Jewish cemetery to the grave of my great-grandfather, Nathan Rottler. This was the first grave I had seen of any of my relatives. This created a direct line through my father, through his Hungarian mother to my Polish great-grandfather. This was the first concrete connection with my roots. This further eased my lack of family connections and my sense of isolation. As a Holocaust survivor living in a country in which you are a refugee and a member of a persecuted minority, you are isolated by several layers of disconnections. You do not belong to the Christian majority. You do not belong to Poland. There is no Jewish community or family to feel connected or attached to in Poland. Although a Jewish Holocaust survivor, you do not feel attached to the English Jewish community. With no accessible known relatives or graves, there are no family or roots to attach to. Language difficulties, particularly a foreign accent and foreign values, generate ways that separate and distinguish you from the indigents. These are the experiences of many refugee children, especially survivors of genocides.

My father died in 1990, a year after Diana. He was very proud of my title of doctor. Our intense rivalry made it difficult for him to admit it openly to me. Just before he died, he was admitted to hospital and we were talking about his time in the Russian Army. He remembered that he had never received any pay or recognition from the Soviet authorities. He was toying with the idea of contacting the Russian embassy and obtaining a service medal. The idea of official Russian recognition pleased him greatly. Because I had discovered so much about our past, I was no longer excluded from his world of survivorship. We were both amused by our discussion and there was an ease and closeness I had never achieved before. He seemed to be recovering from his illness necessitating his hospital admission, and I felt able and obliged to leave for a promised French family holiday I had promised my daughters after their mother died. Sadly, he died two days later.

In the years following my father's death, Josef Schwammberger, the senior Nazi of the Przemysl ghetto, was extradited for war crimes from Argentina and sent to trial in Stuttgart, Germany. My uncle, Zigmund Kellermann, had been his personal slave. He had witnessed many of his crimes.

I joined my cousin, Alfred, to see my uncle give evidence. I sometimes wonder if Alfred was named after me on the assumption I had died in the Holocaust.

This was my chance to look into the face of the Nazi who was responsible for the murder of so many of my family (Freiwald & Mendelsohn, 1994). The courtroom was a modern and light building. I was only a few feet from the dock and Schwammberger's seat. I was hoping for him to be distinctive, ugly, or sinister. When he was brought, in I was shocked to see a short, frail, white-haired old man. He was hard to see because he was so small. There was nothing sinister about him until you looked into his ice-cold, blue eyes. During his evidence, and before my uncle appeared, he was calm and steady in his answers. He was unmoved. When my uncle stood up to testify, he looked at him carefully, and after a while a look of recognition slowly appeared. Then he looked shocked and concerned. He may have remembered my uncle's uniquely advantageous viewpoint to witness his crimes. He was his driver. My uncle gave clear and powerful eyewitness evidence of how he had seen him personally shoot and murder a number of Jewish ghetto prisoners. He was able to give dates and times and locations. He had a fine memory. I am told this ensured Schwammberger received a life sentence. At the end of the court session, we left. Alfred was proud of his father and triumphant at his damning evidence. I was left perplexed. I had no hate for this man. I could not hate some anonymous figure. Intellectually, I knew he was responsible for my maternal grandparents' death, as well as those of my two maternal uncles, Mundek and Abrumek, and of my pregnant aunt, Lolla. Yet this knowledge had no impact. The only person I had hated was my father for the terror and pain to which he had subjected me and our family.

While I was struggling with this dilemma, my cousin, Alfred, asked me what I thought my father would have done had he been here. He suggested that perhaps he would have done what he did at Berchtesgaden (known as Hitler's lair). I had forgotten the story, and Alfred reminded me. When my uncle, Zigu, had taken my parents on one of their several tours of Germany, the coach was just approaching the building when my father shouted, "Stop, stop, I must get out." My father's history of heart disease made my uncle think he was suffering a heart attack. My uncle stressed the urgency to stop for my father. The coach stopped and the doors opened. My father staggered out through the coach full of German tourists, all looking at him for having insisted the coach stop. He staggered over to the wall of the building. He then unzipped his trousers and urinated openly, spraying all over the wall. He then calmly turned and, getting back into the coach, declared loudly in German, "I could not help myself. I had to piss on Hitler's memory."

He was fearless, always doing the unexpected. I find myself struggling with the memory of his abusive cruelty, and at the same time I am filled with amusement and admiration. He was a lovable rogue, and I suppose I had forgiven him after or perhaps even before his recent death.

Zigmund Kellerman, Zigu, and his wife, Dorcha, were good friends of my parents before the Holocaust. My parents remembered lending them my mother's wedding ring with which to get married. Before the war, Zigu had helped his father to drive buses all over the area and knew it intimately. I remember him having laughing eyes, a winning smile, and a fine head of wavy, auburn hair. We were always taught that non-Jewish, Aryan good looks helped you survive.

Zigu had found work under the Russians in their barrack kitchens. While he worked in the kitchen, he and Dorcha never went hungry. He never forgot this lesson. After the war, his constant preoccupation was food. His solution to all health problems was his lovingly cooked cuisine. When Dorcha went into hospital for uncontrolled diabetes, he did not allow her to eat hospital food, but brought in his specially prepared meals. A diabetic diet meant nothing to him. As far as he was concerned, his home cooking cured everything.

After Dorcha died, he talked of nothing but his Holocaust exploits. He never listened to others and he dominated any conversation with tales of his exploits. The mixture of the danger of being Schwammberger's driver, as well as its excitement, were constantly present. He explained that he only survived because Schwammberger had warned him to hide when the liquidation of the ghetto was imminent. His relationship with Schwammberger was a strange mixture of fear and gratitude. Was this an example of Stockholm syndrome as well as identification with the aggressor (Freud, 1938)?

After the liberation, the Polish nationalists were such a threat that he was also obliged to flee. He fled to Germany. When he had settled, he was given compensation from the German government. He took it in the form of buses, his familiar family trade. His solution brought him considerable wealth but no peace. He settled in Central Germany. He still hated the Germans. He attended synagogue regularly but declared he only went to have contact with fellow Jews. He had lost his faith. His mother was a pious woman, fasting and praying one day every week. He was filled with bitterness when he asked why God had not protected her, and instead allowed her to be shot in a mass grave in the woods outside their village.

The lessons of his survival took him to Germany within the enemy camp. His wealth did not protect him from family miseries. His family life was filled with many of the tensions and disputes seen in refugee families today. He had broken off all contact with his closest surviving relative and his relationship with his children was always strained. In 1991, he returned to Poland to commemorate the fiftieth anniversary of the murder of his family. I accompanied him with his sons. He also took us back to Przemysl to show us the cellar where he hid for 11 months and to show me where I was born. I was terrified the whole time.

My parents and I visited him in Germany whenever we could. Dorcha was always talking about the events of the Holocaust. She always returned to the time when some young men who had lived in their apartment block had tried to escape and were hung in the square. All were forced to watch. They talked of lost family and how they longed to find those who might have survived. They were forever searching.

Diana's illness had put all thoughts of psychoanalytic training on hold. At that time, I thought of myself as a child of survivors. I contacted the head of the 45 Aid Society. In 1945, the British government were informed that there were many orphaned children found in the concentration camps. They permitted 1,000 to be brought to England. Eventually, only 732 arrived. They ranged from teenagers to small babies. The youngest were cared for in a house on the edge of Lingfield Park Racecourse. The Jewish carers contacted Anna Freud for advice on how to look after these traumatised orphans (Freud & Dann, 1951). The 45 Aid Society acted like surrogate family to each other, but eventually dispersed, with many lifelong friendships having been made. They continue to meet in annual reunions. Ben Helfgott, their leader, was liberated from the Buchenwald concentration camp in an emaciated state yet he retained great physical and inner strength. He soon became a British champion weightlifter and represented Great Britain in the post-war 1948 Olympic Games. Ben has devoted his life to the support of the survivor community. When I contacted him, he advised me to attend the first gathering of children of survivors in Jerusalem in late December 1988.

In my childhood learned Jewish daily prayer, "Shema Yisrael," Jerusalem was yearned for. Now I was here in the midst of hundreds of fellow children of survivors. On the first day in this beloved city and beloved country where I am not a persecuted refugee, the programme opened with the singing of the plaintive lament "Ailie, Ailie," "Lord, why have you abandoned me?" The women began humming softly and I wept silently. The tears streamed down my face. I was no longer alone. After a lifetime of secret inner struggle. Always solitary. Constantly watchful. I had found a haven. I had come home.

The talks by children of survivors were of lifelong struggles like my own. The groups were filled with those whose parental interactions were also full of pain. I linked with another Alfred whose father had beaten him mercilessly. Soulmates were found in every corner. My silent watchfulness was not needed. I shed my defences and was able to speak openly and freely. My emergence was noticed by my peers. From guarded silence, I began to glow, radiating a warmth and light seen by all around me. The conference ended and I was still dazed by the emotional impact. I returned to London filled with a determination to somehow continue the healing processes I had discovered. I contacted those who had also returned to London and arranged for us to start our own group for children of survivors. We met for eight years. By the time the group ended, several of us had made important changes in our lives. Ann Karpf had completed her book *The War After* and had her first child. David Fainman had become a consultant psychotherapist at a prestigious hospital. Diana had died, and I had remarried and begun our new family.

Eva Fogelman from New York, who ran pioneering groups for survivors and their children, had reminded me I was a child survivor. She encouraged me to talk with the eminent child psychoanalyst Judith Kestenberg. Kestenberg, a Polish refugee, was probably the first psychoanalyst to recognise the suffering of children in the Holocaust. I was now determined to start a psychosocial group for child survivors. In England, I heard a radio programme with Jack Santcross describing his experiences in Bergen-Belsen and his liberation from a train by Russian cavalry. This was our story. I had never heard anyone outside of my immediate family tell it. When I contacted him, Jack wanted to help. He had heard of gatherings of child survivors in the US. He gave me the contact details and I attended my first gathering in the summer of 1989 in California. I was seated on the British table for the Lingfield children who were recording further testimony for Sarah Moskovitz. The early interviews were used for her book *Love despite Hate* (1983). The leader was a feisty, sharp-eyed, tiny lady. She wanted to know what I was doing on their table. I explained my story and she checked every detail. After an intense grilling, she permitted me to join her group of special child survivors who she cared for like a lioness with her cubs.

That was Joanna. I met others who had been on the lost train from Belsen. I cannot forget a young woman who had been in Auschwitz and whose mind and body were still broken by Dr Mengele. She wrote the most moving poetry. The groups for fellow child survivors were intense, powerful, and healing. I still find it hard to describe the experience. For the first time in my life, I was able to safely discuss my innermost pain and struggles with those that shared my Holocaust experience. Simply being in each other's company was healing. I did not think it possible that any experience could surpass the Jerusalem gathering. This proved to be many times more powerful and healing.

On my return to London, I was greatly re-energised but deeply frustrated. I could not wait until next year's gathering. It was so obvious that groups for child survivors of the Holocaust were uniquely healing, yet there were none in England. Ben's 45 Aid Society only met annually for a reunion. I was determined to rectify this and, together with Jack Santcross and another fellow Bergen-Belsen child survivor, John Fransman, I arranged the first gathering of the Child Survivors' Association of Great Britain in September 1989. Jack had a vision of a Holocaust Survivors' Centre. I joined the organising committee, and when Jack resigned I became treasurer and editor of the newsletter. I had by this time met and been interviewed by Judith Kestenberg. I was secretly determined to somehow organise a specialist psychotherapy group for child survivors in London. We began meeting every month and were greatly heartened when the Holocaust Survivors' Centre was opened in North London and the Child Survivor Group was one of the three founding groups of the centre. Soon we were able to find enough participants to form a therapy group conducted by Earl Hopper. Although I played a part in its formation, I knew I needed the group as much as any of the child survivors. When my new wife, Yvonne, became pregnant, we discovered the child was male. We were both shocked and terrified, as well as delighted. Both our pasts had been full of disasters. We shared the fear that if things were going too well, disaster would soon follow. Having our three children two years apart was both wonderful and terrifying. I am still filled with love and wonder when I look back at their births. They were beautiful and happy. They were enjoying the life we had given them. For child survivors, our psychological damage can be so intense that it dominates and controls all our psychic function. It may often prevent us from being available to our children or to be sensitive to their needs. Our own inner scars may obstruct us from sensing our children's needs because our own psychic damage may be evoked, overwhelming and taking us over at a time when our children are asking for holding and sensitive care.

I was still very much involved with the Child Survivor Group and working through my Jewish identity and murdered Holocaust family. I was struggling with my alienation. We named our children after some of my murdered family as well as my newly found Jewish family in France and Israel. I was filled with creative, reparative energy.

In the interim years, I had met some group analysts. They struck me with their warmth and approachability. They lacked much of the arrogance I had all too often felt with psychoanalysts, medical psychotherapists, and psychiatrists. This had a strong impact. My mentor, Colin Woodmansey, was openly dismissive of group psychotherapy; he stated that he did not understand it. Having studied psychoanalytic theory and practice, I felt secure in working with the transference. However, when Diana was becoming more disabled, displaying personality changes that seemed to be affecting our daughters, I arranged systemic family therapy for us all. I was in psychoanalysis at the time and the contrast was considerable. My daughters later reported that they hated it. The focus seemed to try to be open and to have authentic communication about the world we were struggling with, especially Diana's illness and the effect it had on all of us. Diana died soon after in 1989. She was 42 years old.

After the second-generation group had been going for several years, it seemed to be losing its way. We needed guidance, and I was advised by a colleague to consult Earl Hopper, a leading psychoanalyst, which I arranged. I remember being deeply impressed by this consultation. His American accent, his warmth, and his Jewishness, which I had been unconsciously trained to look for, were reassuring and impressive. His tasteful consulting rooms in Hampstead. The interesting paintings on his wall. His obvious intellectual brilliance. He left me with the advice to think about what kind of a group we wanted to have. He declined to take any payment for the consultation, which touched me deeply because I understood it as a sign of compassion for Holocaust survivors in general, and for me in particular. I was also deeply envious.

The strongly held view by most of the group led by Anne Karpf was to continue as a self-help group. I was keen to try to get Earl Hopper to lead us, but this was not accepted. Later I learned of the *Survivor Syndrome* workshop report he had written with Caroline Garland and Lionel Kreeger (Hopper, 2003).

I still hoped to complete a psychotherapy training, and I applied to the Institute of Group Analysis for the qualifying course to train as a group analyst. After the experience of being in the child survivor group run by Dr Hopper, I felt secure enough to join one of his twice-weekly groups.

My father expressed some of his psychic disturbance through his rivalry with me. My achievements were never acknowledged in my presence, and his envy often evoked comparisons with his Holocaust heroism. His obsessional perfectionism was ever-present and persecutory. It was absorbed into my superego as an intense critical faculty that focused on others as well as myself. This was evoked in my group analysis with Dr Hopper. I initially watched him and his technique with great acuteness, checking his technique and insights. I sometimes tried to make observations that pre-empted his possibility for intervention. A successful businesswoman who often missed sessions due to work began to suggest, by her language rather than her direct communications, that she wished to see Dr Hopper for individual therapy arranged around her work. I felt this was about to be suggested by her and I suggested she had this desire.

I believe this rivalry was deeply unconscious, subsumed under my desire to be a good therapist. Actually, I was unconsciously wanting to be as good as Dr Hopper and perhaps I was still reacting to my having been turned down for training by the Institute of Psychoanalysis. Perhaps I was re-enacting my father's internalised envy and rivalry to produce and provoke a crisis and failure in the therapy. This may have been unconscious sabotage. The crisis point came about when I openly challenged Dr Hopper in the group, suggesting he did not understand or empathise with me. Dr Hopper responded in a creative and group-analytic way. He suggested I have a consultation Dr Lionel Kreeger, the senior group analyst and a Kleinian psychoanalyst.

When we met, my rivalry was expressed through my taking a copy of my survivor guilt paper. Dr Kreeger treated me with sensitivity and helped me become aware of my unconscious feelings. He was calm and containing, in contrast to Dr Hopper, who I felt I had provoked into exposing his rage. Dr Kreeger, in my fantasies, I believe represented the benign grandfather I had never had. He enabled me to continue my group analysis with Dr Hopper. However, it meant that beginning my training was delayed by a year. On reflection, bringing Dr Kreeger into this difficult situation was both group-analytic and inspired. I suspect that had I been in the psychoanalytic training, I may have successfully sabotaged it from being rescued.

The abusive humiliations of the children's home experience and my father sensitised me to being assessed. When my first supervisor, who was warm and containing, as well as being a Jewish refugee, retired, I was changed to a new supervisor. The new supervisor seemed constantly critical of me. We clashed strongly and I felt constantly attacked. My past abuse may have played a part in my feeling abused in this supervision. This eventually led to a change of supervisor and another year's prolongation of my training. I owe a debt of gratitude to Liesle Hearst, my first supervisor, Farhad Dallal, and particularly Eva Gottesman, whose final supervision saw me through to my qualification. It followed my traumatic supervision experience and must have been very difficult for her.

A Neo-Nazi patient

When G joined my newly formed training group, what the group noticed was the contrast between his athletic appearance and his sadness. He talked with pride about his sporting achievements and with equal sadness at his failed family life. He attended regularly and benefited from learning from the women about their emotional lives and their emotional intelligence.

After the first year he began to wear military style boots and dressed in T-shirts so his physical fitness could be displayed. He then uncharacteristically missed a session. On his return the following week, when asked, he proudly explained he had been attending an event to support a Holocaust denial historian. This was followed by silence. It hit me like a slap in the face. My countertransference was an overwhelming sense of outrage. It silenced me. I could not wait to get to my therapy session that evening to share my difficulties and to get advice. When I described the events of the day and my disabling rage and outrage I was told by Earl Hopper, my training analyst, to do my job (as my patient's therapist). Hopper knew of my Holocaust childhood. Was I being tested? I spent some hours walking and struggling with my countertransference. Doing my job meant that I must overcome my outrage-induced mental paralysis and think about what had and was happening in my group and with this patient.

G was at home in the world of athletics and strength but the world of strength and its values did not prevent his family breakdown. Understanding slowly emerged. It would seem that his painful family failure had induced a reaction formation of omnipotence turning to racist superiorities and the rejection of inferior people. The idealisation of superiority over weakness.

With the help of the sensitive women in the group he was able to be put in touch with his vulnerabilities and his deep fear and loneliness. He increasingly understood his deep inner fear of helplessness and of abandonment. And how as a consequence, for a while, he came to hate what he saw as weakness. He had used splitting, pursuing the strength while hating weakness. When he was able to explore his childhood trauma he began to work through his encapsulated abandonment. He increasingly explored his childhood trauma and his defensive omnipotence. After about one year his functioning became increasingly emotionally in touch and his omnipotence seemed to disappear.

My initial reaction of outrage might have resulted in my rejection of him through a blocking of my ability to search for psychic meaning. I was struggling in my countertransference with his projections and my projective identification with his omnipotent hate-filled self. Had this predominated I would not have managed to hold him in the group and his need to work through his childhood trauma. Fortunately, through the psychic work we did, he had been able to understand his underlying fear of powerlessness which saved the patient and the group from disintegration.

Psychoanalysis and group analysis

When I look back on my experiences in therapy with my now increased understanding of trauma and its effects on the psyche, much of which has been gained from examination of my own psychic functioning, I realise I have never done so in a systematic and rigorous way. My reflective moments have tended to be reactive to evocative incidents. I will endeavour to do so now.

I have suggested elsewhere that the psyche is organised at three levels of object relations (O/Rs). The primary level is the earliest formed level and is created by internalising the first experience of caring and dependency, the primary caring experience. It is in the realm of the intrapsychic. The secondary group of object relations are the internalised representations of the first relationships with siblings and peers from the extended family and what might be thought of as horizontal relationships, though dependency may

occur. This is the realm of the interpersonal. The third group of object relations are internalised representations of the social. Psychoanalysis focuses on
and works primarily at the level of the primary object relations resonating
through the other levels. When I examine my early experiences, I would
consider excessive experience of annihilation threat as well as neonatal
primal powerlessness to have been present. This I have described as primal
agony (P/A), which I suggest is the most painful emotional experience of
all. Traumatic separation and loss can be seen to have been experienced.
These amount to the traumatic triad (T/T). Insecure attachment and failed
dependency can be seen to have been produced by these early experiences.
As my childhood progressed, it can be seen that parentification as well as
defensive self-isolation developed. The burden of caring for my traumatised
mother became internalised, formative, and developed into a career choice
and a profession. I am like almost all of my colleagues: a wounded healer.

When I began psychoanalysis, I was starved of secure dependency and, of
course, I functioned in my relationships with a degree of personality disorder. Thus, I formed an almost instant strong attachment that was characterised by the insecurity generated by failed dependency and the
watchfulness of the abused child. As my psychoanalysis went on for almost
six years, I am sure Dr Ann Hayman facilitated my increasing feeling of
security. At that time, I was impressed by her seemingly flawless psychoanalytic technique. It took me some 20 years to realise that when you go to
a psychoanalyst, what you get is a psychoanalysis. When in a state of
extreme neediness, you do not think, but yearn for secure holding. Of
course, we explored my fantasies and my behaviour in the transference.
I learned to monitor my psychic process and to reflect on them before
acting on them. However, this was an incomplete and imperfect education,
and it has continued for the rest of my life. Do I look back on this as
a good experience? On the whole, yes. Do I look back on it with fondness?
No. To be fair to Dr Hayman, I must have been a difficult patient. It was
a deeply painful learning experience. The relinquishing of my defences
resulted in my confronting my Holocaust and post-Holocaust pain. It was
also disrupted by Diana's illness, throwing me into survival-mode behaviour.
As I reflect on what I mean by "difficult patient," I think of the effect of
my experience of repeatedly failed dependency, and thus the challenge to
secure my trust. What I have read on the treatment of Holocaust survivors
had been of little help. The prevailing theory was that identification with the
aggressor and one's own aggressive and destructive fantasies caused survivor
guilt and influenced survivors' reactions to their losses, causing the inability to
mourn. Did Dr Hayman contact other psychoanalysts with experience of analysing child survivors? There were some in New York and Israel. I may never
know, and this enquiry might be an example of a disguised sadistic attack to
carry my sense of disappointment, which may have little to do with her.

I had far more overt difficulty in therapy with Dr Hopper, but the benefits I now feel are tangible and great. I cannot recall Dr Hayman addressing

my parentification or my rage and outrage, except when exploring some of my fantasies, particularly one murderous fantasy I repeatedly returned to. She worked in the transference and the symbolic world of my psyche.

My group therapy experiences should be considered in context. It was some years later than my psychoanalysis, and I had explored much more of my Holocaust childhood by then. I believe that Dr Hopper was less constrained by classical theory, being a member of the Independent Group of psychoanalysts as well as having his well-known interest in survivors. However, it should be said that Dr Hayman was a leading member of the Independent Group. My experience of the child survivor therapy group was strongly coloured by the resonances with my dysfunctional survivor family. I found myself frequently overwhelmed by my emotional responses. I recall becoming venomously enraged by an incident in a John Lewis store by a man who I felt was attempting to bully me. I was so enraged that I was prepared to have a fight with this man, who was well over 6 feet. I should add that I am about 5 feet 3 inches in height (1.55 metres). Dr Hopper interpreted this as due to the rage being displaced from him and was evoked by his planned break, a separation anxiety evoked reaction. Perhaps to call it rage or a fight response at a perceived repeated dependency failure would be more accurate. The fact that the group was made up of child survivors allowed our Holocaust trauma to be ever-present and near the surface. It was located in various members at different times and became increasingly manageable. With hindsight, I now see how brave Dr Hopper was in starting this group. We were all deeply traumatised individuals who functioned as severe borderline psychotics, or personality-disordered. We were increasingly contained by the group and Dr Hopper's conductorship so that we learned to listen to one another and reflect more. However, powerful material would be frequently brought in that required all of Dr Hopper's psychoanalytic and group-analytic understanding and technique to contain, unravel, and work with. An important therapeutic factor was the authenticity Dr Hopper displayed in his style of conductorship. Later experience has shown me this is of the greatest importance to those severely traumatised members as they do not readily lower their defences and use their finely tuned antennae to look out for conceit, self-delusion, defensiveness, or dishonesty.

An important issue was rivalry. I think almost all members competed, hoping for the position of favourite. This was skilfully avoided by Dr Hopper. The dynamic of rivalry is often discussed, and rarely has light been thrown on its underlying psychic importance. In a group such as this, anxiety-evoked survival-mode functioning dominates. In my view, rivalry was due to a fear of not being favoured, and thus in an imagined and feared situation where the conductor who represented the omnipotent parent was obliged to choose who would survive. Not being the favourite was associated with increased danger, annihilation anxiety, and powerlessness. Malignant mirroring arose more frequently than usual and I suffered from the unconscious fear of being betrayed. Defensive behaviour by group members that resonated with my family's dysfunction evoked overwhelming emotions in me.

Due to my starting my group-analytic training, I was obliged to leave the survivor group to join a training group after a few years. In the training group, the contrast of my childhood with that of most members caused some tension. It evoked envious attacks and defensive retreat by me. I struggled painfully in all my therapies. How else could it have been?

In a later chapter, I will describe therapeutic child survivor gatherings. These evolved through repetition and reflection to become increasingly effective. Much may be learned from these. However, here I wish to reflect on experiences of my own therapy.

It is my experience as a patient and a therapist that trauma survivors largely communicate by making the therapist feel as they feel through projection and projective identification. These early interactions are ways of testing the therapist to determine if secure dependency, which is longed for, will be available or if they will be failed once again. It requires great skill and sufficient personal therapy and supervision to contain it. The current tendency to entrust such therapy to less experienced therapists is hazardous and may re-traumatise the patient, as well as vicariously traumatising the therapist. Although this idea may have some of its origins in the fantasies of toxicity and contamination that exist in the mind of trauma survivors, what I am suggesting is also a reality.

I gained enormously from psychoanalytic theory and the understanding it gave me in my self-analysis, as well as the means to understand my family, my fellow trauma survivors, and my patients. In recent years, I have worked with trauma victims from all over the world. This has enabled me to develop the theories and some of the understanding I present in this book. My hope is that this legacy may aid those working with trauma survivors such that their suffering may be used creatively.

Notes

1   Michael Rutter, a child psychiatrist at the London Institute of Psychiatry, wrote a seminal volume called *Maternal Deprivation Reassessed* in 1972. This has become a classic.
2   *Muselmänner.* This term was camp slang for those camp prisoners who had lost the will to live and were on the verge of death. They often died where they sat.

References

Freiwald, A. & Mendelsohn, M. (1994) *The Last Nazi: Josef Schwammberger and the Nazi Past.* New York: Norton.

Freud, A. (1938) *The Ego and the Mechanism of Defence.* London: Hogarth Press.

Freud, A. & Dann, S. (1951) An experiment in group upbringing. *Psychoanalytic Study of the Child* 6: 127–169.

Hopper, E. (2003) *The Social Unconscious: Selected Papers.* London: Jessica Kingsley.

Moskovitz, S. (1983) *Love despite Hate: Child Survivors of the Holocaust and Their Adult Lives.* New York: Schocken Books.

Rutter, M. (1972) *Maternal Deprivation Reassessed.* London: Penguin.

Chapter 5

Adaptation and maladaptation

Introduction

In this chapter, I will try to analyse my family by considering the impact of our experiences, beginning with my parents' childhoods. I will then consider our life as refugees and immigrants. Some factors that may have assisted our survival will be sought, and I will explore causations that I believe may relate to our vulnerabilities, adaptations, and resilience. The influences that assisted or obstructed our adaptation to life in peacetime will also be sought. The material that fills this chapter is distinct from the previous biographical material, in that much of it is deeply personal and revealing, and is the result of my lifelong struggle to understand my psychic self and the effects of my Holocaust and post-Holocaust trauma.

Early years

My mother was 15 years old and my father 19 when they first met. Women were said to mature earlier in those hard times. Her early life was certainly not easy. I still find it hard to think of her as little more than a child. They were both small in stature. My mother would barely have reached 4 feet 10 inches and my father 5 feet 2 inches. She had natural, jet-black hair and a slim figure. She was pretty, with well proportioned, petite features. She was bright and had an ease about her. My father had inherited his mother's fine features. He had a luxuriant head of wavy brown hair. As his son, I was oblivious to his good looks. However, when I look at his photos now, it is clear he was handsome, and they made a fine couple. They had married in 1938. Leonia was born later that year.

He was just 20 years old when the Nazis invaded Poland. He was working in the Przemysl station barbershop. This was a fine Austro-Hungarian building. Reflecting on the impact of his birth in London and his childhood move to Poland, I may assume from the warm way he talked about his sisters that they would have made a fuss of their baby brother. He never spoke to me of his early childhood in London and Poland, except that his *zaida* (Yiddish for grandfather) had come to London to his bris, his ritual circumcision, and how his father had died in a typhoid epidemic after returning to Poland. His widowed mother, Gisa, then had no source of income. She had been a homemaker since marrying. She had no trade and she could not feed her children. It was 1927, and Europe was suffering the effects of the Wall Street Crash and the Great Depression. A recession was hitting every country in the Western world and there was no welfare state. Widows in these circumstances found widowers who needed a wife to look after their children, usually with the help of a matchmaker. To avoid starvation, she found and married a widower, Moishe Klein, with three children. In the amalgamated family, there was not enough room for my father. A solution was to find him an apprenticeship to a master barber-surgeon with whom he lived. His pay was his board and lodgings. He never mentioned family visits. He only spoke of his improvised home visits by running away. Being 10 years old, without shoes, walking home was no mean feat. He must have been cold, hungry, and in danger. He hated being separated from his family far more than any risk of danger or punishment. His sharp mind showed in the detail he gave that he always went back to the home of his *bubba*, the Yiddish name for grandmother. This was to avoid the inevitable harsh punishment of his mother and stepfather. In the 1970s, he arranged for his mother's favourite sister, Shari, to visit us in London from Brazil. I remember him asking her if she received the letter and photo they had sent. This showed how old and ill his mother looked. The note on the photo explained her widow-hood and their starvation, having only mouldy bread to eat. Why had she never sent help, he asked. It would have been in 1927. I remember him showing me the picture of his beautiful young mother, who by her late thirties was an old lady, worn out by hardship.

Like many fostered out children, my father idealised his mother. He never openly complained of being sent away from his home and his family, but his description of his repeatedly running away to come home spoke clearly of his unhappiness. He often spoke of how beautiful his mother had been, with her large blue eyes and auburn hair cut short into a bob and her engaging smile. How sadly she had aged before her time. This contrasted with my mother's description of her. She described her as hard and cold. My father was not aware of this contradiction when he told me his mother-in-law, Chaya, took him in without question and treated him so warmly; he was treated better than in his own home. How Chaya would always ask how his day had been. How she respected him and sought his opinion. He described how she always fed him and made him feel welcome and accepted into the family without question. Nevertheless, he still idealised his mother. His face showed deep sadness when speaking of her cruel murder by being burned alive in the synagogue.

Life and trust

Perhaps by the time he was working in Przemyl, he had learned the benefit of wit and charm. He certainly had to learn who he could trust and especially who he should not trust. Knowing he could be soft-hearted, I am sure he would have lent money to gamblers and been caught by their deceptions. He had to learn to read people and not risk his safety with users and deceivers. Gambling was strongly disapproved of in the family. In one of his miraculous ways, he only gambled once or twice a year, and never lost. The first time I saw this, I was a little shocked to see him call the apprentice over very secretly and give him a folded piece of paper with the name of the horse and the race details with his stake money to take to the betting shop. He would never give away any clues to the horse's name, which would double the frustration on the face of the other assistant barber, who would try to persuade him to share the tip. After two hours, the apprentice would be sent to check the result. He always returned with a large grin on his face and the winnings in his hand. Many years after my father died, the apprentice revealed the scam and how he never actually laid a bet; he was always sent with the winnings, ready to return in triumph. He fooled us all for years.

Russian conscription

When the Russians arrived three weeks after the Nazi invasion, some of his adaptations were immediately of benefit. His fluency in all of the languages of the surrounding countries was central. Russians did not tolerate class snobbery. They respected anyone who laboured honestly. They recognised intelligence and were not surprised when they found it in someone from a humble trade. My father was conscripted by the Russians and was quickly promoted to lance corporal. My mother described how he was training her conscripted older brother, many years his senior. His quick promotion demanded respect. He had learned the drills and marching manoeuvres with great speed. She also recalled how her youngest brother, Abrumek, became an ardent communist, a commissar, lecturing and talking on communist theory and politics.

Blitzkrieg

The Nazis had overrun Poland in a few weeks. They were only in eastern Przemysl for three weeks when they withdrew to the west bank of the River San. The new border divided the town following the river. The Molotov–Ribbentrop Pact, between communist Russia and Nazi Germany, had been secretly signed just before the invasion of Poland – a terrible betrayal of the Allies and a huge gift to Hitler. Hitler then knew he did not have to worry about fighting a war on the Eastern Front, so he invaded the Benelux countries and France. He also had the resources to turn the French campaign into a lightning (blitzkrieg) war. The Nazis and Russians spent from September 1939 to June 1941 facing each other across the River San. When the Nazis broke the peace treaty and invaded Russian-occupied Poland, crossing the San, the large garrison retreated in panic. The blitzkrieg tactics meant there were German tanks trundling towards them. The Stuka dive-bombers, with their screaming sirens, were bombing the retreating Russian vehicles. My father was also an interpreter, and he accompanied a Russian colonel retreating in a horse-drawn cart when a bomb blew up the road in front of them. My father was thrown into a ditch, breaking his shoulder. The colonel was killed. He quickly assessed the situation, buried his Russian uniform, and went back to Przemysl to make sure my mother and sister were safe.

Languages and memory

His ability to rapidly learn languages showed he had an exceptional memory. This had unexpected and remarkable benefits. Some 45 years later, I had persuaded him to return to Bergen-Belsen on the anniversary of the British liberation of the camp. I had wanted him to guide us there because I was trying to address my Holocaust childhood. I was desperate to gain some sense of mastery because it was clear it had had a profound effect on me. Yet my only knowledge was of my father's heroic exploits, his work as the camp children's *Lager Friseur*, and our survival. My mother and sister remained virtually silent about their time there. They were intensely reluctant to return. My father somehow persuaded them, telling them it was their duty to go back. However, when asked to go back to Poland, they instantly refused. They would never go back to Poland because they could not bear the terrible memories. When Bergen-Belsen was liberated by the British Army on 15 April 1945, it was universally described as "hell on earth." This was confirmed by the documentary of the innumerable walking skeletal prisoners, one-fifth of whom would die. You see how the mounds of the 40,000 dead were filled, all filmed by Alfred Hitchcock's cameraman with Richard Dimbleby's commentary. Bulldozers were needed to dig pits of 10,000 capacity and used to push the piles of the dead into them. It is a challenge to understand how this was more endurable than a return to peacetime Poland. However, I immediately understood. The murder of their loved ones was still immeasurably more painful and more intensely felt than anything that they endured in Bergen-Belsen.

Belsen return

I had arranged flights, a plush car, and a friendly guest house to stay in. It is hard for me to convey how important I felt my quest to obtain a sense of ownership of my childhood was after my wife had died. After the Jewish service on the first day of memorialisations, my father asked me if I would say Kaddish, the Jewish prayer for deceased relatives, after he had gone. Of course, I concurred. The words of the Kaddish always puts me in touch with my inner helplessness from the task of mourning the countless number who were murdered. I become painfully in touch with my isolation and the few relationships I can turn to.

He then asked if we could drive 400 miles to see our relatives in Central Germany. I was very torn. I wanted to learn about our and my experience in Belsen. It was only early that morning that I had the somatic memories and the emotional responses to return. I explained to my father that we could not see our relatives in Germany as it was too far. My father was disappointed and disgruntled. He reluctantly agreed to go to the official celebrations in the state capital. I was still deeply emotional from my solitary return to Belsen, which I describe later, and was trying to explain to my parents and sister that I had had memories of my camp childhood. They did not understand. My father was not in the least bit interested in how I felt. We were all dominated by our own memories and emotions. We attended the lavish celebration thrown by the government of Lower Saxony. In my usual role of carer, I ensured that everyone had amply filled plates of the rich food. We sat down and found ourselves surrounded by child survivors, who were now adults, with their children, speaking many European languages simultaneously and loudly. My father began to slowly look around him. He then approached a small, dark-haired woman with piercing black eyes. He said, "I know you, I know who you are" in French, the language that she spoke. The woman looked suspicious. "How is that possible if I do not know you?" He replied calmly, "Because you look just like your mother." He went on to give her mother's name. To describe where her mother came from in Poland. How she had fled to Belgium, where they had been captured. He remembered that she had a younger sister. He soon convinced her. The woman was astonished and deeply moved that he could remember her and especially her mother from those terrible times. He went on to repeat this process with a number of other child survivors. His position as children's *Lager Friseur* (barber) meant he had cut their hair many times and remembered them well. It gave huge pleasure to the survivors that he remembered them. It also pleased him immensely. He was a hero again.

Manual dexterity

When conscripted by the Russians, he discovered the value of his manual dexterity when he was trained to fire his rifle. This ensured he was a fine shot. Experience later showed I had inherited his natural dexterity. The first time I picked up a rifle, I hit 12 bullseyes in a row. During his childhood, he had endured starvation, cold, and danger returning home. He must have learned to assess, avoid, and escape from danger. I am sure the shaving of the Russian general took place. It also suggests that he had an addiction to risk-taking that we now call traumatophilia (Hopper, 2003). His automatic response to privation or danger was to confront and overcome it. He functioned by fight rather than flight or freeze. He was preadapted, if that was possible, to the rigours of the Holocaust and the post-war chaos.

Post-war peace

The lesson he learned and the coping strategies he perfected became deeply ingrained in his psyche. Once he had settled in Great Britain, these life strategies caused more problems than they solved. Adaptation to the Holocaust became maladaptation to the peace – for example, his multilingual abilities. A customer who had a strong European accent came into his hairdresser's shop. My father asked him where he came from. He was desperate to show off his linguistic skills. The customer reluctantly replied, "You would not know." "Try me," he responded. My father continued to pressure the customer until he was forced to tell him it was "White Russia." Out came a torrent of White Russian. This did not please the customer. This was the time of the Cold War, and to declare you were a Russian risked provoking an outraged response. The customer could not wait to get out of the shop. My father was so desperate to show off his language skills that he did not care if he embarrassed the customer or if he never came back.

Trust and loyalty

His first long-term job was for Mr Leon, a Jewish barber in London's Jewish East End. Mr and Mrs Leon had helped him to learn English, essential to communicate with the customers. They had been kind and patient. He never forgot a kindness. However, he had learned in the Holocaust that it was safer never to trust or rely on anyone. This drove him to seek financial independence. When Mr Leon suddenly died, his widow was left trying to run the shop. My father was preparing to start his own business. However, he would not abandon Mrs Leon. He did not leave until he had helped to find his replacement. Without this, the business would have folded. He opened up his own tiny barbershop as soon as his replacement started and never looked back.

His cautious mistrust made him so watchful of how and what people said that by his later years, he had fallen out with all his friends and even his only relatives in Germany. He was so sensitive to any criticism that he responded as if his life depended on his never creating justification for criticism. He argued with and rejected even his close friends who may have been trying to help him. When I was 15 years old, I was sent to spend a summer with my uncle, Zigu, in Kaiserslautern in Germany. His three sons were rivalrous and manipulative and tried to make me as uncomfortable as possible. I ended up leaving prematurely and making the long rail journey home on my own. This led to my uncle phoning my father and being critical of me, which my father took offence at, leading to him never speaking to him for the rest of his life.

Manners and modesty

My father never learned English reserve or modesty. He had no tact. He spoke his mind without any thought to the impact or its potential rudeness. He would tell his friends' wives that they were fat or ugly. If any of his friends began succeeding in business and wore a good watch, he would find a way to reject them to avoid his unconscious envy. He did not understand the concepts of tact or modesty. He would give his opinion of his friends' failings but could not tolerate one word of criticism. He did not care if his behaviour was seen as showing off. He was immensely proud of his ownership of his own shop and later his home and his children. Leonia was a beautiful child and grew into a beautiful woman. She was employed as a fashion model for the Jewish owners of the Eastex clothing manufacturers.

Family pride and rivalry

After his first heart attack, I had joined him in his hairdressers. He had a sign over the window, Sid's Hairdressers. Sid was his anglicised name. As soon as I joined, to my excruciating embarrassment, he changed the name to "Sid and Son." My painfully learned, middle-class English modesty and tact from school made me react adversely at his display of pride at my joining his trade and business.

Despite being secretly proud of me, he was highly rivalrous and competitive with my achievements. My sister only recently reminded me that he could not believe it only took me six weeks to learn to cut hair and to work competently enough to earn a full week's takings. He was secretly amazed and proud of my achievement. Yet he never once praised me directly. Later, when I was studying surgery and was answering a rare question of interest, he interrupted me to tell me that he had been taught how to give a chloroform anaesthetic by a Jewish surgeon in Bergen-Belsen to a young man who had acute appendicitis, which he described in lengthy detail. He explained how the surgeon had previously sought him out and asked him if he could sharpen his surgical instruments. He said he would if the surgeon could supply the sharpening stones needed, which he did. He never showed overt interest in my knowledge, nor turned to me for advice or information on his medical care. He never met any of my responses with praise – usually just silence.

Obsessive-compulsive disorder

Today he would have been diagnosed as suffering obsessive-compulsive disorder as well as sadomasochistic personality traits. When I was about 11 years old, I was summoned to stop what I was doing to be taught an important life skill. He decided he wanted to teach me how to polish my school shoes. He had laid out a newspaper, upon which he placed my school shoes, polish, brushes, and a neatly folded cloth. He picked up a shoe in a particular way so that he did not get polish stain on his hands. His hand movements were sure and delicate, doing precisely what he intended with no clumsiness or effort. Everything was neat and effortless. His *goldener-hands* (a Yiddish phrase for a master craftsman). He studied my every look to ensure I was giving him my full and uninterrupted attention and following his instructions. He showed me the military method of moistening the shoe polish with saliva and applying it evenly. His face was a picture of effortless concentration but his intensity was as though our lives depended on this process. He insisted I wait for exactly seven minutes for it to dry. Then he selected a brush for the first polish. He then chose a clean cloth to obtain the high-gloss shine. His teaching style always possessed the underlying threat that if you made an error, he could explode, and it would end in tears with another beating with the strop, the thick hairdresser's belt used to sharpen cut-throat razors. I became, as a matter of survival, a quick and accurate learner. The next Sunday, he took me aside and started to teach me to polish my school shoes using another technique. This was then a double bind. My solution was to ensure I only polished my shoes when he was at work so he could not beat me for any error.

After he died, my mother asked me to sort out his clothes. I found everything carefully folded, hung up and carefully placed. His shoes were still in their original boxes. They all had shoehorns in them and were in cloth bags. They had been polished and had matching socks tidily folded inside them. Each suit was hung up with a matching shirt and tie. His wardrobe looked like the shelves of a menswear shop.

Survival lessons

The hidden motive behind his need to impart to me certain skills and values was to ensure I would survive the next Holocaust. He believed it was inevitable. There was always a small suitcase packed with valuables and money in readiness to flee. He never let us forget that our lives depended on it. The hardship before the Holocaust and starvation during it prevented him from ever throwing away food until it had rotted beyond edibility. He threw nothing away until he was sure it was not usable.

Loss and post-traumatic stress disorder

Despite my mother's tiny stature and her studied, polite manner, she had a seam of steely determination running through her veins. If she decided against something, her decision was backed by a rigidity generated by her mortal fear of making errors. Her greatest vulnerability lay in her fear of losing any of her children or grandchildren. The unthinkable number of our family that were murdered, having no graves, meant they were never fully mourned. This ensured my parents' relationship with the living and those that died was highly dysfunctional. My mother would protect my father by not mentioning the illness or death of a friend. She would eventually speak of it when she deemed it safe, when he or she were not feeling vulnerable, which might mean never. They watched and worried over us constantly. If any of us were ill, they would insist that every avenue of possible medical error was covered because if it was not anticipated or avoided they feared we would die. This we now understand as avoidant behaviour due to post-sraumatic stress disorder. I always assumed I would not live much beyond 40 because all of my relatives had died young and that was when my father had his first heart attack. Tragic, premature death had filled our lives and was the norm. Our miraculous survival meant that danger survival and miraculous escape was the expected outcome. My father eventually survived six heart attacks before he had his bypass. What intensified the pessimism was that there were only my immediate family to use as examples. There was no extended family to compare family traits and illnesses. This intensified the impact of any harmful possibility. This is part of what we now call complex post-traumatic stress disorder (ICD11 F43) (World Health Organization, 2018).

Possessiveness

My father never relinquished his possessiveness or his refusal to share *his* family, as all families do, or should do. After I arranged the family reunion in France, he always talked about *his* family and how successful and intelligent they were. How he shared *his* family's good looks. He was completely oblivious to the fact that this denied the rest of his immediate family access to our extended family, alive or deceased, to be used psychologically as supports. His sensitivity to anything he perceived or distorted into a failure, a criticism, or a sign of betrayal or letting him down meant he rejected all his survivor friends by the time he was reunited with *his* French family. This intense possessiveness was so intense that it became imprinted into our psyche, and I find myself automatically describing them as *his* family, having to correct it as *our* family. At least he was able to enjoy them until his death one year later.

Idealisation and gambling

My mother never criticised her immediate family, always describing them in various idealised ways. Her older and much-beloved brother, Mundek, was described as clever and ingenious, always coming up with schemes and business deals for which she reported he had become well known and respected. She adored her mother, Chaya, and never got over her death. She avoided talking about her because it awakened her unresolved grief and sadness. She belatedly reported that she had a younger brother who was disabled in a traffic accident and died soon after. She was undoubtably ambivalent about her father, who she was openly critical of in her later years. He had been a horse dealer, specialising in the heavy farm horses known as drays. He would regularly travel to Belgium to trade and bring the horses back to be sold in Przemysl. She eventually admitted that he was also addicted to gambling at cards. He would meet other gamblers for his regular games. He was a very stern figure. This could be discerned by my mother's story of having to call him when her younger brother was injured by a speeding car. She had to go to his card-playing club, which we called a *shpeiler* in Yiddish. He was engrossed in a game and was very angry at being called away. She confided that her father had saved up enough money to buy the tiny house they rented, but then, as it always seems to go in these matters, he gambled it away. She lived her long life with my father in relative misery. She was diagnosed at a teaching hospital with a heart abnormality that may have been related to childhood scarlet fever. She always showed an abnormality on her ECG. She frequently suffered chest pain, which was always treated as angina (blood supply shortage to the heart). This meant she was admitted to the cardiology ward for several weeks. I think she benefited most from the respite from my father's domination and aggression. In her eighties, she had an angiography and her coronary arteries were found to be as clean as a whistle. So, we may reasonably conclude her lifelong chest pain was diagnosed wrongly as angina and was simply heartache.

Caution excess

Her Holocaust life made her unduly cautious. She thought about problems carefully and repetitively. Before the end of the Cold War and with the opening up of Poland, my father arranged for our first cousin, Mischka's oldest son, Janush, to come to England. We all loved having him here. He was a nervous but gentle soul, and we all grew to adore him very quickly. Leonia, my father, and me would have loved to have arranged for him to live in Britain. We argued for this vehemently, but my mother adamantly refused, citing the fear that they would become responsible for his upkeep and that of his wife and young family. However, underlying this was a fear that my father would give in to what she felt was his excessive tendency to generosity and spend his and her compensation money from the German government. He had already given much of it to Janush's sister in her earlier visit and to their mother, Mischka, with his parcels. Perhaps she was jealous. However hard we tried, she would not budge. The addition of a family of four to our family group would have doubled the number of possible family attachments available to me, such was my isolation. So, my deep loneliness continued.

The formation and deformation of a Holocaust child's psyche

My conception occurring during my mother's imprisonment in the ghetto could not have been welcome news. My mother spoke of how the women expressed pity for her plight. In contrast, she spoke with joy and humour of how active I was in the womb. My medical experience of pregnant mothers leads me to believe my activity in the womb would have brought relief, if not joy, that I was still alive despite the starvation and disease-ridden conditions. I have described how when six months into the pregnancy, my mother tried to join her beloved mother and pregnant sister, who were selected for deportation to Belzec extermination camp. This has many implications for my mother's mental state and its influence on my gestation. She was devastated by the death of her mother. Her response could have, should have, precipitated a severe depressive grief reaction. Perhaps her only chance of physical and psychological survival was denial and dissociation, thus enabling her to care for Leonia and me, if I survived the birth in these medically dangerous circumstances. This assumption is supported by her behaviour when she met the ghetto policeman 45 years after the liberation, in Paris, which I describe in Chapter 10. When she went into labour, to get to the makeshift hospital in the second ghetto required her to walk many hundreds of yards while in pain. My mother was able to breastfeed despite her starvation in the ghetto. Without her breast milk, I would not have survived a week. I have described how my father would escape from the ghetto to purchase food, which sustained them and must have enabled my mother to continue to breastfeed.

Despite my having a relatively secure source of food, its security depended on my mother's continued survival. Her life was always in danger. The life expectancy in the ghetto was only a few weeks longer than the six weeks of the camps. It is likely that my parents' fight for survival was underpinned by a constant threat of annihilation. This must have been transmitted to my sister and me. Research has shown that babies monitor their mother's heart rate. Altemus et al. (1995) have shown that stress-responsive neurohormonal systems are restrained in lactating women. This implies that fear would be transmitted to the breastfeeding baby. In the year following the murder of my maternal grandparents, several *Aktions* took place in which we were all in mortal danger.

I recall being told that my father built a false wall behind the communal toilet on the landing in which to hide while the Nazis were searching with their vicious dogs. He deliberately flooded the toilet, ensuring faeces covered the toilet floor and leaked on to the landing to confuse the dogs. This discouraged the Nazis from approaching the back of the toilets to avoid spoiling their boots and having to endure the foul odours. The evocation of this memory, I believe, caused me to have an overwhelming panic attack when I was conducting therapy with a Polish hidden child survivor who described being packed in like sardines. I believe a hand was placed over my mouth to prevent me from crying, which if it had been prolonged would have suffocated me. Perhaps this is where I learned that children who cried died (Kellermann, 2003). My sister recalls how she hardly ever heard me make a sound as a child and was shocked when she heard me speak after our liberation. In the past, I had no symptoms such as claustrophobia, but since the panic attack I have had nightmares and fears of being trapped in constricting spaces, such as during the 2018 Thai cave rescue of 12 boys and their football coach.

Pain

Perhaps an adaptation that may have added to my resilience was my ability to tolerate and not fear pain. I have described how my recurrent ear infections were treated by painful injections that I endured without complaint. Perhaps having been beaten with a thick leather strop, always trying not to show any reaction, may have helped. When I became my school's first team goalkeeper, I would dive for the ball, scraping my arms or hips on hard surfaces. This did not prevent me from throwing myself around with all my strength to save the goal. When I was bullied at school, the pain the bullies tried to inflict did not bother me, but the humiliation distressed me deeply. The bullying effectively stopped when, having learned some judo, I threw an attempted bully high into the air over my head, sending him through a large somersault on to the concrete surface of the playground. Despite my diminutive size (I was 5 feet at age 16), I had found a way of dealing with the bullies.

Detachment

Eventual insight into the maladjustments I was being taught by my parents led me to the escape route of detachment. By rejecting my religion, I avoided the guilt of nonconformity with religious requirements. This allowed me to conform with English social behaviour. By recognising my parents' teaching as danger avoidance, I was able to behave more freely.

When I discovered that the dangers they were teaching me to avoid did not exist, I was freed. My newly found atheism greatly reduced the incidences of anti-Semitism because I was less identifiable as a Jew. My inherited Polish features added to my ability to not stand out. This was not the Holocaust, and no one could demand me to drop my trousers to identify me as a Jew. The psychic effects were that I escaped the annihilation anxiety, powerlessness, and primal agony suffered by my parents. However, this came at the price of multiple losses, particularly that of isolation. The fewer attachments I had, the more isolated I became.

Wealth and envy

I have never worn ostentatious jewellery or clothes. The only jewellery I wear is a modest wristwatch and a simple gold wedding ring. I avoided expensive-looking cars. I am very conscious of my fear of envious attacks caused by displays of wealth. This may have been initiated by my father's descriptions of *Kapos* being strung up for collaborating and his sensitivity to the slur that he had prospered in Belsen through collaboration.

Shoes

In Belsen, in addition to being the camp children's barber, my father was forced to work on the *Shoe Komando*. This was a mountain of shoes that had to have the soles manually cut from the uppers. If you did not have waterproof, well-fitting shoes, cuts would appear on your feet, which quickly became infected, invariably causing death in a short time. I have always had a love of high-gloss black leather shoes, which, given my small-size feet, have been a challenge to obtain. Occasionally, I have had to compromise with a larger pair that allow my feet to move more freely in them. I am comforted by a well-fitting shoe that holds my feet firmly. Perhaps this is simply the benefit of having shoes that fit properly. It may also be related to the feel of the strong hands of my father examining my feet to find my injuries in the children's home. I can still feel his firm grip holding my foot, lifting it, when I think back. This feels similar to feel of my shoe holding my foot firmly.

Attachment and separation

Today we understand secure and insecure attachment and separation trauma. After my experiences in the children's homes, I had an intense dread of separation from my family that showed itself throughout my childhood. This continued until my insight into being prepared to survive another Holocaust, and I engineered the enforced detachment from them from the age of 13. After many years, I noticed a long-term problem. When I am engaged in conversation, the interaction with the person I am listening to dominates my attention and excludes other interactions. This means that in social interactions, I struggle with groups of people and find it easier to focus on one person at a time. This often means that when in conversation or engrossed in a task, I forget all others despite their clear importance to me. I believe this is now diagnosed as symptoms of severe borderline personality disorder (BPS) (Bateman & Fonagy, 2006). Research now clearly relates BPS to early trauma.

Stature and fear

My rickets and exceptionally small stature were due to malnourishment and genetics. I never achieved the 8 inches of extra height the statisticians predicted that sons grow taller than their fathers. The effect that rickets had in restricting my walking through pain also had an effect on my ability to run away from danger or enjoy the usual games small boys played. This increased my constant anxiety levels and encouraged the bullies at my grammar school. It forced me to become quick and agile. It may also have forced me to use my brain to manage bullying or potential danger situations that may have increased my resilience. Humiliating bullying clearly had an impact on my confidence and self-esteem. At school, I found myself overcompensating by using my father's self-flattering style, which attracted more bullying in the middle-class English ethos. This was one of the first lessons I learned after my detachment from my parents.

Death, the enemy

When I was a medical student, I felt driven beyond the needs of normal academic requirements to recognise and understand disease processes. I was determined to learn how to reduce suffering and prevent death. When I was a junior doctor, I regarded death, when it was not a welcome release, as an enemy to be fought and defeated. I hated to see patients suffer. I found the suffering of children the most painful to watch. I knew I could not specialise in paediatrics. I was too susceptible to my overidentification and countertransference. Now, in my late years, I am able to use this experience to reassure children, to recognise their fear and treat them, whenever possible, with gentleness and reassurance. I have learned to keep a reassuring distance from a frightened child. To lower my voice and approach them slowly and gently. To read their anxiety signs and win their trust quickly. I have also learned to reassure mothers whose anxiety always transmits to their infants.

Survivorship denial

Throughout my life, my parents repeated their belief that because I was a born in the ghetto and only 8 months old when we were sent to Belsen,

I did not understand what was happening when enduring the trauma of the Holocaust. Thus, I was miraculously spared the suffering they endured – that my blissful childhood innocence protected me. This was a fundamental part of my formative years and had a profound, destructive impact on my psychic development. My parents repeating this was not merely a statement of their belief, but was a communication that I was not allowed to believe there was any possible harmful impact the Holocaust had on me. After the separation trauma of being sent to the children's home, parental communications were not just words to understand, but became orders underpinned by threats – that if I disobeyed, I would be returned to the children's home. This occurred twice more when my mother needed surgery, reinforcing the threat. I was allowed to believe I was the child of Holocaust survivors but not a child Holocaust survivor. This obstructed and delayed my understanding of many of the causes of my inner turmoil and sadness, which I explore here.

Loneliness, warmth, and coldness

During these early years, I suffered constant and intense loneliness. Like all insecurely attached children, I ensured proximity to my mother at all times. I would follow her around to ensure she never left my sight. My sister had outgrown our childish games and had her own friends. I would go everywhere with my mother in silent obedience. I would sit for hours while she talked to her few close friends. Listening and learning about life and relationships through their survival-distorted eyes. There were rarely any children to play with. Proximity to my mother was my priority. In my silent watchfulness, a red flag sign of abuse, I never strayed from my mother's side. On reflection, I can now see how I assessed the warmth or coldness of her friends, particularly the women. Some intuitively realised my insecurity and sent unspoken signals that my need for proximity was acceptable. Others would signal they required distance and boundaries. They protected themselves from closeness and emotional empathy. This, I soon discovered, was synonymous with coldness. This was also true for the men. Fortunately, there were two close family friends whose warmth I benefited from and, like a plant in sunshine, helped me develop strength and grow. Through many years of psychoanalysis and especially group analysis, I have overcome my protective, distancing defences. This has allowed me to use and expose my capacity to empathise and comfort, which is sensed by others as warmth. Thus, I learned the signals in vocal language and body language when others are seeking comfort. Despite my father's cruelty, he also had great warmth, which could impact on others, like the sun suddenly appearing from behind the clouds, warming the body through our clothes. With years of therapy and therapeutic practice, my warmth has increased and become more accessible to those around me, especially for my children. For many years, my carapace of defences (Hopper, 1991) separated my inner warmth from those around me, and I could seem cold. This was intense defensive caution because of my vulnerability. Time has reassured me such that my defences are lowered and only appear when I feel under threat. Sadly, they are still occasionally needed for the vagaries of a turbulent life.

Polish and loss

There was never a word spoken of the impact of the stream of Polish Holocaust survivors pouring out their stories in anguished floods of tears while I lay in bed in the tiny room with paper-thin walls through which I could hear everything. I returned home one day to find it in silence. My mother was sat in total silence, staring into space. Looking outwards but seeing inwards. My frightened cries were ignored. I sat in front of her in terror for several hours. I now understand she was struggling with delayed grief. She could no longer deny the loss of her beloved family when Polish survivor after survivor returned to find everyone had been murdered. Soon after, she pronounced a new family rule. This was underpinned by the constant threat of my being sent to the children's home again if I disobeyed. She did not explain, but pronounced that the Polish language was to be banned from our home. Only Yiddish and English were to be spoken. Polish was soon blocked out of my vocabulary. This had a lifelong impact. I could barely remember a word of Polish. Whenever I tried to learn to speak it again, I could not retain what I was being taught. I would be overwhelmed by anxiety. This lasted until after her death. What, then, were the effects of these dynamics? They created psychic barriers to two essential areas of my developmental experiences. Psychically, they were encapsulated (Hopper, 1991) or compartmentalised. The psychic cost of psychically isolating these large areas of experience is inestimable. Ironically, in my clinical work, I have treated numerous patients who professed to having no memories of their childhood, often to the age of 12. This, I intuitively believed, was because of their psychic need to avoid their traumatic childhood experiences.

Food

Having been starved affected my relationship to food. It was different at different stages of my life. When I was a child, my parents showed great concern for my health. Like most children, I sensed this and refused most food to get my mother's concern and attention. I virtually only ate eggs. I was slow to gain weight or grow. Eggs were rationed and a precious commodity. However, they managed to obtain them. Eggs are still a favourite food. I was taken to various doctors due to my frailty and vulnerability to infections. My mother was even advised by a Jewish doctor to give me bacon because it was a high-calorie food. I recall that when later sent to another children's home, my parents sent a supply of eggs, which I could not eat due to my abject misery. The kindly carer who brought the boiled egg for breakfast was angry with me because I could not eat and wasted it. I became expert at how eggs should be cooked. Scrambled eggs were to be cooked in a saucepan so that they adhered to the sides, producing the delicious crust. I would insist on eating from the pan to ensure I did not miss out on this favourite layer. I preferred soft-boiled eggs when boiled. I loved the flavour of the soft-boiled yolk. As I drive along country lanes, I will look out for fresh eggs sold at the garden gate. They are usually the most delicious.

I have no tolerance for hunger. If I feel the first pangs, I will calculate how far I am from home. If too far, I will calculate how long to get to the next source of food. I have come to realise that wherever I drive, I look out for food sources. I mentally note cafés, restaurants, and takeaway food shops. I am always looking for good food. This way, I ensure I rarely endure hunger for any length of time. The food does not have to be haute cuisine. Bread and butter will satisfy my needs. Modern supermarkets bake the most delicious fresh bread. I believe this relates to the slice of bread that was the daily ration in the camp – 130 calories per day. My father rose at 3 a.m. to shave the *Kapos* for a little butter. The taste and texture of fresh butter with bread remains a lifelong favourite. The watery hot soup with virtually no nutritional value was also a daily staple in the camp. I find myself always looking for soup on a restaurant menu. I make my own soup and will eat it daily. I never tire of it. Sweet soup, which I never knew in the camp or my childhood, has no attraction.

Cold

I have no tolerance for the cold. I always wear a sleeveless vest to keep my back warm, as well as several layers of clothes. This I only relinquish in hot weather. At night, I always ensure my back is warmed by multiple layers of underclothes and bedclothes. I believe that due to the discomfort of rough, filthy, lice-ridden clothes in the camp, I am intolerant to rough-textured clothing. I seek soft-textured clothes such as cashmere jumpers or soft cotton shirts. My parents were also particular about the softness of clothes on their skin, probably for the same reason. I recall that as a child, I was aware of the softness of the angora sweaters my mother wore and their perfumes. My father wore cashmere whenever not working. In his work as a barber, he used a very sweet aftershave, Pashana, normally only available to the professional barber. This was used as an aftershave or post-shampooing treatment called a friction. While he was still working, his hands always smelled strongly of roses.

Weather exposure and powerlessness

In Belsen, the barracks were adapted military stables. They were unsealed buildings. They let in the rain and cold draughts. The windows had no glass and there were inadequate heating stoves sparsely placed. The bunks for four persons held 12. Clothing was no protection from the cold and rain. The barracks were freezing cold with chilling draughts in the winter, airless and hot in the summer, stinking of dysentery and the dead.

The multiple and unpredictable causes of death were so numerous that this impacted as powerlessness to defend oneself or anticipate where the next danger came from. This had the effect of creating an annihilation anxiety-driven lifelong desire to create empowerment against the vagaries of weather, of discomforts and insecurities, and of starvation or being under the control of others. This left us all with a drive to possess our own home from which we could not be evicted. To have heating and double glazing that was capable of protecting us from the harshest of winters. To install cooling methods that allowed for comfort in heatwaves. To have the best refrigerators with stocks of food adequate for any siege, shortage, or unpredictable calamity. This can be understood as seeking mastery and financial independence in all aspects of our lives.

Relationships

Having had precious few friendships, I feel fortunate that my closest friends from grammar school are still alive and remain precious sources of support and trust. Having suffered bullying at school and bullying at home, I was always alert to people's behaviour and their underlying trustiness. This improved when I joined a Jewish youth club and was eventually appointed club captain. By this time, I had spent several years developing my understanding of relationships and social skills. Through my sporting activities at school, I grew physically stronger. I joined the amateur dramatic society and made a few more friends. Slowly, I was acquiring the social skills I needed to have a more normal life. However, my early years of abuse ensured that I was always watchful before trusting anyone. My abuse by the children's home matron has left me hypersensitive to domination by strong women. In the years before my psychoanalysis and group analysis, situations that resonated with my dysfunctional family life caused me to defend through avoidance and flight. Being slow to trust and growing increasingly practised in reading people led me to find it harder to find friends or those with shared values. Many of my values and priorities were chosen when I was an idealistic teenager. They often showed the intolerance of the young and naïve. Thus, it became immensely difficult to find role models. My abuse-honed sensitivity meant that I spotted the errors and inconsistencies of new contacts who I rejected too easily. This might be compared with my father's hypercritical faculties, but it was of a different kind. It was not to diminish others to below my standards, and thus flatter or protect my fragile ego. It was creating a standard to reach for myself, of honesty, integrity, humanity, compassion, and consistency, before realising this was hardly ever achieved by anyone. My mother had insisted that I must grow up to be a *mensch*, a decent human being. *Both* my therapies should have and did increase my self-knowledge. It also facilitated self-examination of my behaviour, emotions, and motives, conscious and unconscious. It also created a need for dialogue that was informed and open, with a preparedness to examine one's inner world. Only after a lifetime of searching, and usually failing, did I realise that these are rare qualities to find.

Having been brought up in a dysfunctional family, these values had serious implications for my relationship with my children. Once I had had children, I had to discover my failings through honest self-examination. Perhaps because of my children's home experience, I was preoccupied to show my children honest communication, consistency, and predictability, especially in their early years. However, life intervened when my wife, Diana, developed her fatal form of multiple sclerosis. Finding myself trying to be a comfort to my daughters and at the same time trying to deal with my own grief meant that I failed this challenge, for which I continue to castigate myself. I had to make special efforts to have quality time together on holidays and weekends. This, I hoped, built the core of a deep relationship. Inevitably, my internalised attachments were few, thus resulting in my deep sense of isolation. When my relationships increase, it results in less isolation and more security. Now, in my later years, I have begun to find the healthy closeness with those precious to me that we all desire.

Endings

My final memory of my father was of our conversation in hospital the day before he died. I was obliged to leave the next day to take my bereaved daughters on a precious French holiday with their godmother. He adored his grandchildren and felt for them having lost their mother. He knew I had to give them priority. We talked about his appendicectomy in a Russian Army hospital and the Russian Army in Przemysl. He remembered that he had never been paid by the Russians nor had any campaign medals. He decided he would contact the Russian embassy, confident of his ability to speak Russian, and that he would obtain service medals and some official recognition. His ease while talking to me about the Holocaust told me he had accepted me as a child survivor. He was proud that he could say those sacred Jewish words "my son, the doctor" to the doctors looking after him. He was chuckling with the pleasure at his new idea when I said goodbye. I felt content. I knew much healing had been achieved. He lived his life listening to no one, doing what he wanted to the end. He died in 1990 aged 73 years.

My mother lived another 25 years. She loved the comfort of her bright and warm bungalow. She luxuriated in not being dominated by my father. I visited frequently and dutifully, helping with every aspect of her life. When in her late eighties she became too frail to live alone, I arranged for her to live in a friendly nursing home. She discovered living alone had been isolating, and as the staff began to know her, they became fonder of her and she became more gregarious. She soon felt they were like family and sank into a happy dementia. She felt secure. Through her dementia, she forgot all her Holocaust troubles and became increasingly happy and gentle, which made me think of her description of her mother. She died six days before her 93rd birthday. Leonia and I stayed with her through those final days. She had a good end and was able to die in the bosom of her beloved family.

During the writing of this chapter late in the history of this volume, I began to read *The Lost* by Daniel Mendelsohn (2013), which is frequently focused on photos of lost loved ones and the recovery of these progressively precious items. He breathed life into the images with his descriptions of these long murdered, precious relative as he meets their peers, their survivor *Landsmänner*. Unconsciously, I found myself looking through my precious photos of my murdered family that I had spent a lifetime researching and recovering. Mendlesohn helped me to understand, through his searches and interviews, that he had brought life back into their lifeless images. As I am writing, I find myself inescapably tearful. I became conscious that through this process of writing, I was internalising faded faces, transforming them into psychic representations of people who now had life by having lived through their relationships with my mother, father, and sister. That I had begun to breathe life into their images and feel a sense of depth of my associations with them. Having unconsciously developed relationships with them, they then increased the number and quality of my inner and most important attachment, thus reducing my loneliness.

Like a frightened, abandoned child, I found myself hanging on to their images as though they were there and they reached out to hold my child's hand. It is warm and I feel safe.

References

Altemus, M., Deuster, P.A., Gallivan, E., Carter, C.S., & Gold, P.W. (1995) Suppression of hypothalamic-pituitary-adrenal axis responses to stress in lactating women. *Journal of Clinical Endocrinology Metabolism* 80(10): 2954–2958.

Bateman, A. & Fonagy, P. (2004) *Psychotherapy for Borderline Personality Disorder: Mentalisation-Based Treatment.* Oxford: Oxford University Press.

Hopper, E. (1991) Encapsulation as a defence against the fear of annihilation. *The International Journal of Psychoanalysis* 72(4): 607–624.

Hopper, E. (2003) *Traumatic Experiences in the Unconscious Life of Groups.* London: Jessica Kingsley.

Kellermann, N.P.F. (2003) *Holocaust Trauma: Psychological Effects and Treatment.* New York: iUniverse.

Mendelsohn, D. (2013) *The Lost: A Search for Six of the Six Million.* New York: HarperCollins.

World Health Organization (2018) *International Classification of Disease.* Geneva: World Health Organization.

Chapter 6

Child survivors of the Holocaust

Groups and groupings, healing wounds

Introduction

Arguably, children were the greatest victims of the Holocaust. Not just the 93 per cent of Jewish children in Europe who were murdered (Krell & Sherman, 1997), but the countless children in the occupied countries who were killed, as well as those who were psychologically and physically injured. Insufficient thought is given to the vast numbers of German children who were orphaned and suffered psychological trauma during their formative years, particularly children of Nazis, who were some of the most severe victims.

For observers, the suffering of children is the most emotionally difficult to endure. It evokes potent responses directed towards protection and healing. It may also evoke defensive avoidance and denial. Perhaps this is the reason that for many years, the suffering of child survivors of the Holocaust was ignored or denied. The denial began with the response of adult Holocaust survivors, who would tell child survivors they were too young to understand or to remember what was happening, and that they were lucky compared to the adult survivors.

Child survivor self-help groups

In the 1980s, the distinguished child psychoanalyst Judith Kestenberg, a refugee from Poland, began to mentor and treat a group of child survivors in New York. Similarly, in California, Sarah Moskovitz, a clinical psychologist, helped a child survivor group form. Moskovitz (1983) began her study of the "Lingfield children," on whose care Anna Freud advised and wrote her famous paper (Freud & Dann, 1951). At about this time, other determined and creative child survivors in North America, such as the Dutch hidden child and child psychiatrist Dr Robert Krell, formed a psychosocial self-help group in Vancouver.

In 1988, the visionary leaders of these groups organised the first gathering of several groups of child survivors. They have met annually ever since. From these small beginnings has grown the World Federation of Jewish

Child Survivors of the Holocaust & Descendants, which now includes in excess of 110 groups in 14 countries.

Why child survivors should form groups at this time is an interesting but unanswered question. Adult survivors have stated they were discouraged from addressing and speaking of their Holocaust trauma by the responses of non-survivor communities. They were encouraged to put the past behind them and build a new life. This they energetically attempted. For some, rebuilding their lives, which included creating new families, was a seductive, reparative defence. It could support a defensive denial that their Holocaust past could simply be put behind them and an unencumbered new life could be created. That the almost impossible burden of mourning could be bypassed. However, time showed this to be false. For most, their Holocaust wounds seemed to have been encapsulated or their lives adjusted so as to avoid painful evocations. The Holocaust wounds had not healed, but had only been covered, scabbed over (Hopper, 1991). Sensitivity to certain cues demonstrated this clearly:

> Most commonly, Holocaust survivors respond with habitual panic when exposed to triggers that in some way symbolise the Holocaust. Such Holocaust associated triggers may include ... crowded trains, medical examination, the yellow colour, gas, [etc.]. In addition, happy occasions such as weddings, Jewish holidays and family celebrations may also evoke sudden grief reactions ... As a consequence there is frequently a contradictory effort both to remember and to forget, both to approach and to avoid the traumatic event.
>
> (Kellermann, 2001, p. 202)

Child survivors' traumata

There is a misunderstanding and oversimplification of the traumatic experiences of child survivors of the Holocaust. Although many suffered more than one type of traumatic experience, for reasons of clarity these experiences will be described as distinct entities.

Kindertransport

In August 1939, the British government granted entry permits to 10,000 Jewish children from Germany, Austria, Czechoslovakia, and Poland. Many were alone. The luckier ones were with a sibling. They were torn from their families. It is painful to imagine their parents' agonising discussions as to whether to send their precious children away or keep them, thus risking their death. The children's ages ranged from babies to 16 years old. Few ever saw their families again. This traumatic separation and loss had lifelong effects (Reed, 1999). Reed's moving documentary captures the anguish and uncertainty of being placed on a train with a label around the neck and one small suitcase with a few precious belongings, photos, and perhaps a last letter. However, this was only the beginning of their traumas. Arriving at London's Liverpool Street Station, a Jewish emergency organisation arranged for volunteers to meet them, as well as foster homes. Some were happily fostered (Josephs & Bechhofer, 1996). However, they were frequently misused and abused.

Kindertransport trauma may be characterised as traumatic exile. Psychically, it was a traumatic separation and abandonment, causing multiple losses and layers of losses. These included loss of parents, family, social network, country, culture, education, childhood, and sometimes language.

The initial response to their traumata may be observed as producing psychic fight/flight/freeze. Avoidance of mourning loss by use of the fight response may evoke psychic detachment from primary object relations, which may produce rage and hate for the lost objects. This is experienced at the deepest psychic levels as failed dependency. Thus, it may evoke an intense drive for new attachments, behaviourally seen as idealisation of new caregivers, with intense assimilation, coupled with rejection, repression, denial, and avoidance of the past.

The freeze response may evoke despair, intense grief, and yearning expressed in dreams and unconscious fantasies. Dissociation may occur, with splitting and narcissistic, hysterical, and phobic functioning developing as a consequence. This may predominate. Negative encapsulation may be used to psychically wall off the unresolved traumatic effects.

As traumatic exile involves the traumatic triad of annihilation anxiety, powerlessness, and loss, powerful defences are mobilised. Defences against powerlessness coupled with defences against loss are likely to produce hypersensitivity to separation and loss. This may produce total silence regarding the past, which is psychic burial. The survivor may develop an intrusive controlling relationship towards all to whom they are attached. In some cases, attachment may be avoided to protect them from further loss, causing coldness and unavailability. The avoidance of intimacy usually causes psychic emptiness, isolation, and often depression.

Security may be sought through avoidance of risk-taking, play, or adventure. Surprises may be avoided and advance warning of future events may be demanded. Life may be constricted by excessive conformity to routine and home life. Powerlessness and dependency may be avoided through self-employment and the acquisition of sufficient resources for long-term security, which may be treated as though they were emergency funds in case the Holocaust restarted. Conscious and unconscious attachment may be made to organisations and employers that have actual or symbolic connection to their lost past. A number of the Kindertransport children were active voluntary workers for, or were employed by, the charity that organised their entry visas: "A Kindertransport child spent his adult life in the confectionary business but never made any connection with the last memory of his father giving him some chocolate before boarding the train" (Reed, 2003).

Hiding

Children were hidden with and without their parents by nuns and priests, resistance organisations, and individuals. This occurred most frequently in France, Belgium, the Netherlands, and Denmark. In Poland, children were often hidden for payment. When the money ran out, the children were usually thrown out or betrayed to the Nazis.

> A Christian neighbour Janka, said to my mother, "Clara, don't go to the ghetto. You'll never get out of there." Janka offered ... to hide us. We packed all we could carry and gratefully moved in with Janka. Late that first night there was a sudden loud banging on the door and a lot of screaming. "Open up. You have Jews in there," a man's voice shouted. To this day I still get goose bumps remembering that sound. Someone from the Gestapo ordered my mother to come with her ... An hour later that same man was back. Now he and Janka chatted in a friendly way, as they proceeded to divide up all our belongings.
>
> (Marks, 1993, p. 16)

Some courageous individuals hid both adults and children for altruistic reasons. For children to survive in hiding required them to show compliance, passivity, and silence. This required intense self-control. Some children were hidden and confined in cramped spaces for long periods of time, without regular meals. They were forced to suffer long periods of uncertainty and annihilation threat:

> One hiding place was a small, empty space, three feet long and one foot deep, below the window which my father had camouflaged to look like the wall. I remember having to sit in there with Pavel for hours, struggling for air and being so scared. Tears were running down my cheeks, but I didn't dare make a sound for fear the Germans would find us. But silently I prayed for my father to come and let us out. Each time he came back, I begged him, "Daddy, please let this be the last time." I didn't think I could take it any more.
>
> (Marks, 1993, p. 16)

This required self-discipline and suppression of anxiety and distress. Control of the instinctual desire to express these or ask for reassurance was essential for survival. In order that the annihilation anxiety and powerlessness was prevented from becoming overwhelming it was probably encapsulated (Hopper, 1991). It also would seem that a core of psychic security

(Garwood, 1998), a secure base (Bowlby, 1998), would have been a psychic necessity to turn to in times of distress. Hiding meant repression of the instinct to cry for help, to protest, and to regress. Regression was not compatible with survival: "children who cried, died" (Kellermann, 2001, p. 209). Psychic turning inwards to existing resources would appear to be the only psychic alternative. Survival does not seem possible without a protective, security-providing object relationship. The fight response was, of necessity, repressed. Psychic flight may have involved psychic reverie that may have taken place under the influence of endorphin release, the endogenous opioids. These reveries are likely to have been idealised, omnipotent fantasies. Dissociation with encapsulation, splitting, projection, narcissism, and hysteria has been observed.

Hiding often resulted in lifelong repression of distress or the need for aid and the avoidance of being noticed. This has been observed to cause lifelong psychic deformation. This had predictable effects on relationships throughout life. The metaphor of a psychic recluse seems apposite. Recluse implies living in self-enforced isolation. Flight, or avoidance of repetition of the trauma, resulted in staying in the background, avoiding being noticed, accepting suffering without protest. Fighting the trauma may cause compensatory activity such as dominance and strident, vocal protest.

In 1991, the first international gathering of hidden children took place in New York. To the amazement of the organisers, rather than the expected 400 participants, 1,600 survivors arrived from all over the world. Despite the organisation being overwhelmed, the participants stated that it was a watershed. They had been in hiding all their lives. They now felt that they could come out of hiding and allow their presence to be felt. Since then, they have organised and have become a powerful presence within the survivor and child survivor community. The Hidden Child Foundation, which was then formed, is led by determined and outspoken former hidden children.

False papers

"My mother used the gems to buy a false birth certificate from a man whose wife had died" (Marks, 1993, p. 16). Surviving on false papers or using a false identity was largely only possible for children 6 years or older. These were mostly girls. Almost all Jewish men were circumcised and thus were often detected when made to drop their trousers by Nazis. Even so, some men survived this way. In many cases, a false identity was imposed by the carer. During wartime, the orphaning of children was common and used as a cover story. Jewish children were taught Catholic prayers as this was a commonly used test. Their new name and behaviour needed to be learned and convincingly repeated if asked by curious adults. This was a challenge to core beliefs, such as being honest and obedient to adults. A whole new set of beliefs needed to be quickly learned. As previously suggested, the lessons of survival form defences and behaviour patterns that are likely to be formative when learned in childhood. They will not readily be relinquished, even with therapy.

False papers required the opposite response to hiding (i.e. danger mastery in the midst of the enemy by acting and lying). This may create a character personified by the metaphors of the gambler, the sentry, or the spy. The gambler always risks trusting his judgement. Sentries are always on guard, checking for friends or foe. Spies trust no one, edit everything, and live by the minimum, necessary disclosure. This causes psychic deformation and creates lifelong problems with intimacy and psychic isolation. Life becomes a total performance. The cost in psychic energy is enormous. Terror and collapse may occur if energy or health fail.

Psychically, this form of survival is consistent with the psychic rejection of all new attachments. Any new relationships seem to focus around a struggle in which dominance or control is sought. The fight-induced rage and hate may frequently be eroticised, creating perverse sadomasochistic relations with underlying contempt. The fight response was utilised in confronting, sometimes seeking, danger. The flight response would seem to fuel secretiveness, constant self-editing, with the loss of spontaneity. The creation of a defensive carapace or false self has been observed (Winnicott, 1965). The freeze response seems of no psychic value but may obstruct reflective processes. Annihilation threat will evoke a drive to conquer and engage with the danger. Powerlessness will evoke action and interaction with the external world. Loss that evokes powerlessness may be the most potent potentially overwhelming trauma, and may be avoided by rationing attachments or separation from what is likely to be an over-controlled existing primary reattachment.

A Jewish, Polish child, at 9 years old, charmed his way into Gestapo headquarters, making himself useful cleaning and polishing their boots. He was eventually sent to Auschwitz, where he survived. Gaining entry to the US, he changed his name to an English one and practised for many years as an accountant, having forged false qualifications. He seemed addicted to surviving by deception, always taking risks that just skirted or crossed the line of illegality. For example, in later life, he never purchased stamps, but reused prepaid envelopes. The psychic price included marrying a gentile, and never having children because, following an argument in which his wife refused to perform a domestic task, he permanently withheld sexual relations. His secretiveness precluded intimacy, and thus lifelong psychic isolation ensued. In his later years, his defences softened, and a degree of trust and dependence was permitted.

Concentration camps

The major causes of death in the concentration camps, other than being shot or gassed, were starvation, disease, cold exposure, and work exhaustion. These were usually cumulative. For infants and younger children, survival was not possible without protection from adults. Death was so common and arbitrary that there were few survival rules other than that reciprocity aided survival (Davidson, 1992). Survival in concentration camps was virtually impossible without the support of other prisoners.

This experience was characterised by extreme, almost constant annihilation threat in the face of almost total powerlessness without any reliable or predictable protective factors or behaviour. The fight response produces rage and a desire for revenge, which was of necessity repressed and psychically transmuted into sadomasochistic fantasies. The victim/victimiser experience may colour the fantasies and thus the play of children.

In Bergen-Belsen concentration camp in play at 2 years old, I was buried alive in sand by other children. This mimicked the observed burial of dead prisoners but reversed the roles of victim and victimiser, thus identifying with the aggressor (Freud, 1937). I was rescued by my mother before harm was done (Carvalho, 1995). The suppression of the fight response necessary for survival creates the psychic necessity of detoxifying the great pool of rage and hate produced. Projection is a commonly seen defence, causing hypersensitivity to threats, hypervigilance, and paranoia.

This experience produces an anxious disorganised attachment pattern (Lyons-Ruth & Jacobvitz, 1999). Mastery is attempted by excessive control described by the metaphor of the air traffic controller. Among the psychic effects observed were intense fear of disease, intolerance of the slightest hunger or cold, and the constant seeking of strong, protective, secure attachment figures.

The child survivor gatherings

Child survivors are relatively few in number, and thus rarely meet another child survivor. In the company of non-survivors, a constant defensive shield is maintained. It is difficult to convey the impact on a child survivor of being among large numbers of their fellow child survivors. There is an ambiance created in which there is an unspoken recognition of survival of the shared massive psychic traumata of annihilation threat, powerlessness, and loss. This reduces the psychic energy needed to maintain the defences required when among non-child survivors. There is a reduction in the need to explain or to defend against the shame that is generated by the unconscious struggle with powerlessness causing self-blame, which turns frequently into shame (Garwood, 1996). This reduction in the need for defences creates an increase in psychic energy and a lifting of the general weight of the psychic burden usually felt. This causes a sense of uplifting and freedom.

The format of the gatherings was developed through the psychodynamic insight of the founders. Their insights and creativity ensure the maximum therapeutic potential. Initially, only child survivors and their partners were allowed. This avoided the hierarchy of suffering and the recurrent problems with adult survivors who tended to deny the suffering of the child survivors or those survivors who were not concentration camp survivors. This was the hierarchy of suffering that was cruelly maintained in the initial post-war survivor community. In recent years, as child survivor numbers and energy reduce due to age and death, succeeding generations play an increasing part.

The gatherings take place over a long weekend in a large hotel. There are rarely less than 400 child survivors, and these days the succeeding generations play an important role.

Child survivors were defined as having been 16 years or less by 1945. Additionally, Kindertransport children who were older were routinely included. In the early years, all participants, speakers, and group conductors were child survivors, with the exception of Judith Kestenberg and Sarah Moskovitz, the organisation's matriarchal figures. No press were allowed. There was an awareness of the primary need for safety and for the issue of loss to be addressed. Most had lost one or both parents. All had lost their country and community of origin. Through their persecution, most had lost years of education. One of the greatest losses was that of their childhoods. Through the survival necessity, they could not play, and only the needs of survival were permitted.

The programme

In the first ten or more years of gatherings, the programme comprised of formal meals, presentations, workshops/groups, and spaces for informal social contact. Shame and helplessness being constantly present dynamics, empowerment through equality and creative activity was a constant feature.

Meals

Meals are designed to foster the feeling of family gatherings with what have been described as siblings of Holocaust trauma. Food is plentiful and of quality. Breakfast is arranged in tables of country of origin. This allows for the use of the lost or seldom-used mother tongue and the possibility of meeting a fellow survivor with shared experiences. Lunches are opportunities to discuss the issues evoked by the morning workshops and groups with friends and newly found surrogate siblings. Evening meals and lunches include talks given by distinguished members, often on a psychodynamic theme. These are usually ended with music and dancing.

Speakers

In the early years, only child survivors would be chosen as speakers. With dwindling numbers, scholars and prominent individuals would be invited to speak, such as Deborah Lipstadt, the historian who was sued for libel in a prominent Holocaust denial case. Over the years, child psychiatrist Robert Krell, a hidden child born in the Netherlands, has become valued for his ability to voice those painful psychic struggles that child survivors find so hard to express. Sarah Moskovitz became the matriarchal figure following the death of Judith Kestenberg, the Polish child psychoanalyst, and often spoke. She had a warm, religious childhood in a large Yiddish-speaking family, the benefit of which resonated and expressed itself in her capacity to express herself in Yiddish poetry, as well as her seemingly endless capacity for warmth and affection.

The groups and workshops

Child survivors tend to feel, as do other survivors of massive psychic trauma, that only those who had shared their trauma could possibly understand their pain. Experience has shown that loss of family seems to be the most powerful and long-lasting trauma. Powerlessness, coupled with annihilation threat, has been described as primal agony, and is the second most common theme. Loss of the capacity for independence generates great anxiety and concern. Thus, workshops on the recurrent themes of loss, ageing, insecurity, separation anxiety, powerlessness, guilt, shame, and self-blame abound under a related title.

In recent years, groups in developmental age bands have been organised – for example, groups for those born between 1941 and 1945, which I was asked to conduct. This means they were between birth and 4 years during their Holocaust trauma. These groups reflect the major differences in the effects of trauma on such young children and reflect the dominant effect of the degree of powerlessness and dependency of their developmental stage. The fact that for some, the trauma was experienced during the period of infantile amnesia poses the substantial problem that their traumatogenic experience affected their whole lives, yet they have only age-appropriate memories (i.e. only somatic and fragmented memories). This makes them dependant on older relatives or carers for narrative, chronological, and family identification details, and all too often they do not even have these.

The next birth age band was between 1940 and 1935. This means they were between 5 and 9 years old during their Holocaust trauma. They then had some time of relative normality before their Holocaust trauma to recall and to psychically use. Thus, their capacity for memory of their traumatic experience was less affected by immaturity and was past the period of infantile amnesia. Their struggle may be characterised by a high degree of need for secure dependency, which they may have had to overcome. Apart from the loss of family and community, this age band struggled with their loss of education and lost childhood as their survival was dominated by the struggle to survive.

The next and oldest age band is characterised by the capacity to act as or even pass themselves off as young adults. They were old enough to have had significant pre-Holocaust family and societal experiences, which may have offered protective remnants and experiences with which to help with their Holocaust survival, their post-Holocaust life, and the task of rebuilding their life. The older survivors have the most pressing struggles with declining strength and capacities and their declining capacity for independent life.

Therapeutic groups

Some years ago, the largely female organisers and therapists decided to include workshops/groups for those that had been abused. The group membership was restricted to those who had suffered abuse and a senior child survivor therapist was selected to conduct the groups. Soon after this, I was asked to conduct these groups, and in recent years was accompanied by Elisheva van der Hal, a senior psychotherapist of great experience from Amcha, the Israeli organisation for the psychosocial care of Holocaust survivors and their families.

Chaya

Chaya, a senior child survivor, had been attending from the earliest days of groups for the abused. She was an independent senior professional who had shown great bravery in her actions that helped save her brother and father. She always described her sexual abuse in terms of being a young, well-developed teenager having to fend off the unwanted groping of two males at different stages in her Holocaust survival and post-war struggle. She did not seem particularly overwhelmed or deeply distressed by these. Despite this, I always ensured she had the opportunity to relate her story again. She attended this recent group, telling her story in her usual way.

Danielle

Danielle was slender and held herself with such rigidity that I thought she was anorexic. She was so thin that she had an almost skeletal look to her face. She seemed so brittle that she would break with a puff of wind. This was the first child survivor gathering she had attended in the US. She had only attended one previous gathering for hidden children.

She described how she remembered being a child in their family villa in the suburbs of Brussels. She saw the Nazi cars driving into their front gate and called out to her father to warn him. Her parents and all her siblings escaped. She and her younger brother were hidden in a dark, unlit cellar. They had to wait for the farmer to come and feed them. They felt helpless, like animals. They slept on straw, and there were mousetraps to catch the many mice with whom they shared the cellar. She recalled her brother being beaten because he would release some of the mice from the traps. She did not explain where her mother and father and her baby brother were hidden. She explained that they were eventually taken by the Nazis to a transit camp and within a few days were transported to Auschwitz, where they were murdered. She was left with her sister and her brother. After the war, they went to live with her paternal grandmother. She never felt wanted. She described herself as being hated and blamed by her grandmother and aunt. She could not forget her grandmother, saying that if her son, their father, had not had children, he would have escaped. So, it was their children's fault that both her mother and father had died. This was the environment she was brought up in from the age of 10 years. Her brother could not cope with the hate and blame, and committed suicide soon after the liberation. This, she explained, is why she had no idea how to bring up children. Eventually, she married a British civil servant. She has three sons and four grandsons. She thinks her grandsons are wonderful. They are a great comfort to her.

She looked gaunt. She admitted to not eating much, not looking after herself, not letting people get close. Her comforts in life were art, culture, and music, and especially ballet. She could not describe a close relationship, except to her grandsons, who she thought were brilliant. They thought she was wonderful because she was a Holocaust survivor. When they studied the Holocaust at school, they could talk about her experiences. This gave them the best stories and it was fascinating for them. She had avoided her Holocaust experiences until now and the earlier hidden child conference.

The therapeutic challenges in her presentation were considerable. How much ego strength did she have? What was she looking for? She did not seem to know what she was looking for. What kind of intervention would be helpful? Thinking of her gaunt, constantly controlled demeanour, I suggested that perhaps she was looking for some peace of mind. I talked to her about the huge amount of psychic energy it required to maintain self-control, to constantly edit what she says, to constantly not give away information that she feels may be dangerous. This, she immediately recognised, was the way she functioned. I explained how exhausting this was, and how frightening and threatening it was to begin to feel older and more tired, and thus less able to maintain this constant vigilance. She acknowledged this. She explained how she works out daily in the gym to keep fit. She seemed to digest this as others were speaking, and she began to look freer, less tense, less strained, and less frightened.

After she had finished, Chaya began to weep, quietly at first and then uncontrollably, in deep anguish. In the many years I had known her, I had never seen her so distressed. Asking her why she was so distressed, she explained that she felt guilty about her mother. She explained that they had been warned the ghetto was being liquidated, and if they were to survive they must escape to the Polish side. Her mother was too ill to escape with them. Her mother insisted they escape and leave her. They never saw her again. Chaya berated herself for leaving her mother, repeating tearfully, over and over, that she should have stayed with her.

After some time, I made an interpretation regarding her powerlessness to save her mother and her defensive self-blame causing her to feel survivor guilt. In all the 20 years she had been attending the gatherings, she had not addressed this trauma. Now the trauma of being a young woman, left without another female family member to survive with her father and brother, to negotiate the post-war chauvinistic world without the guidance or protection of her mother, could be understood. How it intensified the loss she was not allowed to speak of. She was expected to be uncomplainingly grateful for survival, and only in the mainly female group for the abused could she hope to be understood. Until now, she had suppressed the traumatic loss of her mother. She was almost 80 years old and still she carried this encapsulated trauma. Only with the resonance with the Belgian survivor was the encapsulation ruptured. Perhaps she too had contemplated the escape of suicide.

Therapeutic challenges

The setting and work is unconventional and unpredictable, generating technical challenges. The participants are not vetted and the handling of difficult situations is left to the more experienced clinicians. An unexpected therapeutic challenge occurred in the early 1990s. A silent member of the youngest age-limited group thanked me after the group and wrote to me, saying she was looking forward to next year's gathering and my groups. At the following gathering, she sought me out, telling me how much she was looking forward to the group. I was pleased and flattered. In the lobby of the conference, displays were allowed for those promoting their books or artwork. A physically disabled and very vocal, disturbed-sounding woman who was using crutches was declaiming her trauma as a young child in Auschwitz, who in my mind I dubbed the "disabled woman." At first sight, she seemed to be high on drugs or delusional, or both. She proclaimed in a wild way, shouting at passers-by how she was tattooed under her breast with the name Auschwitz and what terrible traumas she had suffered. The organisers were uncertain as to how to handle this situation. They could see she seemed deeply disturbed and suspected she was not a Holocaust survivor, but had a need to be seen to be one. They were unsure as to what to do and so did nothing. My admirer and the "disabled woman" were seen to become friends and were seen in each other's company between events. After the first of the two scheduled groups for the youngest child survivors, in which my admirer had been silent, an outspoken, astute participant approached me and declared that my admirer was not a child survivor, but an "impostor." She asked me to exclude her from our final meeting. I asked how she could be sure, and was told the alleged imposter's US birth certificate had been seen.

This created some immediate dilemmas. As a medical practitioner, did I have a duty of care to our "impostor"? She had gone to great lengths and expense to get what she believed she needed. If I excluded her, would she be psychically harmed? What of the child survivors who felt betrayed that an imposter, and thus a voyeur, was in the group? Would it sabotage their sense of safety and obstruct the possibility of any thera-peutic benefit?

At the first opportunity, I asked the "impostor" as gently as I could if she would not participate in my next group. She seemed to accept this without question or protest. I felt guilty, but felt my first and greatest duty was to the child survivors who had never had a therapeutic experience with others who had been traumatised in the Holocaust at a similar, tender age. On my way to check that the room was ready for the next group, I walked passed the "impostor," who was talking to the "disabled woman." She seemed calm and unaffected.

The group began to assemble and finally numbered 43 members, a median if not a large group. Some had been deeply moved by our previ-ous session and were looking forward to the next session. One of the more apparently outgoing and jolly members said she needed to share something with us. She had waited until the second group to tell us that her son had recently committed suicide. I felt stunned and filled with sadness. I had recently remarried after my widowhood and my new wife had just given birth to our first son. The group was also silent and shocked. It is hard to imagine a more devastating trauma that could occur to a Holocaust survivor. The silence seemed endless and heavy. I felt the group were feeling para-lysed by their helplessness and seemed to be looking to me to manage this group trauma. I felt helpless and struggled with my own associations and countertransference. This was not the time for interpretations, so I simply said how terrible it was to hear of her loss and how dreadful it must have been for her. I then stated how all of us who have children dread what she has had to suffer and how words do not seem enough at this time. After a brief pause, another survivor described how they had lost a child through AIDS. Others then came forward with their history of similar losses. They described how awful it was but that it could be survived. Life must go on.

By this time, the group had been going for about 20 minutes when the "disabled woman" barged into the room, noisily slamming the door with her crutches and making her way to a chair. The group stopped and watched as she struggled to get a chair placed in the circle of the group. I felt anxious and uncertain. The group seemed fearful. Was I projecting my fear on the group? She seemed oblivious to what was going on in the room. As soon as she was seated, she began speaking loudly. A torrent of claims of her suffering and experience in Auschwitz poured out. It was a psychic evacuation. The outburst was confused and she seemed delusional. What was going on here? Was she psychotic? Was she having a psychotic breakdown? What to do? My dilemma was that I was torn between protecting the group or the "disabled woman." I felt my primary duty of care was to establish if the lady was psychotic and needed emergency psychiatric admission. I asked her if she would like to talk to me outside on her own. Sitting near me was another experienced psychotherapist, who I asked with a meaningful look to take over the group while I took her outside.

When we left the room and sat down, I expressed concern for her distress. She immediately began to calm down. She slowly became coherent. I was greatly reassured that she was quickly capable of rationality and was in touch with reality. When I was confident she had regained her equanimity, I found myself thinking of how I could leave and return to the group. I then noticed the "impostor" sitting nearby. I went over to her and explained that her friend had become upset, and asked her if she would sit with her to look after her. She seemed pleased that I had asked her to be of help, and they immediately engaged in conversation.

I then returned to the group. I was told that while I was outside, the talk was of concern for the "disabled woman." When there was a pause in the group, I asked how the group felt about what had happened. They asked how she was. I assured them she was calm and composed when I had left her. They felt it was the right thing to do to have taken her out.

In the group was a senior religious scholar. He seemed to be struggling with his need for help and his need to be in authority. Perhaps seeing the distress of the "disabled woman" had resonated with his inner core of distress. The group was sensitive to his dilemma and encouraged him to care for his own needs. He became emotional and then quiet. The group returned to the theme of helplessness, which I linked to the suicide of the group member's son and the "disabled woman." The group stayed with these themes until it came to an end. When the group ended, there was a warm sense of containment and cohesion. The group members felt close and heard. They lingered, seemingly not wanting to leave the room, and expressed gratitude to each other.

Although the group had ended, I was still preoccupied with the "disabled woman." What was my duty of care? What if she returned home to break down or commit suicide? So, I called the senior psychotherapist among us and explained what had gone on. The reflective space created allowed me to recall that one of the child survivors was a senior psychiatric nurse from the disabled woman's home city. When I spoke to her, she said she knew her and would ensure she was not just left without care, but would ensure she was secure and safe when she returned.

Imposters

The problem of those pretending to be Holocaust survivors continued. Those pretending to be older child survivors would find themselves being interrogated by curious survivors with similar histories in the search for some connection. Generally, survivors are unabashed in confronting and questioning each other. There is always the hope that a lost relative or friend will be found. The older impostors were soon found out. The impostors claiming to be too young to have coherent memories could evade the usual questioning. I first met what I believed to be two imposters in Brussels in the early 1990s. A man and woman from Berlin attended a gathering of hidden children. The woman claimed she had been in Buchenwald concentration camp. Her story was disjointed, contradictory, and unconvincing. How do I know she was an imposter? I do not know, but I felt I sensed in her demeanour and emotions differences from the other child survivors. Perhaps an absence of fear. It is not easy to define the effects of early Holocaust trauma so that they can be recognised. However, there is something about the way we speak of our trauma that suggests a deep, underlying fear of our own emotional response. Perhaps it could be a fear of being overwhelmed. In my experience, there was always a sensitive identification with other group members in which, in a group, we listen to the trauma of others and resonate to it. This seemed to show itself in our demeanour as well as our language. It is difficult to define but it is recognisable. So, when I hear someone who may be an impostor, there is an incongruity, rather like wrong notes in a familiar tune. Sometimes one notices the imposter watching carefully for a response in contrast to the sense one has with authentic survivors, who live and relive their trauma when they tell their story. One does not sense any artifice or effort to be convincing. Of course, after the exposure of the fraud perpetrated by the Swiss man Binjamin Wilkomirski claiming to be a child survivor of a concentration camp, imposters may not now be such a surprise.

Hidden, unhealed wounds and countertransference

In August of 2011, I attended a gathering of child survivors in Warsaw, Poland.

It may be helpful to remind the reader that I had had a six-year psychoanalysis and ten years of group analysis, a full group-analytic training, as well as many years of therapeutic work and supervision to work with my countertransference. Despite this, it was a particularly difficult challenge for me. My childhood spent in Poland was not lengthy. I was born in the ghetto of Przemysl on 29 October 1942. I have previously explained that I was taken to Bergen-Belsen concentration camp in Germany at the age of 8 months. Our return to Poland nearly two years later in May 1945 was only for approximately three weeks before we fled. My first return in adulthood was in 1991 when I returned with my uncle, Zigu, for the fiftieth anniversary of the murder of his family. He returned to show two of his sons where he had hidden for 11 months as well as to show me where I had been born. During the whole time in Przemysl, I was intensely anxious. There were times when I was terrified for no identifiable reason. I did not feel this anxiety when visiting Auschwitz on our way back. When I asked my father to take us back to Bergen-Belsen concentration camp, he agreed, but stated he could never go back to Przemysl ghetto in Poland because the memories were too terrible.

I had returned in 2008 to Kraków to give a presentation with the child of a Nazi at a trauma conference and to guide a tour of Auschwitz by psychoanalyst and group analyst colleagues. At the British airport departure lounge, I inadvertently dropped my passport, which was picked up by a passer-by who returned it. I kept directing my wife towards the arrival gates, becoming increasingly confused and anxious. Eventually, my wife had to take over the management of the journey, holding my passport and directing me correctly through the required security checks. I became most anxious when we arrived in Kraków. I found myself looking at the faces of passers-by, looking for a familiar or family face. I was expecting danger, and as I write I feel my alertness increasing as though I am now in danger and must be on guard. Eventually, we found a Jewish-style restaurant. Only when eating hot soup and some childhood favourite food did I begin to calm down.

I returned to Poland in 2010 for a gathering of child survivors. For this trip, I had decided to take our three teenage children to Poland to see the ghetto in which I was born and to go to Auschwitz. My level of anxiety was frequently very severe. During the conference, I conducted a number of groups for child survivors. In one group, a woman who had been in hiding in France described how she and several relatives had been packed like sardines in a coffin-like space while the SS were hunting them with dogs. She described how her father had told her later that he had held his hand over her mouth. Had she made any noise, he would have suffocated her. I found my reaction to being in her presence unprecedented. I had never felt like this in the past 20 years of conducting these groups. I found her presence terrifyingly unbearable. I did not understand it. When the group ended, I asked my co-conductor, Elisheva van der Hal, for supervisory support. We considered the history of my time in the ghetto that I had been told of. The room my mother and I had slept in was shared with nine others. It had high ceilings and large windows. It did not fit. The cattle truck we had been transported in to Bergen-Belsen had been crowded but not packed like a sardine tin. The bunk in the barracks in which we had slept six side by side was considered, but there was air and space at the head end of the bunk. We considered the cattle truck that we were transported all over Germany in for two weeks being strafed by Allied aircraft, from which we were liberated by Russian cavalry. This was packed, but not so cramped that I could not breathe.

Then I remembered being told that during one *Aktion* when the ghetto was being cleared, we had all hidden behind a false wall my father had built behind the toilet on the landing between the staircases. He had blocked the toilet so that it had overflowed with excrement so that the dogs would be confused and SS troops would avoid the excrement on the floor, thus not searching carefully. On repeating this memory, my overwhelming anxiety dissipated. I was a baby, a few months old. Had I been held and a hand put over my mouth to prevent me crying? Had I sensed the danger and fear? I will never know for certain, but my anxiety reduced when I recalled this incident. Did this memory simply create a coherent narrative and a sense of mastery through which to channel my fear? If this anxiety was due to a memory, how was it retained in the psyche such that it could still have such power to overwhelm me? This would seem to be another clear example of an encapsulated "memory." It adds weight to the argument that trauma memory may be encapsulated such that the toxic affects created are contained and continued psychic development is permitted.

The question remains: What was my psychic purpose in returning to Poland with my family? After some time in our East End London home, my mother had forbidden the use of Polish for the reason that it reminded her of Poland and her agonisingly painful memories. In my psyche, this became associated with being sent to the children's home. This was repeated twice when my mother required lengthy medical treatment. Thus, speaking Polish being forbidden, the Polish I knew was soon largely banished from my memory. In my various attempts to recall my childhood Polish, I was obstructed and overwhelmed by great anxiety.

The time in the ghetto was such an important part of our story but I felt no sense of mastery or ownership of it. I believe that I wished to give to our children an experience that allowed them to have a sense of ownership of the history they inherited. I also needed to feel a greater sense of possession of my time in the ghetto. That it was a place of which I had traumatic experiences, and not just a place I had been told of or read about. I also found myself saying a few more words of Polish, which was now less filled with anxiety.

These examples of retained anxiety suggest that it is not necessary to seek every traumatic memory or to heal every wound. It may be possible that we may be able to function to high degree despite severe trauma being psychically contained and encapsulated.

From the theory of FFF and the clinical vignettes given, it would seem it is essential for healing to facilitate the fight reaction. This is to stop the survivor being a victim. It is for them to choose how they fight. To fight is to gain mastery and to choose where and how their life is to be rebuilt. To stop or reduce flight and freeze is to regain the capacity to grow and to heal. The survivor may have benefited from the therapist's guidance but the achievement is theirs.

Healing processes

The survivor gatherings are important therapeutic modalities. They heal through group processes that resonate with lost life aspects due to Holocaust trauma. It was so intensely traumatic because of the multiple and repeated losses that were inflicted, which were intensified exponentially by the accompanying annihilation threat/anxiety and powerlessness. Trauma causes a loss of good objects due to failed dependency and an intense sense of psychic isolation often experienced as loneliness. The finding of those with shared traumatic history acts as a reparation for loss of family. The large banquet-like evening gatherings act as reparation for loss of family and community. An important healing experience is when a survivor who shared a traumatic experience is found. This feels like the finding of a lost sibling who one thought was dead.

In 1995, at the Montreal gathering, a short Polish man came up to me and asked, "Are you from Przemysl?" I replied, "I was." He insisted that I must go with him to speak with his wife. He led me through some rooms to a corner, where a thin and anxious-looking woman was sitting. He then introduced me to his wife, Ariella Lowenthal Mayer.

She asked what my Holocaust experience was. I explained that I had been born in the Ghetto and at 8 months old I was taken with my family in a proper rail carriage, and not in a cattle truck, to Kraków, to Montelupich Prison, the Gestapo headquarters, where my father was interrogated to determine whether he had been born in London. After three days and the murder of a large proportion of our fellow prisoners on the train, we were taken to Bergen-Belsen concentration camp. Ariella explained that her parents were murdered and she had been orphaned in the ghetto. She was taken in by her uncle, Dr Mayer, and was taken in the same carriage as my family to Kraków. She remembered my sister and father and my mother carrying me. She remembered that after arriving in Belsen, my father, who was allowed to move around the camp as he was a *Lager Friseur* (barber), came to her barrack and surreptitiously dropped a piece of bread on her bed. This meant life for another day. She recalled how he did this on other occasions, risking his life as it was forbidden and punishable by being shot on the spot. She never forgot his kindness. Sadly, my father had died earlier that year, so she was unable to thank him. After this, Ariella would always attend the gatherings and seek me out so we could sit and talk. We both had a special place in each other's hearts and minds. When I first met her, I remember my knees felt weak and almost gave way, as they continue to do when I recall our first meeting. She was very traumatised and suffered with constant anxiety, which she shared with me after her supportive husband suddenly died the next year.

This event was healing in many ways. Throughout my childhood and adult life, I was told I was too young to remember, and thus was unaffected and unscarred by, the Holocaust. The Holocaust was kept as a family story in which I did not participate. Ariella validated my presence and experience of the Holocaust. We shared the experience and validated the truth of the terrible past for each other. We told the same stories independently, and thus we could turn to each other, if it were needed, to say unspeakable and indescribable traumas had occurred and we had been there together. The story of my father's kindness had a special value as it enabled me to hold on to an idealised image of my father, which acted as an amelioration for the memories of the cruelties he had inflicted on me.

Child survivors are ageing and dwindling in numbers. This has had an impact on the clinical focus of the work. In a recent gathering that followed the shooting at the Pittsburgh synagogue, in which a Holocaust survivor was murdered, there was a distinct drop in attendance. The therapeutic group was for survivors only and included a range of ages such that some were adults or teenagers during the Holocaust. The title was "What do I need to tell my children and grandchildren before it is too late?" It was introduced by Elisheva van der Hal. She explained her background of being a young hidden child in the Netherlands and now being the senior therapist at the Jerusalem branches of Amcha. She gave the title of the group theme again. It began with two French sisters who were keen to tell us how they were hidden. They were matter-of-fact about the death of their parents. They did not want to linger on this pain. They then described how they had got to the US and made a good life. They ignored the theme and just wanted to tell their survival story. So, Elisheva carefully repeated the theme to help them think about what is important to pass on to their children. I found myself wondering about how much I had told my children. Had it been enough? Had it been too much?

An older man who had survived an extermination camp described how his children were not interested in his survival story. He would attend gatherings every year but none of them wanted to join him. He had taken them into the business and now they showed some interest, he said. He hinted that he knew this was only to avoid upsetting him as he was now their employer.

Then a man who had been a refugee from Germany expressed his deep distress. He was a Kindertransport survivor. He was hurt and angry that his children denied him the title of Holocaust survivor. They called him a Second World War survivor. He felt bitter and reminded us all that his entire family had been murdered. The French women were keen to advise him that if he brought his children up to be religiously Jewish, they would be interested. Another suggested the March of the Living, which takes mainly young people around the key sites of the Holocaust in Poland. It is reputed to be a life-changing experience. "That would work," he said. Another told of her miraculous escape from the Warsaw ghetto. The sad man continued to complain that his children were not interested. Some sitting near him tried to comfort him, and his expression softened and lifted from their empathy.

A survivor talked about being asked to give talks at schools by a very enlightened black teacher. The teacher had asked her, when she had finished speaking, how it was that Jewish people had recovered to some degree and had achieved so much, whereas black people, the teacher felt, had achieved so much less.

This had a discordant quality, out of tune with the rest of the discussions. Elisheva sat up, startled, and we looked at each other at this communication. It was like someone had rung a loud bell. What did it mean? My mind was suddenly working overtime. I asked the group if they thought if Jews were not white and inconspicuous, could we have avoided anti-Semitism more successfully? The group suddenly became animated. The men talked about how in business, they had repeatedly met anti-Semites who did not recognise them as Jews and were openly anti-Semitic. Another talked of how he had specialised in Jewish business and would not do business with corporations if he found them to be anti-Semitic. Another told of how he had been recognised as a Jew but the anti-Semitic slurs were not hidden. These stories were told over and over with fervour. The women then started to talk about bringing up their sons to marry Jewish women. Some women told how they had told their sons that if they married non-Jewish women, they would treat them as if they did not exist. This went on with vigour. I began to think of the social unconscious. I recalled that the murder of 11 Jewish members of the Pitsburgh synagogue, including a Holocaust survivor, had just taken place. I then asked if we had taught our children enough about how to spot dangers from anti-Semites in the US, remembering the bombs being sent to Jewish targets and the murders in the synagogue. Immediately, the room became more animated. The French women could not be contained. They stood up, declaring, "You must bring your children up Jewish and to marry Jewish spouses and they will be OK." The gentle businessman was reassuring. He had never encountered anti-Semitism that affected his business. Another said he would not deal with anti-Semites. We had come to the end of the group. The time had flown by, and a sense of calm descended on the group. Someone remembered that the gathering organisers had employed extra armed security, which was announced. We may have felt consciously safe, but unconsciously the deep well of annihilation anxiety, still deeply unconscious, had been reawakened, and in the group we had made it conscious and less toxic. The unique dynamics produced by the gathering's large numbers of child survivors were once again having their healing effects.

Discussion

Large gatherings create psychodynamic security from a community composed of the dispersed fragments of the originating community with whom there is shared traumatic experiences. This provides security at many psychic levels, including the social unconscious (Hopper, 2003).

The gathering as a form of treatment does not lend itself to the measurement of its effectiveness. The caution created by survived persecution will obstruct the completion of surveys. However, one measure of its effectiveness is the regularity with which child survivors attend this not inexpensive event over 30 years together with the anecdotal reports of the benefits. How effective is this approach? These unanswered questions must wait for further explorations. Some of the described trauma survivors or their children are appearing in our consulting rooms. It is hoped that this exploration will assist in the work.

References

Bowlby, J. (1998) *Attachment and Loss: Separation*. London: Pimlico.

Carvalho, L. (1995) Personal communication.

Davidson, S. (1992) *Holding on to Humanity: The Message of Holocaust Survivors – The Shamai Davidson Papers*. Ed. I. Charney. New York: New York University Press.

Freud, A. (1937) *The Ego and the Mechanisms of Defence*. London: Hogarth Press.

Freud, A. & Dann, S. (1951) An experiment in group upbringing. *Psychoanalytic Study of the Child* 6: 127–169.

Garwood, A. (1996) The Holocaust and the power of powerlessness: survivor guilt an unhealed wound. *British Journal of Psychotherapy* 13(2): 243–258.

Garwood, A. (1998) Psychic security, its origins, development and disruption. *British Journal of Psychotherapy* 15(3): 358–367.

Hopper, E. (1991) Encapsulation as a defence against the fear of annihilation. *The International Journal of Psychoanalysis* 72(4): 607–624.

Hopper, E. (2003) *The Social Unconscious: Selected Papers*. London: Jessica Kingsley.

Josephs, J. & Bechhofer, S. (1996) *Rosa's Child*. New York: I.B. Tauris.

Kellermann, N.P.F. (2001) The long term psychological effects and treatment of Holocaust trauma. *Journal of Loss and Trauma* 6: 197–218.

Krell, R. & Sherman, M.I. (Eds.) (1997) *Medical and Psychological Effects of Concentration Camps on Holocaust Survivors*. New Brunswick, NJ: Transaction Publishers.

Lyons-Ruth, K. & Jacobvitz, D. (1999) Attachment disorganisation: unresolved loss relational violence, and lapses in behavioural and attentional strategies. In *Handbook of Attachment: Theory, Research and Clinical Application* (Eds. J. Cassidy & P.R. Shaver), pp. 667–695. New York: Guilford Press.

Marks, J. (1993) *The Hidden Children: The Secret Survivors of the Holocaust*. New York: Bantam Books.

Moskovitz, S. (1983) *Love despite Hate: Child Survivors of the Holocaust and Their Adult Lives*. New York: Schocken Books.

Reed, S. (1999) *The Kindertransport* [documentary film]. London: Golden Reed Productions.

Reed, S. (2003) Personal communication.

Winnicott, D.W. (1965) Ego distortion in terms of true and false self. In *The Maturational Process and the Facilitating Environmental: Studies in the Theory of Emotional Development* (Ed. D. Winnicott), pp. 140–152. New York: International University Press.

Chapter 7

The Holocaust and the power of powerlessness

Survivor guilt an unhealed wound

Introduction

The following three chapters are what I consider to be my early Holocaust writing. There can be no doubt that all my writing is influenced by my Holocaust experiences, but these can be clearly seen to have Holocaust trauma as their focus. In the early 1990s, I attended a conference on the subject of the treatment of Holocaust survivors. I had founded the Association of Child Holocaust Survivors of Great Britain and co-founded the Holocaust Survivors' Centre in London, where we child survivors met. I was asked to offer supervision to social workers that worked with Holocaust survivors at Shalvata, Jewish Care's counselling and therapy centre. At this time, there was no consensus regarding the most appropriate treatment for Holocaust survivors.

A presentation was given by the distinguished author of a book on Holocaust survivor trauma. The basis of the book was his interviews of a number of concentration camp survivors. A number of prominent camp survivor participants were eagerly awaiting his presentation. He began by reading the survivors' stories. He was a skilled presenter and his delivery captured their sadness and pain. Their suffering was deeply moving. He continued in this mode, retelling story after story like an actor. He spoke in the first person as though he was the survivor. An Auschwitz survivor sitting next to me and I were becoming increasingly frustrated. His repetition of immensely painful histories eventually seemed excessive. The virtual absence of any psychological or theoretical insights was frustrating. I concluded that if he did not or could not offer an explanation of this enigmatic psychic response by trauma survivors, then they remained ill understood. I left the presentation determined to address this problem. I immediately began writing when on holiday a few months later with my new wife, Yvonne, and our first son, Aaron, who was then 10 months old. I completed the first draft. Soon after this, I met Yael Danieli and was invited by her to give the first public presentation of the paper at the International Society for Traumatic Stress Studies conference in a panel with Marvin Hurvich, the psychoanalytic authority on annihilation anxiety, and

Ilani Kogan, the Israeli psychoanalyst and authority on Holocaust trauma intergenerational transmission (Garwood, 1996). Being the first paper I had written and being unsure of its quality, I sent it to Charles Rycroft, the famous academic and author of *A Critical Dictionary of Psychoanalysis* (Rycroft, 1995). He replied promptly, briefly stating that the central thesis seemed valid. I had always believed that psychoanalysts, and in particular *The International Journal of Psychoanalysis*, were leading pioneers in the development of theories of psychic function. I thus sent the paper to Professor Joseph Sandler, who replied promptly, suggesting I send the paper to *The International Journal of Psychoanalysis*. I had little knowledge of specialist journals or their idiosyncrasies. The editor, David Tuckett, informed me that the paper was initially accepted by the British reviewers. The cautious editor then sent it for further review to American reviewers. It was eventually rejected on the basis that I was not a psychoanalyst. Ironically, the paper was selected by the recent editor of *The International Journal of Psychoanalysis*, Paul Williams, for the book *Terrorism and War* (Covington et al., 2002).

The traumatogenic triad of annihilation anxiety, powerlessness, and loss were central issues in my first paper. The birth of our first son seemed to evoke what I now believe were unconscious memories of powerlessness and annihilation threat, which I believed he experienced in the neonatal period. This created the hypothesis for the article on the power of powerlessness, which was written shortly after. The early hypothesis was presented in the survivor guilt article but more fully developed in the succeeding article. It was accepted by group analysis but took six years to be eventually published in the special edition on Earl Hopper's approach to the social unconscious.

The article on psychic security arose out of the article on the power of powerlessness. Thus, there is some overlap in the text and theorisation. It has become an almost automatic process for me to look outwards from deep psychic processes to make links with individual and group behaviour as well as to look inward to increasing depths of psychic function. In my countless contacts with patients in primary care, I had been struck by the different apparent degrees of psychic security exhibited. This paper flowed readily from its predecessors, incorporating a number of approaches, including the evolutionary and biological, instinctual ones that are needed by practising physicians. Although the instinct for the preservation of the species may be thought to underpin Freud's Oedipal and drive theories, even though Freud was not a Darwinian, but a Lamarckian, the instinct for the preservation of the self, the survival instinct, can be seen to be of importance in the face of annihilation threat. First, principal thinking is deeply engrained in medical education, and inevitably produces a search for simple, clear theories, which may be seen reflected in my theorisation. It can also be seen that despite the first paper being written before my group-analytic training, the social, interpersonal, and family context is essential to my understanding of massive psychic trauma.

The Holocaust and the power of powerlessness: survivor guilt an unhealed wound

Reading the psychodynamic literature on Holocaust survivors, my increasing sense of dissatisfaction prompted the writing of this paper. Numerous authors present deeply moving material from survivors' lives and then offer some explanation of psychic function. The theoretical bases of these explanations were usually derived from classical psychoanalytic theory. It became increasingly clear that current theory did not satisfactorily explain Holocaust trauma and its psychic consequences, which led me to the formulations offered. There is an implicit but unstated belief that only material obtained from the clinical setting has value or reliability. This view asks us to believe that behaviour in everyday life is not motivated by the same emotions and psychic processes demonstrated in the therapeutic setting and that survivors only show their true inner selves in therapy. In the standard literature, material from therapy or psychoanalysis is presented; the context and interpersonal setting are often needed to give it solidity but are lacking. It is for this reason that I have drawn on my experience of being a child survivor of the Holocaust, a child of survivors, as well as the many subsequent years of contact with the world of survivors, to attempt to make the mental processes of the Holocaust survivor more accessible and comprehensible. None of the material is presented as though derived from the clinical setting. This is a considered choice. If compared with clinical material in the now extensive literature, it will be seen that there is no qualitative significant difference. There are strikingly few detailed case histories and reports on psychotherapeutic work available (Grubrich-Simitis, 1981). Almost all the material presented was taken from my family's direct experience, in which I have been a participant as well as a witness. My survivor relatives, like the vast majority of survivors, would not seek therapy or psychoanalysis. However, much of the material was presented during my own analyses. In my attempts to understand my own psychic processes and formative experiences, both during and after the Holocaust, I have had what I believe is a rare, if not unique, opportunity to explore, as a participant, an analysand and a psychoanalytic psychotherapist, a complete nuclear survivor family's entire post-Holocaust life, and their struggle with their massive psychic trauma, which would never have become available for study as clinical material. It is unlikely that in the clinical setting the precise chronology, and completeness of detail, as well as the complex interactions described, which are open to verification, would ever have come to light. These efforts have produced the ideas and conclusions presented. In traumatised families, one member often takes the role of the healer. It is in this spirit that this paper was written.

When psychoanalysts and psychotherapists attempt to understand the effects of the Nazi Holocaust on its survivors, they are faced with inherent difficulties. The experiences of the survivors are unimaginable. Even if the survivor's suffering is graphically described, the listener's self-protective conscious and unconscious defences prevent them from subjecting themselves to that degree of suffering. Thus, the Holocaust survivors' experiences and psychological processes tend to be imbued with a mysticism and fear that may inhibit full and free analysis. As the survivor is so often held in awe, what tends to be overlooked is that they entered the nightmare world of the Holocaust as ordinary human beings and were forced to endure extraordinary events. The mental mechanisms available to them were no different from those available to all human beings. Although the full intensity of the experiences and suffering of the survivor is unimaginable, it may still be examined and understood.

Survivor guilt

It should be stated clearly that not all survivors suffer guilt, nor has the extent to which it is suffered been fully investigated. There appears to be little consensus as to the psychic determinants of its formation or the mental mechanisms involved. This has confused the efforts and compounded the well-recognised difficulties of those working with Holocaust survivors (Chodoff, 1980; Danieli, 1981; Kren, 1989). Survivor guilt does not fit classical theory, which maintains that the creation of neurotic guilt is related to the fulfilment or feared fulfilment of instinctual impulses or infantile unconscious wishes (Rycroft, 1995). Thus, survivor guilt has been widely viewed as being guilt for behaviour that Holocaust survivors would not have engaged in under ordinary circumstances (Ornstein, 1989). The important early theory was Anna Freud's (1937) concept of "identification with the aggressor." This proposes that identification with the aggressor reinforces and increases the intensity of the guilt. Bettelheim (1943), a psychoanalyst who spent a year in Dachau and Buchenwald in 1938, was an important but misleading influence. His description of behaviour in the camp was unremittingly negative and denigratory in tone, omitting the important place of reciprocity described by Frankl (1987) and others. Most recent theorists have held the classical view that survivor guilt is a form of pathological mourning in which the individual felt guilty for aggressive feelings towards the lost object, these feelings being suppressed. These death wishes became linked with the actual destruction of the object. Niederland (1981) later suggested that survivor guilt was a reaction to simply having survived. More recent views have considered its adaptive aspect. Distinction has been made between various types of guilt. Carmelly (1975) distinguished passive carriers who felt guilty about their survival from those who felt guilty about actual immoral acts. Robert Jay Lifton (1967) studied Hiroshima survivors, coining the term "death guilt." Lifton (1979) later differentiated between moral and psychological guilt and considered classical writing as having described the latter. He viewed moral guilt as an adaptive experience that helps individuals see their shortcomings, which, when not worked through, can lead to psychopathology. Grubrich-Simitis (1981) suggests that extreme trauma can be cumulative (Khan, 1974, pp. 42–68), causing permanent changes in psychic structures through deprivation of external narcissistic supplies, leading to narcissistic depletion, which causes grave and permanent changes to the ego-ideal. Klein (1984) considered that guilt maintained a link to Holocaust survivors' past and those they lost, thereby serving a healthy adaptive purpose in maintaining a sense of belonging to their lost family and to the Jewish people.

Survivor guilt development

All the above theories appear to offer some degree of understanding of survivor guilt, the more recent adaptive theories being of greatest value. However, they do not adequately explain its perplexingly high incidence in survivors, nor its formation, intensity, and persistence. Some were forced to act in ways for which guilt was entirely appropriate. For them, all causes of guilt will be linked and add to the intensity of the guilt associated with these acts. Others did not lose their parents yet still suffer survivor guilt. The classical theories of guilt direct thinking away from the actual experience and towards the phantasies generated in the unconscious. These may intensify and reinforce the response to the experience but did not determine the psychic mechanisms and consequences. In the formation of the established views, the existing theories have been inadequate, and new hypotheses are required and are offered below. It may be that the manifest horror of the concentration camp experience obstructed clear analysis and distracted from the pre-camp experience that gives the clues enabling the survivor guilt puzzle to be solved. It is also essential to the understanding of survivors' post-Holocaust functioning.

The four essential components to Holocaust survivors' trauma are: (1) threat of annihilation; (2) powerlessness; (3) object loss; and (4) torture. The latter would be considered by some to be a combination of powerlessness and threat of annihilation. All four reinforce one another, but powerlessness in the face of annihilation threat is of the greatest importance.

The majority of Nazi Holocaust survivors were confined in the ghettos of Eastern Europe. Many were the fitter, younger Jewish inhabitants of the thousands of adjacent smaller communities, their parents and younger siblings having been murdered. The ghettos were formed in the major towns adjacent to the railway and were walled off from the non-Jewish part of the town. They were inhumanely overcrowded and unsanitary. Anyone attempting to leave was shot on the spot. A *Judenrat*, a Jewish administration of Jewish elders, was immediately formed by order of the Nazis. They were made to maintain lists of the ghetto's population, from which they were forced to make the selections for deportation to camps or for immediate murder by shooting.

Some elders resisted, well aware of the fatal consequences (Freiwald & Mendelsohn, 1994). They were forced to distribute the progressively reduced starvation rations, leading to death from malnutrition and disease.

Death from "natural causes" such as starvation and typhoid fever was the norm. Early mornings brought the sight of those that had thus died together with victims of random shootings and hangings by one or two Gestapo who had dropped in for a visit the previous evening. In the distorted faces of these adults and children strewn around, I would recognise those of kin, friends, and teachers. *Aktions*, or raids, were routine and culminated in the victims being murdered by machine-gunning, and were succeeded by the more "efficient" deportation to the death camps. Although the fate of those deported was not known for certain, though suspected by those left behind, a deep depression always hung on the emptied ghetto streets for days after (Rosenbloom, 1988).

These carefully planned and developed programmes of systematic terrorisation, ghettoization, and concentration camp internment – intended to impoverish, humiliate, deceive, and enslave – made the Jews feel they were in part responsible for their own fate. They were led to believe that if they obeyed, worked, and were useful, they could buy a little more time and survive. The true purpose of these systems was to ensure that virtually no Jew had enough food, luck, or resourcefulness to escape death. To have survived despite all this, the survivors were made to feel they had had more than their fair share of luck, usefulness, resourcefulness, or food (Leon et al., 1981). Thus, they were made to feel they had survived by eating the food or using the lucky chance that might have kept their loved ones from death – that the price of their survival was the death of their loved ones and fellow Jews.

In the face of their cumulative losses and these inescapable yet impossible choices, of the mental mechanisms available to adapt or defend against their powerlessness, *self-blame* and consequential guilt were almost inevitable. It is my view that "survivor self-blame" had the initial primary and principal function of reducing the pain and anguish of intolerable powerlessness in the face of annihilation risk and overwhelming loss. Being forced to be totally passive and helpless in the face of the Holocaust was perhaps the most devastating experience for the survivor.

Resistance to healing and mourning

Survivor guilt has persisted primarily because survivors are unable to grieve and mourn their losses successfully. Whenever losses are remembered, the overwhelming feelings of powerlessness and annihilation fears that were experienced at the time of the events, together with the highly effective defence of self-blame, are mobilised with others described below. This effectively obstructs working through, and thus the mourning process. The unconscious tension between the fundamental need to mourn and the overwhelming feelings of powerlessness and annihilation anxiety that would then have to be endured generate effective defences to alleviate the psychic pain. It can be seen that if effective defences are not mobilised, then the unremitting intensity of feelings of self-blame and guilt would be likely to cause intense and possibly psychotic depression with suicidal feelings, culminating in suicide, which sadly has been observed.

The effective mourning of loss has long been understood as fundamental to mental health. It is well established that the mourning of a single important loss can be difficult, often needs facilitation, and frequently, when to some degree unsuccessful, leads to psychopathology. When the losses were unnatural, cruel, often unprepared for, and frequently multiple, then the difficulties of mourning are increased exponentially. Mourning at the time of the losses was virtually impossible as survivors were involved in their own life-and-death struggle. On liberation, the understandable priority was to rebuild their lives, and they were encouraged to look forward and put the past behind them. Delay in mourning is known to increase the difficulty and reduce the likelihood of success. It may be that "the mourning cannot be finished in one lifetime. It will take generations. Over six million Jews died, the enormity staggers one" (Kestenberg, 1995).

A unifying hypothesis

The theories

The classically based theories of survivor guilt are largely of the superego. These include Oedipal murderous phantasies towards lost objects, identification with the aggressor (Anna Freud), and cumulative trauma damaging the ego-ideal (Grubrich-Simitis). The separation of moral and psychological guilt (Lifton) separates conscience and superego and is self-contradictory. Guilt for simply having survived (Niederland), or death guilt (Lifton), is descriptive rather than explanatory. Most of the remaining theories are reparative-adaptive theories maintaining links to the lost past (Klein). At first glance, powerlessness in the face of loss has little obvious connection with the classic concepts of Oedipal murderous phantasies or identification with the aggressor and the other reparative-adaptive theories. However, further examination reveals links. The postulate that the central traumatising experiences were powerlessness in the face of annihilation risk, reinforced by object loss, would lead one to predict that the defences generated would be primarily omnipotent phantasies as a response to powerlessness, encapsulation as a response to annihilation threat and anxiety, and attempted reparation of losses. The psychic self-empowerment necessary for self-blame is achieved through omnipotent fantasy. Both Oedipal murderous phantasies and identification with the aggressor may be viewed as defensive omnipotence. Cumulative trauma and damaged ego-ideal imply regression to a primitive, malleable state. The traumata, undefined in the writings of Khan and Gru-brich-Simitis, producing psychic changes through altered internal objects and ego-ideal are congruent with the unifying hypothesis. The intense psychic energy generated by the unconscious memories of annihilation threat will be directed into any defence or psychic process at any level that will diffuse it. Self-blame is the response to memories of primal powerlessness, which will cause guilt at the level of the superego and ego-ideal, and remembered actions or humiliations will be found to become its vehicle.

The important issues of rage and shame deserve some discussion. When an annihilation threat is experienced, the instinctive reflex response of fight/flight is generated (Cannon & de la Paz, 1911). In a neonate, neither flight nor fight are possible, nor can internalisation of an object occur until memory develops. This increases the intensity of the instinctual fear gener-ated. Primal psychic agony is experienced, which sensitises the individual to powerlessness, and annihilation threat in later life is postulated as a new developmental hypothesis (Garwood, 1996). In the adult Holocaust victim, the rage generated by the fight response to annihilation threat could not be expressed without increasing the threat and anxiety (Danieli, 1985). Thus, it was invariably directed towards self by intensifying the self-blame and guilt (Woodmansey, 1966). The superego is conceived as deriving its energy from the child's own aggression; as a result, the sense of guilt is influenced directly by the extent to which the individual expresses his aggressive feelings by taking it out on himself in moral condemnation (Rycroft), or by identifica-tion with the aggressor. Many survivors suffer feelings of shame. Self-blame and shame are functions of the self-observing aspect of the psyche, the superego and the ego-ideal. Survivors, when attempting to integrate the humiliation and degradation they suffered, will find remembered experiences of denigration to act as vehicles for self-blame, causing shame.

The traumata

It is a commonly held belief that the concentration camp was the most trau-matising Nazi Holocaust experience due to its manifest dreadfulness and was presumed to be the major aetiological experience of so-called survivor syn-drome and survivor guilt. It is observed that the dreadful screaming night-mares together with the other florid symptoms commonly suffered by concentration camp survivors diminish in frequency and intensity with time. However, the memory of their losses usually remains unbearably painful. Eitinger (1971) studied 227 non-Jewish Norwegian concentration camp sur-vivors and found that guilt was not a significant characteristic in his subjects. Thus, incarceration in a concentration camp may not always cause survivor guilt. He suggested that the absence of a hero's welcome for the Jewish sur-vivors accounted for their survivor guilt. This may have had some reinfor-cing effect but does not provide a convincing explanation.

Although the great majority of the European Jewish population were concentrated in the East and were forced into ghettos, many survivors came from the Netherlands, France, Belgium, and Denmark, where ghettos were the exception. The Jews of Germany and Austria never suffered ghettoisation during this period; however, many suffer survivor guilt.

I have proposed that powerlessness in the face of annihilation threat and loss are the essential traumata required to generate the defence of self-blame and thus survivor guilt. These traumata can readily be found in the experience of the Jews of Northern and Western Europe. In Germany and Austria, increasingly anti-Jewish laws and public humiliation were intended to disempower, impoverish, and terrorise. Some 10,000 Kindertransport children from Germany, Austria, and Czechoslovakia were torn from their families and put on trains to Britain by anguished parents desperate to save their children's lives. In the other occupied countries, deportation to camps took place rapidly without the formation of ghettos. In the camps, disempowerment, infantilisation, humiliation, starvation, torture, and murder were the daily fare. Many children were hidden in these countries and were totally dependent for their survival on their protectors. Most suffered the loss of one or both parents. Thus, the combination of powerlessness, annihilation risk, and loss can be found in experiences of survivors of ghettos, the camps, hiding, Kindertransports, and refugees from Germany and Austria.

Adaptive and maladaptive defensive behaviour

Survivors' post-Holocaust behaviour shows successful adaptive as well as maladaptive defensive patterns. These may be defensive, reparative, and adaptive at the same time. They can be described as *searching, silence, living in the past, readiness for disaster, overprotectiveness, intrusiveness, boundarylessness, dependence phobia*, and *control excess*.

These have been described separately for the sake of clarity but may be seen to coexist and overlap.

In the survivor family previously described, the man and woman showed two well-recognised patterns of behaviour. He, characteristically, turned to action and was constantly searching for survivors. There is a well-described post-Holocaust symptom-free interval in survivor syndrome. Williams and Kestenberg (1974) suggested this was due to survivors still hoping and waiting to find some remnant of their families in fantasy, thereby delaying the full impact of the losses. This observation would support the thesis of the effectiveness of the denial and the attempted reparation in actively searching together with the other defences used to minimise the attendant anguish in this initial post-Holocaust period when the losses had to be faced.

In his constant searching, the man had discovered on one of their many trips to Israel that there might be a surviving *Landsmann*, a fellow exile from their home community, who was a pre-war friend and a ghetto policeman living in Paris. Forty-five years after their liberation, they found him. On meeting, the conversation was entirely between the men, with the wife a silent onlooker. Their conversation was confined to the confirmation of who had died and how they had died. Eventually, they came to the death of his wife's parents. Although the ghetto policeman had reported having seen her father's body in the square, she was unable to retain this. She became confused, and on later questioning said that she could not remember what he had said. Her husband was most careful to protect her from this affirmation of her losses, being uncharacteristically gentle and sensitive, allowing her this defence.

The defensive behaviour of searching is common. It is not usually seen by the survivor as consciously searching for surviving family members, but logically must include that possibility. It is clearly reparative, bringing a reduction of the sense of loss and, if the *Landsmann* knew their family, it brings an affirmation of their pre-Holocaust family and life. This may facilitate a degree of healing nostalgia and is generally felt to be of great comfort. However, while searching goes on, powerlessness and loss are denied, and mourning is to some degree blocked.

His wife behaved in an entirely different manner, showing passive stillness, silence, and avoidance of anything to do with her losses, avoiding any mention of her murdered parents, sister, and brothers. This silence was so complete that their children were not told the names of their murdered grandparents, aunts, and uncles until some 45 years after the war. The survivor who never talks of the Holocaust or their lost family is repeatedly described in the literature. The example given typifies this behaviour, which demonstrates the defence mechanisms of repression, confusion, and denial. It may also demonstrate encapsulation of annihilation anxiety (Hopper, 1991). Both survivors described were always highly protective towards one another when dealing with any loss. The serious illness or death of a friend or acquaintance would be carefully kept from one another for as long as possible, sometimes permanently, in a clear manoeuvre to protect the other's feelings, and perhaps their own. The link to the avoidance of facing loss is clear.

A couple survived in hiding for 11 months in a camouflaged cellar, often starving and losing their firstborn son in a fire. They live in the past, maintaining the same lifestyle since the Holocaust. The husband had learned while under the Russian occupation of Poland that working in a hospital kitchen meant he and his family never went hungry. His post-war daily routine would begin at dawn, when he would prepare food for the day. He made soup, a meat dish, and vegetable dishes – always enough to feed his family, with much to spare. His conversation was almost solely on the subjects of his exploits and experiences while the personal slave of the SS commander of his town, the recently convicted Joseph Schwamberger (Freiwald & Mendelsohn, 1994), and while in hiding. His wife would also talk of little else other than the ghetto, her home community, and her murdered family. They seemed to be living as though still in the ghetto, frozen in time. They believed the cause of any illness was due to "bad" or inadequate food, and the cure: his special cooking.

Holocaust survivors are commonly observed to hoard food and hide money, jewellery, and valuables, living with a suitcase packed and ready to flee from disaster (the Nazis). This is another form of living in the past. The freezing of the Holocaust lifestyle expressed in readiness for disaster can be seen as an attempt to avoid the finality of these massive and cumulative losses as well as a defence against annihilation anxiety. If the Holocaust has not ended, then, in fantasy, there is still a chance that some relative may return. Whereas if the reality is of 50 years having passed without the return of the loved one, then their loss must be faced.

Many married survivors are inseparable from their spouses. The extent to which they are never parted, almost fused together, is underestimated or goes unrecognised. There are numerous descriptions in the literature of survivors marrying quickly after their liberation and living unhappily but inseparably. The large and growing literature on the second generation frequently describes the overprotectiveness of survivor parents. Difficulties of physical as well as psychological separation are significant and often central problems. Intrusiveness and the lack of boundaries are also frequently described. Fusion, clinging, and physical proximity as protection from danger are all defences against annihilation anxiety, separation, and loss.

Powerlessness being one of if not the most traumatic experience of the Holocaust, then empowerment if not omnipotence may be sought. This may be found by the achievement of wealth and financial independence as well as control within the survivors' lives. Many, if not most, survivors are self-employed. Often their spouses and families are involved in their business. Control can be equated with power so that control over their lives, spouses, and children avoids the return of feelings of powerlessness. However, this is usually over-control due to excessive unconscious anxiety, and thus brings great tensions and sometimes catastrophic rebellion in their partner or children, driving them away.

Self-healing

Many survivor responses to their traumata have been adaptive, highly successful, and healing. This is achieved through *safety*, *effective mourning*, and *the creative reparative response to loss, reparation, and memorialization*. Thus, the rebuilding of a family and a place in a new community with the gathering of the surviving remnants of their community was observed to be undertaken with intense energy.

Through searching, fellow survivors were found. In Israel and New York, where substantial numbers were located, *Landsmannschaften*, the

Yiddish name of associations of fellow countrymen and townsmen, were formed. Most survivors will recount being implored by a dying relative or fellow Jewish victims to survive and bear witness so that they had not died in vain. The recording of their testimony then became of paramount importance. Many wrote an account of their experiences and of their community before the Holocaust, which would be amalgamated with others and published as a *Yiskor* book, giving them permanence. *Yiskor* is the Hebrew word for "remembrance." The testimonies would usually include their last contact with their murdered loved ones, memorialising them. The therapeutic value of documenting these testimonies has been eloquently described (Krell, 1985).

In the year following the liberation of Bergen-Belsen, 1,000 babies were born to the survivors. They formed the World Association of Bergen-Belsen Survivors and still meet annually to commemorate their liberation. In 1945, the British government, discovering many orphaned children in the concentration camps, agreed to bring 1,000 of them to England. In the event, only 732 came. They were housed in ex-army camps and children's homes (Moskowitz, 1983). They formed strong bonds, acting as surrogate siblings and parents, and formed the 45 Aid Society, keeping in close touch ever since. They were unusual in being brought over as a group. Most survivors dispersed, forming small clusters. Recently, they have increasingly felt the effects of their isolation. As a consequence, shared experience groups have formed. In England, associations of Holocaust survivors include groups of camp survivors, child survivors, hidden children, and Kindertransport children. After these groups formed, the need for a meeting place was recognised and a centre was founded. Shared experience groups are particularly healing. The Child Survivors' Association of Great Britain exemplifies these well. Most of the members had rarely met a fellow child survivor before coming to the group. It does not replace family and community in any immediately obvious way. There is a mixture of child survivors, hidden children, and Kindertransport children. What is shared and especially valued is the reparation of their enforced isolation as a consequence of their attempts at normal life. The almost universally expressed feeling that they are not understood by non-survivors is addressed. They are drawn together by a usually unspoken recognition of shared wounds and losses, without shame, explanation, or justification of their needs, perhaps as it could be in a healing family.

Memorials are of the greatest importance. A 14-year-old survivor of a community of 1,100 Jews in Galicia hid when the Nazis came to his village, Bzezov. On returning, he discovered that his entire family together with the other Jewish villagers had been taken to the Jewish cemetery and murdered. Initially, he was overwhelmed and immobilised with grief. When he recovered, he vowed that they should never be forgotten. He was captured by the Nazis, survived a number of camps, and eventually emigrated to Israel. There, he formed *a Landsmannschaft* of the handful of survivors of his community scattered around the world. Being a close community, all had been to the village school and knew each other's murdered families. As the fiftieth anniversary of the murder of his family approached, he became energised and worked frantically to realise his goal. Rather than meet in Israel, as in previous years, he arranged to meet in the village of their birth. He organised the building of a memorial on the sight of the mass grave and had a road and bridge built over the stream. He arranged a solemn ceremony in which the Israeli ambassador and a number of Polish high officials, including the Cardinal of Galicia, participated, observed by hundreds of the Polish villagers. Finally, Kaddish, the Jewish memorial service for relatives who had died, was recited.

At the Chamber of the Holocaust on Mount Zion, Jerusalem, Israel's first Holocaust museum, there are hundreds of plaques commemorating survivors' murdered relatives. They are understandably precious as there are no graves and few have known resting places. There are hundreds of plaques commemorating the destruction of the Jewish communities, their dates, carved in Yiddish, the language of these destroyed communities. Yizkor, the service of remembrance, is recited annually on the anniversary. It may be no accident that the museum is part of a *yeshiva*, a Hebrew college where Jewish law and tradition is studied and its students supported by the community, thus replacing one of the thousands of lost Yeshivot. Memorialisation and naming of perished family give them a permanence that combats the fear that they will be forgotten and lost forever. This act of reparation is a fundamental one, its importance recognised and ritualised in most religions and societies. Recently, the famous Nazi hunter Serge Klarsfeld (1994) published a book naming the 11,104 Jewish children deported from France, most never to return. It contains 1,500 photographs. He states, "We wanted to save the memory of these children from oblivion … It is not a book of death but a book of life."

Successive Israeli governments have clearly understood this fundamental need, many ministers and members of parliament being Holocaust survivors. In Israel, a day of Holocaust commemoration, Yom Hashoa, is a solemn national day of mourning. Moving ceremonies take place, including a two-minute silence, which is respected throughout the country. On the roads, all vehicles are found at a standstill, with their passengers and drivers standing in respectful silence when the announcing sirens are sounded. In addition, for the whole day the names of some of the millions that died are read out over loudspeakers throughout the country so that their names are spoken even when their last surviving relative has died. Thus, they are never lost to oblivion. These are creative responses to the massive losses, which for some Holocaust survivors will be sufficient to enable adequate healing.

Yad Vashem, the Israeli Holocaust memorial and museum, has a Hall of Remembrance and a Hall of Names. The latter is where the names of those whose death had been witnessed is inscribed in books and treated with great reverence. Recently, a new memorial, the Valley of the Lost Communities, has been built. The deep significance of these memorials can be seen on the faces of the survivors present.

The Hassidic Jewish community, recognised by their black hats, long coats, and sidelocks, frequently used to depict the archetypal Jew, continue to use Yiddish as their day-to-day language. It is believed that this community includes many Holocaust survivors. Little is known of them. However, it may be speculated that in this historically frozen, highly protective community, where every aspect of their day-to-day life is laid down by Jewish law and tradition, Holocaust survivors may effectively insulate themselves from the past as well as slowly heal through the many rituals in the Jewish liturgy for mourning and loss. The history of the Jewish people includes many periods of great suffering that are commemorated in the liturgy, thereby giving numerous opportunities to mourn. It is the view of some writers that the ability to retain a strong religious belief has a powerful effect in assisting self-healing (Marcus & Rosenberg, 1989). Although this has not generally been linked with the psychic process of alignment with a deity, an omnipotent power may be seen as a defence against powerlessness and annihilation anxiety.

Therapeutic implications

Working as a psychotherapist with those who have suffered severe traumatisation as well as many severely borderline psychotics has been of great benefit in considering the therapeutic implications for those working with survivors and their children. The proposed additions to psychodynamic theory offered and their therapeutic implications merit discussion. Therapists will be presented with the difficulty of containing and working with the effects associated with annihilation anxiety, powerlessness, and multiple losses. These echo the neonatal dependent state and generate the most primitive and painful of emotions, and the most difficult to endure, for the patient and the therapist. The countertransference may be so powerful as to be overwhelming and crippling (Danieli, 1981).

The taking of a history may be essential to establish and communicate that the Holocaust trauma and its importance in the current difficulties are recognised by the therapist. This avoids the conspiracy of silence invariably complained of by survivors, who complain that their Holocaust experiences were avoided or barely touched on during their analyses. The initial task of making the therapeutic setting a safe one will inevitably be more difficult. Consistency will be of greater than usual importance. Survivors have learned not to trust too quickly as the price for error could be death. They are invariably extremely watchful, with finely tuned antennae. Thus, annihilation anxiety will colour the therapy from its onset. The defences developed at a time of existential annihilation threat will not readily be challenged or relinquished. Focusing on and communicating the recognition of these feelings and the reasons for them are likely to speed the development of the therapeutic alliance.

The start, end, and breaks between sessions are likely to be the centre of a struggle for control as they may be painfully experienced as a reminder of past powerlessness, and thus be deeply persecuting. Trust and dependency are likely to be slow to develop, and when they do, the dependency is likely to be of great intensity. Thus, breaks between sessions as well as longer breaks will be experienced with the attendant anxiety and power given them by the actual object losses experienced in the Holocaust. Defensive pre-empting and lengthening of the breaks may be more common than usual. The pain of powerlessness will need to be focused on repeatedly in its various manifestations. If feelings of loss and mourning are generated, then the attendant anguish, rage, hatred, and desire for revenge will be present in the transference. They will be of greater than usual intensity and much more difficult to bear in the countertransference.

The success of the working through of this intense grief may largely depend on the capacity of the therapist to tolerate, contain, and work through the projected countertransference powerlessness, annihilation anxiety, and feelings of loss. Many, if not most, attempts at therapy with survivors do not succeed.

At a conference, a therapist despondently gave the example of a child survivor who asked, "How can you help me if you cannot bring my mother and father back?" The psychotherapist expressed feelings of helplessness and of being deskilled. He may well have felt in his countertransference the survivor's overwhelming powerlessness and despair. Another psychotherapist, a hidden child survivor, described treating a child survivor who at 9 years of age had thrown herself into a ditch to avoid being shot with her family, hiding there for some days, immobilised with fear. The therapist described an attempt at psychodrama in which he offered his hand to help her out of the ditch in which she was still metaphorically hiding. He repeatedly implored her to take his hand but she was unable to do so. Her annihilation anxiety may simply have been too great. Had the countertransference powerlessness led him to need to be active? Would recognising the patient's annihilation anxiety and powerlessness, and communicating this to her and persisting with this approach, have been more effective and helped her psychically leave the ditch? Focusing on the survivor's powerlessness and annihilation anxiety in all its manifestations is probably only possible if the analyst or psychotherapist is able to recognise its place in the traumatisation, and thus in the countertransference, and thereby free themselves of its paralysing and deskilling effects.

In a large group the author held with children of survivors, the focus being on guilt, traumatic and painful material was presented of parental suffering and traumatising behaviour towards the participants. The tension in the group rose as successive participants related their experiences and expressed their feelings of guilt (and unconscious powerlessness). Nearing the end of the session, when the tension had risen to a great intensity, the author offered the interpretation that their intense guilt was a response to their powerlessness in the face of the immense burden they felt in the face of their parents' loss and suffering. The tension in the group diffused almost instantaneously, as though the valve of a pressure cooker had been released.

Self-styled specialists in working with Holocaust survivors are appearing. They often offer eclectic and short-term contract therapy. The idea that these psychological traumata can be treated by short-term therapy can clearly be seen to be unrealistic for the reasons given. The term "eclectic therapy" may be a rationalisation of the therapist's "acting in" as a consequence of their inability to tolerate the countertransference powerlessness. Without the foundation of an appropriate qualifying training, together with considerable skill and experience and probably supportive supervision, therapy is likely to fail. As survivors are likely to be easily disillusioned and then despair of help ever being available, particularly as they usually come to therapy only with great difficulty and often in crisis, never to return if let down, then referral for therapy should be restricted to those appropriately trained and experienced.

Discussion

It might well be asked: Why is a paper on the psychological effects of the Holocaust being written *50 years* after its end? When so many survivors have died and most of those remaining will not come to therapy, or are probably too old to benefit from it? What is its relevance today? Part of the answer is self-evident. The extensive specialist literature reflects how ill understood the effects of the Holocaust have been. This is particularly true of survivor guilt. There are relatively few detailed accounts of lengthy analyses or therapies of survivors. During my research, I discovered papers that stood up well to examination in the light of survivors' experience. Some added significantly to my understanding. Most presented moving experiences of survivors and then offered little or no insight or understanding. Some authors engaged in veritable intellectual contortionism, attempting to use classical theory to explain survivor guilt. Most survivors complained of the conspiracy of silence during their psychotherapy, which avoided their Holocaust experiences. It also seemed self-evident that the only likely source of understanding of Holocaust trauma would come from psychoanalytic and psychodynamic concepts, as non-psychodynamic theories seemed superficial and largely descriptive rather than explanatory. Detailed discussion of the application of psychodynamic or psychoanalytic theory or of mental mechanisms was invariably superficial, and discussion of technical implications was conspicuous by its absence. These conflicting observations led me to believe there were fundamental omissions in current psychoanalytic theory, and thus prompted my attempt to identify clearly the essential traumatising experiences and the nature of the difficulties of understanding them and their psychological consequences. The question of why these traumatising experiences – annihilation threat, powerlessness, object loss, and torture – were so powerfully traumatising led me to the omnipotent defence of self-blame and consequential survivor guilt, as well as the developmental theory of the sensitising experience of neonatal powerlessness, annihilation threat, pain, cold, and hunger, and their link with the self-preservative instinct and primal agony.

It became increasingly apparent that these explanations could and should help explain the psychological sequelae of other traumata such as the birth of a sibling, bereavement, rape (Hill & Zautra, 1989), incest, sexual abuse, and other forms of post-traumatic stress. Sadly, history is repeating itself. The wars, genocides, and human rights abuses of North Korea, Vietnam, the former Yugoslavia, South Africa, South America, and Rwanda have produced many traumatised survivors.

With the passage of 50 years, the numbers of Holocaust survivors are dwindling. The child survivors will be the last witnesses of the Holocaust. Fortunately, they seem more open to psychodynamic therapies. The literature on survivors and the transgenerational effect is substantial and growing (Eitinger & Krell, 1985). The avoidance of powerlessness and loss is usually transmitted. The subject of therapy for survivors and the transgenerational effects, although discussed briefly, is one that requires lengthy and separate consideration. However, the issues of powerlessness, annihilation anxiety, loss, and self-blame as a response are likely to be central. The extent of the transmission to subsequent generations is now recognised (Bergmann & Jucovy, 1982), and the massive task of mourning is passed on (Wardi, 1992). Thus, sadly, this paper may have particular relevance for many generations.

References

Bergmann, M.S. & Jucovy, M.E. (1982) *Generations of the Holocaust*. New York: Columbia University Press.

Bettelheim, B. (1943) Individual and mass behaviour in extreme situations. *Journal of Abnormal Social Psychology* 38: 417–452.

Cannon, W.B. & de la Paz, D. (1911) Emotional stimulation of adrenal secretion. *American Journal of Physiology* 28: 64.

Carmelly, F. (1975) Guilt feelings in concentration camp survivors? Comments of a survivor. *American Journal of Jewish Communal Services* 52(2): 139–144.

Chodoff, P. (1980) Psychotherapy of the survivor. In *Survivors, Victims, Perpetrators* (Ed. J.E. Dimsdale), pp. 205–218. Washington, DC: Hemisphere.

Covington, C., Williams, P., Arundale, J., & Knox, J. (Eds.) (2002) *Terrorism and War: Unconscious Dynamics of Political Violence*. London: Karnac.

Danieli, Y. (1981) Countertransference in the treatment and study of Nazi Holocaust survivors and their children. *Victimology: An International Journal* 5(2–4): 355–367.

Danieli, Y. (1985) The treatment and prevention of long term effects and intergenerational transmission of victimisation: a lesson from Holocaust survivors and their children. In *Trauma and Its Wake* (Ed. C.R. Figley). New York: Brunner/Mazel.

Eitinger, L. (1971) Acute and chronic psychiatric and psychosomatic reactions in concentration camp survivors. In *Society, Stress and Disease* (Ed. L. Levin), pp. 219–230. New York: Oxford University Press.

Eitinger, L. & Krell, R. (1985) *The Psychological and Medical Effects of Concentration Camps and Related Persecutions on Survivors of the Holocaust: A Research Bibliography*. Vancouver: University of British Columbia Press.

Frankl, V.E. (1987) *Man's Search for Meaning*. London: Hodder & Stoughton.

Freiwald, A. & Mendelsohn, M. (1994) *The Last Nazi: Joseph Schwamberger and the Nazi Past*. New York: W.W. Norton.

Freud, A. (1937) *The Ego and the Mechanisms of Defence*. London: Hogarth Press.

Garwood, A. (1996) The Holocaust and the power of powerlessness: survivor guilt an unhealed wound. *British Journal of Psychotherapy* 13(2): 243–258.

Grubrich-Simitis, I. (1981) Extreme traumatization as cumulative trauma. *Psychoanalytic Study of the Child* 36: 415–450.

Hill, J.L. & Zautra, A.J. (1989) Self blame attribution and unique vulnerability as predictors of post rape demoralization. *Journal of Social and Clinical Psychology* 8(4): 368–375.

Hopper, E. (1991) Encapsulation as a defence against the fear of annihilation. *The International Journal of Psychoanalysis* 72: 607–623.

Kestenberg, J. (1995) Personal communication.

Khan, M.M.R. (1974) *The Privacy of Self*. London: Hogarth Press.

Klarsfeld, S. (1994) *Le Mémorial des Enfants Juifs Déportés de France*. Paris: Les Fils et Filles des Déportés de France.

Klein, H. (1984) The survivor's search for meaning and identity. In *The Nazi Concentration Camps: Proceedings of the Fourth Yad Vashem International Historical Conference* (Eds. I. Gutman & A. Saf), pp. 543–552. Jerusalem: Yad Vashem.

Krell, R. (1985) Therapeutic value of documenting child survivors. *Journal of the American Academy of Child Psychiatry* 24(4): 397–400.

Kren, G.M. (1989) *Healing Their Wounds: Psychotherapy with Holocaust Survivors and Their Families*. (Eds. P. Marcus & A. Rosenberg). New York: Praeger.

Leon, G.R., Butcher, J.N., Kleinman, M., Goldberg, A., & Almagor, M. (1981) Survivors of the Holocaust and their children: current statement and adjustment. *Journal of Personality and Social Psychology* 41: 503–516.

Lifton, R.J. (1967) *Death in Life? Survivors of Hiroshima*. New York: Simon & Schuster.

Lifton, R.J. (1979) Victimization and mass violence. In *The Broken Connection* (Ed. J.E. Dimsdale), pp. 113–116. New York: Simon & Schuster.

Marcus, P. & Rosenberg, A. (Eds.) (1989) *Healing Their Wounds: Psychotherapy with Holocaust Survivors and Their Families*. New York: Praeger.

Moskowitz, S. (1983) *Love despite Hate: Child Survivors of the Holocaust and Their Adult Lives*. New York: Schocken Books.

Niederland, W.G. (1981) The survivor syndrome: further observations and dimensions. *Journal of the American Psychoanalytic Association* 29: 413–425.

Ornstein, A. (1989) An interview. In *Healing Their Wounds: Psychotherapy with Holocaust Survivors and Their Families* (Eds. P. Marcus & A. Rosenberg), pp. 105–116.

Rosenbloom, M. (1988) Lessons of the Holocaust for mental health practice. In *The Psychological Perspectives of the Holocaust and of Its Aftermath* (Ed. R.L. Braham), pp. 341–352. New York: Columbia University Press.

Rycroft, C. (1995) *A Critical Dictionary of Psychoanalysis.* London: Penguin.

Wardi, D. (1992) *Memorial Candles: Children of the Holocaust.* London: Tavistock/Routledge.

Williams, M. & Kestenberg, J. (1974) Introduction and discussion in workshop on children of survivors. *Journal of American Psychoanalytic Association* 22: 200–204.

Woodmansey, A.C. (1966) The internalisation of external conflict. *International Journal of Psycho-Analysis* 47: 349–355.

Chapter 8

Psychic security

Its origins, development, and disruption

Introduction

Many of the ideas presented in this chapter are used in Chapter 9 on the power of powerlessness. That paper was written before I began training as a group analyst, and was accepted for publication early in my training by Malcom Pines, the then editor of *Group Analysis*. However, this was not published for some six years after its acceptance. The history of the power of powerlessness is relevant here. I sent the early version of this paper to Eric Rayner, the distinguished psychoanalyst and author of *The Independent Mind in British Psychoanalysis* (Rayner, 2020) and works on Matte Blanco. I was shocked and flattered when he rang me and invited me to meet him to discuss the paper. He was remarkably generous and positive regarding my ideas. He sent an early version of the paper to a colleague in Paris, who was the editor of the journal *Devenir*, who wanted to publish it if I could arrange for its translation. Thus, I found myself trapped. Senior figures felt positively about the paper but I would have to offend one of the leading figures in group analysis, my future chosen training discipline, if I withdrew the paper from *Group Analysis*. I felt saddened by the final rejection of my survivor guilt paper by *The International Journal of Psychoanalysis* and felt there was no point in sending the paper on the power of powerlessness to them. Becoming increasingly frustrated, I developed the ideas further and wrote the psychic security article using the same basic supportive ideas and research. As a trainee of the Institute of Group Analysis, I was eligible to enter the *British Journal of Psychotherapy* essay prize competition, which it was awarded. These papers emerged out of my observations as a family doctor and a psychoanalytic psychotherapist. The empirical approach often anticipates researchers and authors. The current version of the paper includes recent supportive references. The original paper and other papers presented here were informed by my grief reaction to the death of my wife, Diana. While editing this paper, my mother died. I have included some observation of my grief reaction to her loss as they link to my developmental experiences, which I describe in the opening chapter.

Psychic security: its origins, development, and disruption

The concept of post-traumatic stress disorder (PTSD) has been belatedly recognised by its inclusion in DSM-III (APA, 1980). It has spawned a substantial body of specialist literature in which, despite Freud having written *Psychoanalysis and War Neuroses* in 1919, psychoanalytic theory is given scant attention. Freud (1917–1919) suggested that war neurosis was a form of traumatic neurosis characterised by "an alienation of the self, social withdrawal, irritability, recurrent dreams and flashbacks repeating the details of the experience, and severe anxiety." Moore and Fine (1990) state that "efforts to relate the disorder to personality structure and function and to explain the symptomatology in terms of defences, gains and somatization have not been entirely satisfactory." Traumatic neurosis is described as having two forms: the first being where trauma acts as the precipitating factor revealing a pre-existing neurotic structure; and the second where the trauma is a decisive factor in the actual content of the symptoms (i.e. ruminations over the traumatic events, recurring nightmares, and insomnia). The symptoms appear as a repeated attempt to bind and abreact the trauma; such fixation to the trauma are accompanied by a more or less general inhibition of the subject's activity. Psychoanalysts, when speaking of traumatic neurosis, are generally referring to the second form (Laplanche & Pontalis, 1988).

A trauma implies an injury, but what has been injured? The clinical picture suggests this is *psychic security* (Sandler, 1960). In this chapter, I wish to suggest this is a psychic entity, and to explore and describe the concept, its development, psychic elements, organisation, and disruption.

During my researches into Holocaust trauma, it became clear that the central traumatising experiences were: (1) annihilation threat; (2) powerlessness; and (3) object loss (Garwood, 1996b). Pondering on why these were so powerfully traumatising led me to focus on the earliest experiences of annihilation threat and powerlessness, the instinct for self-preservation, and thus to the hypotheses that follow.

Primal annihilation anxiety and powerlessness

When exploring primal experience and psychic function, there is a tradition that uses material from the psychoanalyses of adults and children in which the analysand has suffered early trauma, to which many of the psychic processes observed are correctly related. However, there is a limitation in this retrospective approach due to the possibility of bias. Recent research gives us an increasing body of data from which to extrapolate prospectively.

(This opening section on early development duplicates much of the early section of Chapter 9 on the power of powerlessness. It is presented here to support a further argument: that humankind has evolved developmental processes to achieve independent function in order to reduce the risk of the consequences of abandonment and predation. Readers who have read Chapter 9 may wish to proceed to the section on object loss.)

Birth trauma

Obstetricians remind us that the second most dangerous event in our lives is our birth, the most dangerous being the event causing our death. Birth involves traumatic and precipitous changes in the neonate's world and would appear to be the biological signal that it has been expelled from the security of the womb and must now fight for survival armed only with its instinctual inherited capacities. Otto Rank (1929) felt that "the affect of anxiety is a consequence of the events of birth and a repetition of the situation then experienced," which was dismissed by Freud (1926) as simplistic and invalid. However, the proposition that birth is a trigger calling into play instinctual behaviour and drives is supported by observed physiological changes. These include changes in the lungs with the first breath and the gut circulation on cutting the umbilical cord, which, together with the first experience of hunger and cold, would seem to be sufficient to trigger this signal. Brain compression during birth seems to be a normative biological process, except in caesarean section, which is a recent and probably insignificant influence in evolutionary terms. The neonate's cranium is formed from separate bones that are overlapped by compression in the birth canal, gradually separating postnatally. This undoubtedly produces pain, which causes the release of catecholamines, which in turn is opposed by endogenous opiate production, the recently discovered endorphins, some of which are 200 times more powerful than morphine, thus enabling the neonate to calm quickly. Kelly (1982) has shown that these behave as an agonist/antagonist system. They are released in response to stressors such as pain and counteract the effects of adrenaline, and in this way calm the baby and reduce or eradicate their pain and anxiety.

Hunger, cold, and pain

The human neonate is totally dependent on mother for survival for longer than all other primates. Thus, it has an instinctual expectation of mother's presence, her capacity to provide food and protection, and consequently an instinctual response to mother's absence. This is indicated by reflex behaviours that assist survival, including the Moro,[1] the grasp, the startle, and the rooting reflex (Illingworth, 1987). However, these do not imply psychic object representation at birth.

For the neonate, warmth, food, and comfort mean contact with mother. Significant discomforts, such as hunger, cold, and pain, signify non-contact with mother (i.e. mother's absence). To the neonate, having no sense of time, mother's absence means gone forever, and the response generated by self-preservative instinct will evoke annihilation anxiety, producing the reflex cries of distress intended to alert any carer to the neonate's distress. Until memory is developed, the experience of mother as a source of protection and nourishment, a protective good object, cannot be internalised and is not available as a container of the neonate's anxiety. Thus, hunger means potential starvation, cold means loss of mother's body heat, and these imply abandonment or her death, while pain implies an attack on the body's integrity, an annihilation threat. Only after memory is developed and a need-satisfying, safety-providing object is internalised will significant discomforts cease to be experienced as life-threatening abandonment.

Recent research has shown that for the first two years of life, infants have levels of adrenaline and noradrenaline averaging twice that of adults, suggesting levels of anxiety greater than that of adults. These fall to adult levels by the third year (Candito et al., 1993). Massage of preterm infants lowers these levels (Acolet et al., 1993). Catecholamines released by the autonomic nervous system are a reflex response to threat, causing the fight/flight reaction (Cannon & de la Paz, 1911) driven by the self-preservative instinct. It is observed that by their third year, infants have internalised their key objects and acquired sufficient mobility and language to explore the wider world, and that a battle to control mother takes place, colloquially described as the "terrible twos." As their abilities increase, their instinctually driven levels of alertness and anxiety seem to reduce, reflected by the reduction of catecholamine levels to adult norms.

Fight/flight is not possible for the powerless neonate. The fight/flight reaction provokes a massive increase in excitation and anxiety, implying a massive increase in somatic and psychic energy. Being anxiety related to annihilation, the greatest of all threats, we must assume it will be nearly as dreadful as is possible. The existing descriptions include primitive agony (Winnicott, 1974), nameless dreads and great awe (Bion, 1962), and aphanisis (Jones, 1927). I would like to suggest that *primal agony* may be more apt as it suggests this is the first experience of psychic pain of such intensity.

For the proposed experiences and psychic processes to be seen as developmentally normative ones, it must be demonstrated that all neonates suffer significant hunger, cold, or pain. It might well be argued that with caesarean deliveries, the pain of brain compression is avoided. For the first three days, the mother's breasts produce colostrum, which has little nutritional content, rather than milk. However, bottle-fed neonates may get ample nutrition from birth. Despite these modern advances, there still appear to be some experiences and physiological processes that are constants. The change at birth from mother maintaining its body temperature *in utero* to the cold exterior, and the neonate having to expend three-quarters of its energy to maintain its body temperature, seems to be a potent physiological and psychological shock that causes the neonate to cry and inflate the lungs, which starts the cascade of physiological circulatory changes previously described.

Neonates cry to alert mother to their hunger or discomfort. Although among tribal peoples babies may be given the breast as often as every ten minutes, once the neonate is asleep it generally does not waken until hungry. Deep sleep occupies most of its existence during the neonatal period. Significant hunger must be experienced to awaken the neonate from deep sleep, demonstrating its presence and power as an unpleasant stimulus. From birth, the neonate must struggle to breathe for the first time, adding to its energy needs and thus its hunger, and must maintain its body temperature, which it has difficulty in doing. Its energy and food needs increase dramatically, causing frequent hunger. Primal agony would seem inevitable until mother has responded.

These arguments, in addition to supporting instinctual drive theory, suggest infants are instinctually object-seeking (Fairbairn, 1954) and secure object attachment is a primary psychic need (Bowlby, 1981). Additionally, they suggest that annihilation threat and powerlessness are potentially traumatising experiences throughout life due to our being sensitised to the primal agony of annihilation anxiety and powerlessness.

Object loss

Why loss is so potentially traumatising needs further exploration. When the neonate's memory is sufficiently developed and mother responds promptly and appropriately to the neonate's cries, meeting the neonate's needs, the internalisation of a representation of a security-providing good object begins. Once formed, it would seem to provide a shield against primal annihilation anxiety and powerlessness (i.e. primal agony). Significant separation then becomes equivalent to psychic abandonment and the removal of the protective shield that would cause the re-experiencing of annihilation anxiety and powerlessness. Thus, one part of psychic security is achieved through benign object formation at the cost of psychic sensitisation to object separation and loss.

Encapsulation as a defence against annihilation anxiety

(This argument and vignette is used in Chapter 9 on the power of powerlessness, and readers may wish to bypass it.)

The affects and energy produced by the instinct for self-preservation seem to be like free radicals. They seek to attach to available objects, which are the psyche's equivalents of molecules. At a molecular and cellular level, this must also be true. Before object formation, annihilation anxiety has the quality of free radical energy and must be initially contained as there are no objects with which to attach. This is achieved through encapsulation (Hopper, 1991) as this would seem to be the only psychic option at this phase of development. Once objects have formed, some of the encapsulated annihilation anxiety may then be bound, fixed, and detoxified through integration with them. However, it would seem that some of the anxiety associated with primal agony is never bound to an object and needs containment by encapsulation, which is part of the mechanism by which we are sensitised to powerlessness and perceived annihilation threats.

The following material seems to illustrate and support the concept of encapsulation of annihilation anxiety particularly clearly and is the reason I have taken the unusual step of including it as it is taken from my childhood. I was born in a Nazi ghetto in Poland and at 8 months of age was taken with my parents and older sibling to Bergen-Belsen concentration camp. Throughout my adult years, I had seen photographs and heard horrific details of Bergen-Belsen without conscious anxiety, even though death and annihilation threat had been ever-present from birth and throughout my first two and half years of life. In 1990, 45 years after our liberation, my entire nuclear family of four survivors returned to commemorate our survival. Arriving at Belsen, we visited the camp grounds and the museum, with its horrific photographs of our past. I was told many details of my time there but did not experience any emotional reaction. Awaking very early the following morning, I decided to return to Belsen alone to shoot some video footage. A few minutes after starting the journey, I found myself overcome by intense feelings that I could only describe as "dreadfulness." I was forced to stop until I regained some equanimity. Having recovered sufficiently, I continued the simple journey but constantly took wrong turnings. On arriving, I was unable to leave my car. I had become alert, sharp-eyed, and acute of hearing, conscious of movements of birds and the sound of voices, and felt a sense of relief that at last I had some emotional reaction to my terrible childhood. Walking into the grounds and reaching the site of the entrance to my part of the camp, I felt my stride beginning to shorten and slow. My shoulders and head dropped and my legs weakened until I had to stop. I found myself rooted to the spot, unable to lift my head or move. I felt so weak as to be barely able to support my weight. My eyes kept scanning the ground in front of me in repeated arcs. I was conscious of people walking past, but could not move or look up at them, and felt a sense of menace from those that moved quickly. This lasted for some minutes, eventually dissipating.

Reflecting on these experiences, I believed I recognised them as an age-appropriate, somatic memory of how I had felt as a weak and starving child in Belsen, scavenging for food, suffering from rickets, barely able to stand or move, constantly terrified.

On returning to London, my reaction to photographs of Belsen changed. I would tremble uncontrollably and those terrible feelings returned. I concluded that my memories and their associated affects had until now been encapsulated. Annihilation threat and terror were a constant presence from my birth, and thus the memory demonstrated the breaching of the encapsulation since birth, the normative period of infant amnesia, as well as the psychic organisation producing security.

Bion's (1962, 1970) ideas regarding containment are relevant here, particularly the notion of the capacity by mother to contain anxiety, which the neonate eventually internalises, creating its own internal container. Segal's (1981) work, discussed in Garland's (1991) valuable article on trauma and the breaching of the walls of the container, leads logically to the concept of encapsulation as a defence against the fear of annihilation.

Psychic security

Thus, encapsulation of the annihilation anxiety, security-providing object formation, and secure attachment are the psychic elements and organisation providing psychic security. These are maintained throughout life for psychic security to be optimised.

Throughout life, the body has the physiological potential to produce annihilation anxiety through the fight/flight reaction. The psychic apparatus for effective encapsulation and benign attachment and diffusion of annihilation anxiety is always being tested. In the event of a perceived threat such as a debilitating illness, the encapsulation of this unconscious memory of primal agony will be strengthened or weakened, depending on the intensity of the perceived threat and the effectiveness of the response of the security-providing mechanisms and objects. These instinctual physiological and psychological systems for processing annihilation threats have evolved through the biological certainty of life-threatening events, which begin at birth and end in death. If the system fails or is disrupted, then traumatic neurosis, anxiety states, or PTSD may result.

Physiological systems are evolved, instinctually derived, and have survival value. There would seem to be survival value in a balance between vigilance for annihilation threats and psychic security. Insufficient vigilance will increase the risk of death through carelessness or overconfidence. This is seen in teenage drivers. Insufficient psychic security will cause the use of excessive psychic energy in constant anxious internal and external vigilance, seen in phobics and described as hypervigilance, a major symptom of PTSD, which reduces or prevents many activities, thus depleting energy needed for pursuit and retention of sexual partners and the capacity for creativity and mastery of the external environment.

The system I am proposing functions as follows. A threat is perceived and excitation is caused, mediated through the fight/flight response, producing catecholamine release and the psychic response of annihilation anxiety. Initially, this anxiety is free-floating like free radicals. Attachment to a safety-providing object will be attempted to detoxify it. If an effective safety-providing object is available, the psychic representation of the anxiety-producing stimulus will be confronted by the security-providing object and will be detoxified. If this fails, the psychic representation is likely to be split and the residual toxic anxiety will be incorporated with a malign object, represented by conscious concepts such as bad luck, the devil, and a vengeful god, or unconsciously represented by the punitive superego or a phobic symbol. These processes are not instantaneous, which is demonstrated by the repetitive ruminations observed in those having suffered a degree of psychic threat. Thus, there is a need for a containing mechanism for the annihilation anxiety until it is fixed. This is achieved through attempted encapsulation, which uses standard defence mechanisms such as repression

Object loss and security disruption

I wish to suggest that existential object loss disrupts the encapsulation and object relations that provide psychic security. Object loss is a psychic trauma provoking powerful, often overwhelming psychic processes due to our forced confrontation with mortality. Powerlessness to undo the finality of the loss is experienced and evokes our primal instinctual annihilation anxieties, which give grief its extraordinary psychic power. Thus, loss, powerlessness, and annihilation anxiety are instinctually and psychically linked (Garwood, 1996a). Bowlby (1981) suggests that the links between actual object loss and infantile annihilation anxieties are clear.

Most authors agree there are specific stages of grief (Bowlby, 1961, 1981; Kubler-Ross, 1970; Lindemann, 1944; Murray Parkes, 1986), the first being shock, which may include disbelief, numbness, denial, physical collapse, violent outbursts, and dazed withdrawal (Pincus, 1974). If the only certainty after birth is death, why is shock the reaction in the face of this fundamental truth? I would suggest that our formative psychic years and much of our adult psychic life and energy are spent in developing and maintaining psychic security from annihilation threat and psychic abandonment by the attempted development and maintenance of benign internal objects and object relationships, as well as existential physical security, which gives protection from unpredictable natural threats. When loss occurs, despite all of these psychic and existential defences, we are forcibly confronted with mortality, reminding us of our own. Thus, shock is the reaction to the traumatic disruption of our defensive organisation and denials.

This is followed by a phase of turmoil and protest. There is a struggle to re-establish psychic equanimity. Denial of the loss, incredulity, anger, and reproach of self, the loved one, and the medical attendants for allowing the loss to have occurred are common. Blame predominates being an omnipotent self-empowering defence as it implies "I (they) chose wrongly: I could have done something: I can do something and if I only tried hard enough I will find what it is" (Danieli, 1981).

Classical theory suggests resolution is achieved by relinquishing the object. However, observation suggests the object is not relinquished, but remains active and important in our internal world. These are now described as continuing bonds: "The [bereavement] survivor holds the deceased in long memory … an inner representation of the deceased is normal rather than abnormal" (Klass et al., 1996, p. 491).

The hypothesis offers an alternative resolution. Although we attempt to maintain benign security-providing objects, internal objects usually produce both security and insecurity. On death, the memory of the object's problematic behaviour, if not indelibly ingrained, will be repressed and the object is idealised (Murray Parkes & Prigerson, 2010), giving it a nostalgic glow. The events following Princess Diana's death exemplify this. It becomes more benign and more likely to provide security and narcissistic supplies unconditionally and on demand, increasingly coming under the psychic control of the bereaved. This, I suggest, is the ideal resolution. However, this may fail to take place or may only partly be achieved.

Object loss and suicide

If mother provides an effective protective, need-fulfilling environment and adequate narcissistic supplies, then cumulative trauma (Khan, 1974, pp. 42–68) will have been avoided. This experience having been internalised will be successfully turned to for comfort. However, if the mother is unable to provide sufficient security for the infant, then turning to the comforting object will also evoke anxiety that may exceed the object's comforting capacity, causing the anxious attachment described by Bowlby (1981).

Clinicians will be familiar with the sadly common occurrence of rejection in a relationship causing suicide. This contrasts starkly with those that respond with optimism for their future. The despairing individual suffers the anguish of an overwhelming experience of loss, abandonment, and thus unconscious annihilation anxiety. Sufficient comfort is self-evidently not available from the maternal object. Annihilation anxiety will cause the fight/ flight reaction. The fight reaction produces murderous rage, which will increase the unavailability of any comforting capacity of the object, increasing the sense of loss. Flight will be self-defeating as it increases the separation. In the face of this anguish and powerlessness, empowerment will be achieved through self-blame and self-punishment to the point of self-destruction, unless the destructive cycle is somehow broken. Attachment trauma was shown in 86 per cent of suicidal patients in a study by Adam et al. (1996).

Psychic security, infant development, and PTSD

It is observed that infants strive with great determination, which is instinctually derived, to gain motor control, strength, and coordination to effectively communicate and achieve mobility. They seem driven to explore and understand their world to achieve autonomy and self-reliance. The instinct for self-preservation would appear to drive this quest for empowerment over dependency and vulnerability, giving protection from abandonment and the risks of natural threats. The infant seems to be driven to learn to scavenge for food and avoid danger by hiding and running, as though it were living in the hunter-gatherer community when these instinctual drives were evolved. The games of chase and hide and seek are probably universal. The drive to develop a secure relationship with mother seems remarkably strong, is observed throughout life, and if achieved early will facilitate independence. It is observed that children may achieve psychic security in the first three years of life but, if insecurely attached, may exhibit insecure symptoms and behaviour that may continue throughout life.

Biological systems invariably have an underlying organising principle. One is suggested by the symptoms of PTSD. Infants are observed to re-enact situations of distress or anxiety during play, usually taking the position of authority. Their omnipotent play fantasies are efforts to achieve psychic mastery and empowerment, thus reducing anxiety, their subjective powerlessness, and the power of perceived threats. Play repetition is constantly observed. Repetition compulsion was used by Freud (1926) to describe an innate tendency to revert to earlier conditions. He saw it as relatively uninfluenced by the pleasure/unpleasure principle, and used this characteristic to differentiate mental operations that are more primitive in a biological, evolutionary sense than those regulated by the pleasure principle. Repetition would seem to be necessary for effective internalisation. Stern (1985) suggests research shows neonates seek patterns of repetition in events that perhaps make the world more predictable. The repetition of obsessive behaviour observed in infants and children and the repetition of themes in therapy may indicate that repetition is fundamental to psychic integration.

Freud (1920) stressed how active repetition in play of previously unpleasurable experiences that have made a great impression upon the child enables him to gain mastery over the situation, diminishing the strength of the underlying anxiety. Freud also linked the repetition compulsion in play with some of the intransigent phenomena revealed in his analysis of shell-shocked adults, phenomena that contributed to his hypothesis of the death instinct.

The following vignette would seem to illustrate repetitive anxious play in search of mastery:

A 2{1/2}-year-old child with gastroenteritis was suffering diarrhoea, severe weakness, hunger, and abdominal pain whenever she ate. While being cuddled by her mother, she spontaneously associated to the words "sticking plaster," then recalled having had her fingertip amputated in a door. It regrew. She then remembered a traumatic allergic reaction to nuts that necessitated hospitalisation. When having her bath, she played with cups of water, repeatedly saying she was eating nuts. This seems to illustrate play provoked by weakness and hunger, which in fantasy she had the power to overcome.

The repetitive nature of the symptoms of PTSD and morbid ruminations would seem to be an effort to psychically master the threat and painful affects contained in the memory of the trauma. Recurrent distressing dreams are part of the process of attempted integration of the experience. Flashbacks, the intrusive, unchanged memories seen in traumatic neurosis, are clearly not object-attached and support the suggestion that they are insecurely encapsulated. These processes seem to be psychically similar to anxious childhood play.

The pattern of processes described seems familiar. The re-enactment of the dependent child beside the safety-providing maternal object also describes the analysand on the couch. The analysand presenting the current problem over and over again echoes the child's attempt at play, integration, and mastery.

Conclusion

In this theoretical exploration, I have taken as my starting point traumatic neurosis and its recent recognition in the form of PTSD. I have attempted to address the question of what has been traumatised in these conditions and have suggested it is a psychic entity, which I have called psychic security. I have then attempted to describe its elements, organisation, development, and disruption. Having explored the place of the self-preservative instinct, birth trauma, and neonatal powerlessness in the face of annihilation threat provoked by neonatal cold, hunger, and pain, I have suggested these cause primal agony that sensitises us to powerlessness and annihilation anxiety. The self-preservative instinct drives the neonate to be object-seeking and to attempt to internalise a benign security-providing object. If successful, it shields us from annihilation anxiety, powerlessness, and primal agony. Significant separation removes the shield, allowing the full force of these unconscious memories and affects to re-emerge. This gives separation and loss its power. Encapsulation of the annihilation anxiety and powerlessness is a containment mechanism, making it psychically possible to turn to the benign safety-providing object and avoid primal agony. Object loss thus becomes a psychic trauma, provoking powerful, often overwhelming psychic disturbances seen during grief, which parallels those of PTSD.

These developmental hypotheses offer some possible clinical and theoretical implications. They suggest the drive for psychic and existential empowerment, mastery, and control is derived from the self-preservative instinct. Disorders in which anxiety, excessive control of self and others, and omnipotence predominate may be rooted in the earliest phase of secure object relations development. These include the anxiety disorders such as phobias but also, less obviously, eating disorders, obsessive-compulsive disorders, and forms of hysteria. Their resistance to treatment may be explained by their psychic link with annihilation anxiety and the self-preservative instinct.

Technique has developed empirically from the understanding, sometimes more intuitive than theoretical, of the need for a secure setting and boundaries. Understanding, and thus interventions, may become more sensitive to the place of powerlessness, separation, and loss. Dynamics that resonate with primal powerlessness and annihilation anxiety are likely to become important aspects of the therapeutic process that need to be recognised, contained, and worked through. The theses suggest that we have all been sensitised to primal powerlessness and annihilation anxiety and defend against their psychic effects. Thus, working at these levels involves the most painful counter-transferences (Danieli, 1981).

A full exploration of the implications would require separate and lengthy discussion. However, it can be seen that the thesis may provide an alternative to the death instinct in that aggression and murderous rage may be generated by the instinct for self-preservation through the fight response in situations of imagined or actual threat, and killing for pleasure may be an omnipotent response to powerlessness and annihilation threat by taking power over the life and death of self and others.

Postscript

When Murray Parkes (1986; see also Murray Parkes & Prigerson, 2010), a leading authority on bereavement, published his authoritative work, in the 1972 edition, he devoted approximately two pages to the reliving of trauma and the continued relationship with the lost object. It is not in the index, which I highlight in the early version of this paper. In the 2010 edition, authored with Prigerson, the third chapter is entitled "Trauma," the fourth "Attachment and loss," and the fifth "Continuing bonds." They discuss fight/flight/freeze and begin to explore the concept of psychic fight/flight.

During the final compilation and editing of this book, my mother's health suddenly deteriorated. She went into a coma and died. She was six days short of her 92nd birthday and had been suffering with progressive dementia for the last few years such that she did not recognise me. In recent weeks, she had been constantly confused and rambling in various languages, mainly Yiddish and Polish.

I believe it may help to illustrate and follow some of the psychic impact of this loss by my charting my reactions. Through the biographical details I have previously given, I have offered a context as well as some data to form a sense of the quality of the security and nature of my attachment to my mother. This should help understand my grief reaction and relate it to the theoretical propositions presented.

When I was first told she was in a coma, I felt a deep and anxious need to be with her. It was my own anxiety I was struggling with. Having rushed to see her and from my medical training, I could see she was deteriorating but was not in immediate danger of dying. Her quality of life had now rapidly deteriorated and she was suffering constantly. After I left her, I was racked with feelings of anxiety. I was nearly overcome by the desire to rush back and be with her in case she should suddenly die. This was a deep and childlike state that was only just controlled by turning to my medical knowledge and experience, which told me she was stable, deteriorating steadily but not in immediate danger.

She soon deteriorated to the point where she was in her final struggle. I found myself preoccupied with the desire to convey to her she was not alone, and that my sister and I were with her. I did not want her to feel alone. I wanted her to know I would not abandon her. Her being in a coma and her lack of response did not produce a rational diminution of this desire, and I repeatedly spoke to her, telling her I was with her. My medical training only served to prevent me from denying the pain of her struggle to breathe, and thus I was unable to diminish my recognition of her suffering. I retain and return to the image and sound of her fighting for breath hour after hour. I was torn between my desire for her to show the determined fighter she was and for her pointless struggle, which I knew she would inevitably lose, and her suffering to end.

After her struggle was over, I was exhausted, tormented, and overwhelmed. I could not bring myself to think clearly. I just wanted to be left alone. I felt numb and intensely lethargic. I avoided conversation or social contact. On reflection, I recognised this as a dissociation, perhaps to the abused, silent, watchful child part of my psyche. I was avoiding the memories of this recent trauma. I was in flight; I did not and could not simply return to being the disciplined and committed doctor. Intermittently, I felt a sense of relief that my lifelong feelings of responsibility for my mother's welfare and recent care were at last ended. In these early days, I would often switch off by dissociating.

One of my empirical observations of my patients in grief was their preoccupation with death and their mortality. This is found in most descriptions of grief, and doctors are warned to look out for the delusional belief that the bereaved may develop: that they are suffering from the same fatal illness as their loved one. I have suggested that being confronted with loss forcibly reminds us of our own mortality, and thus psychic effort must be made to reconstruct and repair our psychic processes, which give us more optimal psychic security.

In my grief, I found myself returning to the memory of my mother's life and her fighting for breath. I oscillated between a sense of helplessness, as I knew this final struggle was unavoidable, and a wish that it should not be prolonged, as well as a sense of admiration for the fight still displayed by this tiny woman who was my mother. At this time, there was a news item of a burglar who became stuck in a chimney and died, being discovered many weeks later. It reminded me of the carefully designed, terrible, tiny, suffocating cells in Auschwitz and my own fear of dying and fighting for breath. I became increasingly vulnerable and sad. Yet this feeling was coupled with a great sense of relief that I no longer had to constantly be watchful for my mother and protect and look after her. My lifelong burden of parentification (Chase, 1999) was lifted from me.

I found comfort in listening to soothing Mozart arias such as *Porgi Amor*, as well as gardening and homemaking. The latter two would increase my existential psychic security.

When I was approximately 5 years old, my mother declared she did not want to hear the sound of Polish in our home and we were to speak only English or Yiddish. This caused an association in my mind with speaking Polish and traumatic separation, such as being sent to the children's home. Several times during my adult life, I met with Polish survivors, colleagues, and recently a long-lost cousin. All previous attempts to speak Polish were quickly thwarted by overwhelming anxiety, distress, and exhaustion. I had owned a Polish language course with a speech cassette for 20 years. I began to try to obtain Polish conversation lessons to enable me to speak to my Polish cousin who spoke little English. One month after my mother's death, an attempt to have lessons with a Polish survivor floundered. However, I found myself able to listen to the audio lessons and begin to reabsorb and recognise the language. Initially, I was still distractible, flitting to other tasks such as tea-making; however, I was able to think clearly enough to order a modern version after listening to the sample speech and lessons. This had a CD that I would be able to listen to in the car.

In my bereavement, my fear of abandonment had to be faced. My sense of responsibility associated with annihilation anxiety due to my early survival being dependent on my mother's survival was a severe burden that I was able to shed. This had diminished and was now tolerable.

Elsewhere, I suggested observation shows that psychic change is driven by biological forces, such as the drive for developmental progress seen in infants. In adolescents, there is observed a biologically driven force for the acquisition of sexual partners in search of attachment or object relations that replace the primary or mother–child object relations. The instinctual sexual drives cause a plasticity of the adolescent psychic organisation that seeks, let alone allows, change. The loss of my mother in life created psychic changes in me that I believe echoed the plasticity of adolescence such that I found myself examining my key attachments to ensure their security and dependence strength. This mutability parallels what we seek to produce in therapy.

I found that in my grief, I oscillated between various increasingly early psychic stages. I was regressing through deeper and earlier aspects of my maternal object relations. I was remembering and re-experiencing the feelings of being abandoned in the children's home. I also found myself increasingly sensitive to early tactile and olfactory cues such as the memory of the softness of my mother's touch. Early food, which was the difference between life and death, such as bread and butter, became a focus. I also found myself purchasing and hoarding food. I dissociated, frequently inhabiting a solitary, perhaps narcissistic, encapsulation that allowed me to escape into an intellectual escape. My capacity to think clearly in crisis, the silent, watchful child, had frequently been my saviour. This oscillated with increasing vulnerability and a sense of abandonment. My escape to music often brought tears. Perhaps the sound of a sweet, soothing voice resonates with safety and being held physically and psychologically.

Note

1 *The Moro reflex*. This is a primitive reflex seen in the neonate up to 4–5 months of age. When the child experiences a sudden movement or change of position and feels there is a loss of support, the child throws out its arms and straightens its legs as though to brace itself for a fall. It then displays distress by crying.

References

Acolet, D., Modi, N., Giannakoulopoulos, X., Bond, C., Weg, W., Clow, A., & Glover, V. (1993) Changes in plasma cortisol and catecholamine concentrations in response to massage in preterm infants. *Archive of Disease in Childhood* 68: 29–31.

Adam, K.S., Sheldon-Keller, A.E., & West, M. (1996) Attachment organisation and a history of suicidal behaviour in adolescents. *Journal of Consulting and Clinical Psychology* 64(2): 264–272.

Bion, W.R. (1962) *Learning from Experience*. London: Heinemann.

Bion, W.R. (1970) *Attention and Interpretation*. London: Tavistock.

Bowlby, J. (1961) Processes of mourning. *The International Journal of Psychoanalysis* 42 (3): 17–40.

Bowlby, J. (1981) *Attachment and Loss*. Harmondsworth: Penguin.

Candito, M., Albertini, M., Politano, S., Deville, A., Mariani, R., & Chambon, P. (1993) Plasma catecholamine levels in children. *Journal of Chromatography* 617: 304–307.

Cannon, W.B. & de la Paz, D. (1911) Emotional stimulation of adrenal secretion. *American Journal of Physiology* 28: 64.

Chase, N.D. (1999) *Burdened Children: Theory, Research, and Treatment of Parentification*. London: SAGE.

Danieli, Y. (1981) Countertransference in the treatment and study of Nazi Holocaust survivors and their children. *Victimology: An International Journal* 5(2–4): 355–367.

Fairbairn, W.R.D. (1954) *An Object-Relations Theory of the Personality*. New York: Basic Books.

Freud, S. (1917–1919) *Psychoanalysis and War Neuroses*, vol. XVIII.

Freud, S. (1920). *Beyond the Pleasure Principle*. S.E. 18: 34.

Freud, S. (1926) *Inhibitions, Symptoms and Anxiety*, S.E. 20: 161.

Garland, C. (1991) External disaster and the internal world: an approach to psychotherapeutic understanding of survivors. In *Textbook of Psychotherapy in Psychiatric Practice* (Ed. J. Holmes), pp. 507–532. London: Churchill Livingstone.

Garwood, A. (1996a) *The Long-Term Effects of Traumatic Stress: Holocaust and the Power of Powerlessness – The Unsolved Enigma*. Presented at the Second World Conference of the International Society for Traumatic Stress Studies, Jerusalem.

Garwood, A. (1996b) The Holocaust and the power of powerlessness: survivor guilt, an unhealed wound. *British Journal of Psychotherapy* 13(2): 243–258.

Hopper, E. (1991) Encapsulation as a defence against the fear of annihilation. *The International Journal of Psychoanalysis* 72(4): 607–624.

Illingworth, R.S. (1987) *The Normal Child*. London: Churchill Livingstone.

Jones, E. (1927) Early development of female sexuality. In *Papers on Psychoanalysis*. London: Bailliere, Tindall & Cox, 1950.

Kelly, D.D. (1982) The role of endorphins in stress-induced analgesia. *Annals of the New York Academy of Sciences* 398: 260–271.

Khan, M.M.R. (1974) *The Privacy of Self*. London: Hogarth Press.

Klass, D., Silverman, P.R., & Nickman, S.L. (1996) *Continuing Bonds: New Understanding of Grief*. London: Routledge.

Kubler-Ross, E. (1970) *On Death and Dying*. London: Tavistock.

Laplanche, B. & Pontalis, J. (1988) *The Language of Psycho-Analysis*. London: Karnac.

Lindemann, F. (1944) The symptomatology and management of acute grief. *American Journal of Psychiatry* 101: 141–148.

Moore, B. & Fine, B. (1999) *Psychoanalysis: The Major Concepts*. New Haven, CT: Yale University Press.

Murray Parkes, C. (1986) *Bereavement: Studies of Grief in Adult Life*. Harmondsworth: Penguin.

Murray Parkes, C. & Prigerson, H.G. (2010) *Bereavement: Studies of Grief in Adult Life* (4th edition). London: Penguin.

Pincus, L. (1974) *Death and the Family*. London: Faber & Faber.

Rank, O. (1929) *The Trauma of Birth*. New York: Harper& Row, 1973.

Rayner, E. (2020) *The Independent Mind in British Psychoanalysis*. London: Routledge.

Sandler, J. (1960) The background of safety. *The International Journal of Psycho-Analysis* 41: 352–356.

Segal, H. (1981) *The Work of Hannah Segal*. London: Aronson.

Stern, D. (1985) *The Interpersonal World of the Infant*. London: Routledge.

Winnicott, D.W. (1974) Fear of breakdown. *The International Review of Psycho-Analysis* 1: 10–17.

Chapter 9

Life, death, and the power of powerlessness[1]

Alfred Garwood[2]

Introduction

In this chapter, I endeavour to explore and clarify how the simple starting point of the biological given, the instinct for self preservation, in part explains man's response to life, death, and powerlessness, and how sensitisation to primal psychic agony has shaped the development of man's psyche and civilisation. General practice exposes the clinician to major events of life from birth to death. Training now addresses the social and psychological aspects of the patient's "management." The broad mixture of disciplines and experiences struggled with in primary care has shaped and informed this chapter. In addition, the hypotheses and arguments are derived from my researches into Holocaust trauma in which annihilation threat, powerlessness, loss, and the self-preservation instinct are central.

My starting point will be the neonate's formative experience at birth and in the following days. Supportive research will be offered as well as what seem to be some far-reaching implications. The hypotheses support and appear to cross the boundaries between classical drive theory, attachment theory, and object relations theory.

Instincts

The study of human embryology can evoke wonder and amazement as we observe stages resembling lower-order vertebrates (gill folds), providing compelling evidence for evolutionary theory and man's animal nature (Hamilton et al., 1957) and which, with the isolation of the gene, has now made evolutionary theory irrefutable. Gaddini (1992, p. 48) reminds us that psychoanalysis is based on the study of the psychical derivatives of instinct and its path has hitherto been indissolubly linked to the progress of its psychological knowledge of the instincts. It would seem self-evident that evolution and its instinctual sequelae affect all levels of physiological function, including the psychological. Freud (1920) described instincts as "at once the most important and the most obscure element of psychological research" (p. 34).

However, "Nowhere throughout Freud's writings is Darwin's theory of natural selection debated; instead it is passed by as though it had never been proposed" (Jones, 1957, p. 332). Perhaps thus the absorption of evolutionary theory by psychoanalytic theory has so far been slow and limited, despite notable work on the subject (Bowlby, 1981).

Primal experience

Analysts can only explore early trauma retrospectively. This has important limitations due to the risk of bias. In the past, little research was available. Recent research gives us a substantial body of data from which to extrapolate prospectively.

Neonatal hunger, cold, and pain

The human neonate is totally dependent on mother for survival for longer than all other primate offspring. Thus, it has an instinctual expectation of mother's presence, her capacity to provide food and protection, and consequently an instinctual response to mother's absence, indicated by reflex behaviour such as the grasp, startle, and rooting reflexes (Illingworth, 1987). However, these do not imply psychic object representation at birth. Warmth, food, and comfort mean contact with mother, while hunger, cold, and pain mean noncontact with mother and mother's absence. Having no sense of time, mother's absence means gone forever, provoking instinctually derived annihilation anxiety and producing reflex cries to alert any carer to the neonate's distress.

Until memory is developed, the experience of mother as a source of protection and nourishment, a protective good object, cannot be internalised and is not available as a container of the neonate's anxiety. Thus, hunger means potential starvation, cold means loss of mother's body heat, implying abandonment or her death, and pain implies an attack on the body's integrity, an annihilation threat. Only after memory is developed and a protective object is internalised will significant discomforts cease to be experienced as life-threatening abandonment.

Research shows that infants in their first two years have levels of adrenaline and noradrenaline (catecholamines) averaging twice that of adults, suggesting increased anxiety, falling to adult levels by the third year (Candito et al., 1993). Massage of preterm infants lowers these levels (Acolet et al., 1993). Catecholamines released by the autonomic nervous system are a reflex response to threat, causing the fight/flight reaction (Cannon & de la Paz, 1911) driven by the self-preservation instinct. By their third year, infants have usually internalised their key objects, acquired sufficient mobility and language to explore the wider world, and at that time a battle to control mother takes place, colloquially described as the "terrible twos." As their abilities increase, their instinctually driven levels of alertness and anxiety seem to reduce, reflected by the reduction of catecholamines.

Fight/flight is not possible for the powerless neonate. The fight/flight reaction provokes a massive increase in excitation and anxiety, implying a massive increase in somatic and psychic energy. Anxiety related to annihilation, the greatest of all threats, may be assumed to be as dreadful as is possible. Existing descriptions include primitive agony (Winnicott, 1974), nameless dreads and great awe (Bion, 1962), and aphanisis (Jones, 1927). I would like to suggest *primal agony* may be more apt, as it implies the first psychic experience of such intense pain.

Birth trauma

Obstetricians remind us that the second most dangerous event in our lives is our birth, the most dangerous being the event causing our death. Birth involves traumatic changes in the neonate's world, signalling that it must now fight for survival armed only with its instinctual inherited capacities. Physiological changes suggest birth is a trigger, calling into play instinctual behaviour and drives. These include changes in the lungs with the first breath and the gut circulation on cutting the umbilical cord, together with the first experience of hunger and cold, which together would seem to be sufficient to trigger this signal. Brain compression during birth seems to be a normative biological process, except in caesarean section, a recent and probably insignificant influence in evolutionary terms. The neonate's cranium is formed from separate bones that are overlapped by compression in the birth canal, gradually separating postnatally. This produces pain, causing the release of catecholamines, opposed by endogenous opiate production, to which I will return.

Maternal heartbeat

The foetus can hear its mother's heartbeat and a neonate cries less when held near its mother's heart. Mothers have an innate tendency to carry the child on the left side: "In short, the maternal heartbeat, with respect to the foetal nervous system, occupies a place of primacy and may be associated with a feeling of well being" (Salk, 1973). While *in utero*, the foetal adrenaline levels reflect mother's. Elevation causes raised maternal heart rate heard by the foetus. Raised adrenaline levels cause increased anxious excitation in the foetus, which is likely to be deeply unpleasant. It is likely that this relationship is instinctual.

Primal omnipotence

Pain, hunger, and cold, and thus primal agony, will be experienced from birth and before the maternal object and the sense of separateness has formed. The neonate's psychic response to powerlessness and the annihilation threat – primal agony – is likely to be attempted empowerment by omnipotent phantasy. At birth, the libidinal cathexes are all internally directed and this situation changes gradually (Freud, 1937).

Introjection, holding, retaining, and internal representation of affective experience describe memory and object formation (Stern, 1988). This suggests that primal agony drives the development of memory and internal objects. Introjection, owning and fusing with oneself, is not only an omnipotent defence, but a function of the mind's immaturity.

Recent discoveries shed light on primal omnipotence. Babies distressed by pain or hunger eventually go to sleep. This is not mere exhaustion. Research demonstrates an agonist–antagonist system involving endorphins (Kelly, 1982), endogenous opiates, some of which are 200 times more powerful than morphine. They are released in response to pain and stressors, counteracting the effects of adrenaline, calming the baby by reducing pain and anxiety. Stern (1985) suggests that neonates look for patterns of repetition in events, perhaps making the world more predictable. The repeated experience of primal agony, seemingly magically eradicated without mother, may be the primal experiences of omnipotence.

For the proposed developmental psychic processes to be seen as normative, it must be demonstrated that all neonates suffer significant hunger, cold, or pain. It can be argued that with caesarean deliveries, brain compression is avoided. Although for the first three days the mother's breasts produce colostrum, which has little nutritional content, bottle-fed neonates get ample nutrition. However, there still appear to be some experiences and physiological processes that are constants. The change from *in utero* to cold exterior and the neonate having to expend most of its energy maintaining its temperature is a potent shock, causing crying and inflation of the lungs, which then starts the cascade of circulatory changes. Neonates cry to alert mother to their distress. Although among tribal peoples babies may be given the breast every ten minutes, once asleep they generally do not waken until hungry. Deep sleep occupies most of their existence. Significant hunger must be experienced to provoke crying. Hunger usually wakes the neonate, demonstrating its presence and power as an unpleasant stimulus.

Therefore, there can be no doubt that, from birth, the neonate must suffer cold and maintain its body temperature, which it has difficulty in doing. It must also struggle to breathe for the first time, adding to its energy needs. Thus, its need for food increases dramatically, causing frequent hunger, which produces sufficient discomfort to waken it and provoke crying.

The internalisation of primal experience

The subject of the internalisation of earliest experience is complex and contentious. Theoretical propositions must be speculative.

Although there may be some sense of self prior to birth, this is somatic rather than psychic. The foetus acquires, through its developing nervous system, an awareness of body sensations, its degree of comfort, discomfort, freedom, and restriction.

At birth, the neonate has no experience of the external world, and thus can have no memory of the external world (Gaddini, 1992; Stern, 1988). Research suggests that the first signs of memory, and thus psychic development, can be seen after a few days. Until the neonate has memorised and internalised the experience of mother, no sense of psychic separateness can be developed. When a sense of separateness has developed, it implies a sense of space and boundary between self and maternal object, requiring internal representation of both self and mother. Thus, the psychic sense of self, mother, and separateness are likely to develop at the same time.

As nascent memory emerges, there will be internalisation of mother, both as a need-fulfilling object, together with the discomforts, including primal agony, that provoke her response. The effects associated with these events will also be internalised and remembered. Brierley (1937) suggests that in the beginning, the object is indistinguishable from the effect. Thenceforward, as objects come to be recognised as outside the self, they are known mainly from the particular pattern of effects evoked in and around them. The reassurance and comfort of the maternal presence, the warmth and odour of her skin and milk, and the sound of the maternal heart will be internalised together with the annihilation anxiety that was experienced during the interim until the maternal response was elicited. Research shows the 3-day-old neonate can recognise the smell of its mother's milk. In the first month of life, they show interest in and preference for the smell of their mother's milk (MacFarlane, 1975), the sound of the human voice (De Casper & Fifer, 1980), and the sight of a face (Stern, 1985).

Encapsulation as a defence against annihilation anxiety

One must now ask why the memory of the primal agony and annihilation fear is not also recalled whenever the need-fulfilling behaviour of the mother is recalled in later life, since both were internalised at the same time and are linked. It seems reasonable to assume that the internal representation of the primal agony and maternal comforting response are initially recalled together but eventually are effectively psychically separated. The memory of the primal psychic agony is repressed and, when psychic development allows, split off. Bion's (1962, 1970) ideas regarding containment are helpful here, particularly the notion of the capacity to contain by mother, which the neonate eventually takes into itself, creating its own internal container.

The discussion so far has been from the point of view of the neonate before it has a sense of separate mother. It is recognised that one of the most powerful and emotional experiences for mothers is the cry of their distressed neonate. Although the neonate is initially incapable of projection, the mother is capable of introjective identification and association. It would seem that the power over the observer of the neonate's cry lies in its capacity to evoke unconscious memories of our own experience of powerlessness and primal agony. The mother's response will reflect her capacity and psychic organisation to respond to these most powerful memories. Segal's (1981) work, discussed in Garland's (1991) valuable article on trauma and the breaching of the walls of the container, leads to the important concept of encapsulation as a defence against the fear of annihilation (Hopper, 1991).

The following material seems to illustrate and support the concept of encapsulation of annihilation anxiety particularly clearly, and is the reason I include it, as it is taken from my childhood.

I was born in a Nazi ghetto in Poland, and at 8 months was taken with my parents and older sibling to Bergen-Belsen. Throughout my adult years, I had seen photographs and heard horrific details of Bergen-Belsen without conscious anxiety, even though death and annihilation threat had been ever-present from birth and throughout my first two and a half years of life. In 1990, 45 years after our liberation, my entire nuclear family of four survivors returned to commemorate our survival. Arriving at Belsen, we visited the camp grounds and the museum, with its horrific photographs of our past. I was told many details of my time there, but did not experience any emotional reaction. Awaking early the following morning, I decided to return to Belsen alone to shoot some video footage. After a few minutes driving, I found myself overwhelmed by intense feelings that I could only describe as "dreadfulness." I was forced to stop until I regained some equanimity. Having recovered sufficiently, I continued the simple journey but constantly took wrong turnings. On arriving, I became fixed in my car. I had become alert, sharp-eyed, and acute of hearing, conscious of movements of birds and the sound of voices, and felt a sense of relief that at last I had some emotional reaction to my terrible childhood.

Eventually, I walked into the grounds and, reaching the site of the entrance to my part of the camp, I felt my stride beginning to shorten and slow. My shoulders and head dropped and my legs weakened until I had to stop. I found myself rooted to the spot, unable to lift my head or move. I felt so weak as to be barely able to support my weight. My eyes kept scanning the ground in front of me in repeated arcs. I was conscious of people walking past but could not move or look up at them and felt a sense of menace from those that moved quickly. This lasted for some minutes, eventually dissipating.

Reflecting on these experiences, I believed I recognised them as an age-appropriate, somatic memory of how I had felt as a weak and starving child in Belsen, scavenging for food, suffering from rickets, barely able to stand or move, constantly terrified.

On returning to London, my reaction to photographs of Belsen changed. I would tremble uncontrollably and those terrible feelings returned. I concluded that my memories and their associated affects had until now been encapsulated. Annihilation threat and terror were a constant presence from my birth, and thus the memory demonstrated the breaching of the encapsulation since birth, the normative period of infant amnesia, as well as the psychic organisation producing security.

Encapsulation and object loss

For encapsulation to be viewed as normative, further evidence is required. This is found in examining object loss, grief, and mourning. I wish to suggest that object loss disrupts the encapsulation and object relations that provide an individual's degree of psychic security from annihilation anxieties. The great psychic energy generated is derived from the self-preservation instinct.

Bereavement may be defined as the loss through death of a person to whom there was attachment. Object loss is a psychic trauma, provoking powerful and often overwhelming psychic processes due to our forced confrontation with mortality. Powerlessness to undo the finality of the loss evokes our primal instinctual annihilation anxieties, giving grief its extraordinary psychic power. Thus, powerlessness, annihilation anxiety, and loss are instinctually and psychically linked (Garwood, 1996a). Adult psychic processes provoked are likely to be omnipotent defences such as manic denial and empowering self-blame (Garwood, 1996b). Bowlby (1981) suggests the link between actual object loss and infantile annihilation anxieties is clear.

Most authors agree there are stages of grief (Bowlby, 1961, 1981; Kubler-Ross, 1970; Lindemann, 1944; Parkes, 1986): initially shock, which often includes disbelief, numbness, denial, physical collapse, violent outbursts, and dazed withdrawal (Pincus, 1974). If the only certainty after birth is death, why is shock the reaction to this fundamental truth? I would suggest that our formative psychic years and much of our adult psychic energy are spent developing and maintaining psychic security. This is security from annihilation threat and psychic abandonment by the attempted development and maintenance of benign internal objects and object relations and existential physical security. This gives protection from unpredictable natural threats. When loss occurs, despite all of these psychic and existential defences, we are forcibly confronted with mortality, reminding us of our own. Thus, shock is the reaction to the traumatic disruption of our defensive organisation and denials.

Turmoil and protest follow in a struggle to re-establish psychic equanimity. Denial, incredulity, anger, and reproach of self, the loved one, and medical attendants for not preventing the loss is common. Blame predominates, being an omnipotent, self-empowering defence, as it implies "I (they) chose wrongly: I could have done something: I can do something and if I only try hard enough I will find out what it is" (Danieli, 1981).

Classical theory suggests resolution is achieved by relinquishing the object. However, general practice experience suggests that the object is not relinquished, but remains active and important in our internal world. Although we attempt to maintain benign securityproviding objects, key objects usually produce both security and insecurity. On death, the memory of the object's problematic behaviour, if not indelibly ingrained, will be repressed and the object will be idealised, giving it a nostalgic glow. The events following the death of Diana, Princess of Wales, exemplify this. The object becomes more benign and more likely to provide security and narcissistic supplies unconditionally, on demand, increasingly coming under the psychic control of the bereaved. This, I suggest, is the ideal resolution, which may fail to take place or may only partly be achieved.

The almost universally observed denial of our mortality, particularly during adolescence, and reaction of shock and turmoil in response to loss support the hypothesis that the encapsulation of the neonatal experience of primal agony and annihilation anxiety is a normative process, the encapsulation being traumatically breached by object loss.

The nature of the capsule is of importance. As the annihilation anxiety it encapsulates influences psychic function, the formation of psychic defences, and life strategies, it seems permeable. Its integrity seems to be maintained by standard defences such as repression and omnipotent phantasy. However, the cost in psychic energy may be enormous. The extraordinary power of object loss attests to the psychic importance of its maintenance. The flashbacks of the Holocaust survivor or Vietnam veteran exemplify its breaching. In situations of powerlessness, separation and feared loss such as analytic breaks, overwhelming affects may be released and psychic equilibrium disrupted. Extreme annihilation threat and powerlessness, as in Holocaust trauma, provoke omnipotent, self-empowering defences and defensive existential organisation, demonstrating the capsule's permeability. These defences reseal and maintain the encapsulation. These psychic disturbances and defensive strategies have now been dubbed "post-traumatic stress syndrome" (Garwood, 1996a).

Psychic security, powerlessness, and object formation

I have suggested that all neonates suffer the combination of annihilation threat and powerlessness, generating primal agony. This experience sensitises us to later powerlessness and the unpredictability of natural threat. The self-preservation instinct and this sensitisation drive us towards empowerment and security through developing benign internal object relations and mastery of our environment, which is successful adaptation. Psychic security is preserved through encapsulation of the primal annihilation anxiety and primal agony.

These hypothetical constructions appear to be novel but relate to Sullivan's (1953) theory of security. He initially defined security as freedom from anxiety and saw the need for power as an antidote to the helplessness caused by early parental disapproval, later suggesting that security was the avoidance of anxiety entailing the search for power. The need for security becomes the infant's dominant concern and continues throughout life. Fairbairn (1943) suggests that the earliest months of life are characterised by the perpetuation of the mental state *in utero*, the child being in such total merger with mother as to preclude differentiation from the maternal body (p. 275). The inclination to merge with mother is derived from total unconditional helplessness and dependency. Although Bowlby's (1981) theories of attachment are closely linked to this, and the self-preservative instinct would clearly seem to underlay attachment to minimise risks of predation, his theorisation starts when attachment has already developed. His concern with separation, deprivation, and attachment are closely related.

If the mother provides a protective, need-fulfilling environment and adequate narcissistic supplies, then cumulative trauma (Khan, 1974) is avoided. This experience having been internalised as part of the maternal object, it will be successfully turned to for comfort. Rejection in a relationship causing suicide is common. The despairing individual suffers overwhelming loss, abandonment, powerlessness, and thus annihilation anxiety. Suicide seems the only solution when the anguish is intolerable and psychic comfort is unavailable. Annihilation anxiety provokes fight or flight. The fight reaction produces murderous rage, increasing the unavailability of internal objects, increasing the sense of loss. Flight is self-defeating, increasing separation. In the face of this powerlessness, empowerment is achieved through self-blame and self-punishment to the point of self-destruction, unless the destructive cycle is broken.

This contrasts starkly with those who respond with optimism towards their future by turning to secure internal and external objects, thus obtaining adequate narcissistic supplies.

Primal agony: creativity or despair?

Why do some respond to powerlessness with despair and others go on to creative achievement? A number of factors seem relevant. When neonates are hungry and cry but are ignored, some will continue trying to obtain comfort for much longer than others. In general practice, one regularly sees deprived children persistently seeking potential good objects, despite many failures and disappointments, and they continue to do so as adults. We call this resilience. This may relate to the fight part of the fight/flight reaction, and reflects the strength of innate aggression and the self-preservation instinct, which, when directed and controlled, we call determination.

Psychic organisation and the quality of attachment to the primary object has a clear influence. Children, when struggling with a withholding parent, may try various strategies until they succeed. The child's intelligence and inherited potential for creativity would seem to be involved. However, the response of the parent may well signal hope and thus encourage creative alternative approaches.

If neonatal distress is ignored, this encourages despair, whereas speedy, appropriate responses create an object relationship and optimism. Despair is hopelessness, which is another form of powerlessness. Ignoring the neonate may signal potential abandonment. However, food must be given and the prolonged wait may condition the neonate to wait and be passive rather than active. Thus, the speed and pattern of response to cries of need in the neonate may condition the neonate to be optimistic and active rather than passive and despairing when abandonment potentially seems to have taken place.

Powerlessness and self-empowerment

Observation of primitive tribes suggest that when humankind's instinctual behaviour was developing, neonates were carried in constant contact with the mother's breast, thus smelling her milk and hearing her heart, confirming mother's availability to meet essential needs.

Infants strive with remarkable determination to gain motor control, strength, coordination, and to communicate. They explore and try to understand their world, achieving increasing self-reliance. The instinctual energy associated with self-preservation drives this quest for empowerment over dependency and vulnerability. Mobility, control of carers and their environment, minimises vulnerability to abandonment and natural threats. The infant strives to be able to feed itself, to run and hide, to recover mother if separated, as though it lives in the hunter-gatherer community when these instinctual drives evolved. The games of "chase" and "hide and seek" are probably universal. It can be observed that the drive towards a facilitating relationship with mother is remarkably strong throughout life, and early achievement facilitates independence and individuation. Its aim is maximal empowerment over the child's world.

Individual development and society

Group analysis has fuelled research on humankind's social nature and the influence of the social on the psyche. The developmental theories proposed suggest the psyche has generated the formation, development, and shaping of society. The response to powerlessness and primal agony is a sensitisation causing a striving for empowerment and mastery generating adaptive and maladaptive psychic processes throughout life. Creativity, inquisitiveness, and inventive energies are thus derived. Vulnerability to natural threats has driven primitive man's search for empowerment through the invention of tools, fire, the wheel, and the creation of shelters. Humankind's search for meaning is a striving to understand, and thus master, the unknown and all its hazards.

This extrapolates to today's quest for scientific understanding and the harnessing of nature's power to overcome its restrictions. The conquest of Everest and other peaks may be seen as the omnipotent denial of annihilation threat, the power of nature, and man's diminutive place therein. Within science, cosmology, the attempts to understand the creation of the universe, the ultimate event of power, may be seen as an omniscient quest. Existential power may be sought through acquisition of great wealth and position. The building of phallic symbols of power, such as skyscrapers penetrating the horizon, forcing their way into view, is common.

Self-preservative, instinctual energy is cathected at the Oedipal level. It is prerequisite that the individual survives to sexual maturity to preserve the species, suggesting that the self-preservation instinct generates energy more powerful than, and underpinning, libidinal energy. The power to procreate is also the power to defend against, deny, or make reparation for annihilation threat and loss. Creativity has long been recognised as the response to loss. Painting and sculpture, in representational form, may be the fixing of life in magical imagery, conferring a form of immortality. Power may be sought through the development of large families, tribes, societies, and nations, and predominance within them by the building and use of armies for conquest. Empowerment through the military machine and political processes has led to dictatorships, emperors, and world wars. Intellectual empowerment has led the quest to understand and control the outer world through science and technology, the inner world of the body through medicine, physiology, and pharmacology, and the mind through psychiatry, psychology, psychotherapy, and psychoanalysis.

The universal phenomenon of religions with their omnipotent deities exemplifies the quest for protection from annihilation threat and powerlessness. In monotheistic religions, obedience and compliance with the perceived wishes of the deity achieve the deity's favour and the reward of eternal life, the mastery of the finality of death. Heaven and eternal life also undoes the death of parents and loved ones with the promise of reunion.

Acknowledgement

Without the selfless support of my wife, Yvonne, this paper would never have been written. For their generous encouragement and helpful comments on earlier drafts of this article, I am indebted to Kannan Navaratnem, David Vincent, and especially to Eric Rayner. Lastly, I wish to thank Earl Hopper and Tony Garelick, who have generously shared their ideas and wisdom, which I have absorbed specifically and by a process of osmosis that has played an invaluable part in my struggle to understand my inner and outer worlds from which this paper emerged.

Notes

1 *Group Analysis.* Copyright © 2001 The Group-Analytic Society (London). SAGE Publications (London, Thousand Oaks, CA and New Delhi), 0533–3164 (200,103)34:1;153–167;016138 from the SAGE Social Science Collections. All Rights Reserved.

2 Alfred Garwood is a general practitioner, psychoanalytic psychotherapist, IGA
   Qualifying Course member, Founder of the Association of Child Survivors of the
   Holocaust of Britain and co-founder of the Foundation for Holocaust Survivors.
   Author's Address: 14 Monkhams Avenue, Woodford Green, Essex IG8 OET,
   UK.

References

Acolet, D., Modi, N., Giannakoulopoulos, X., Bond, C., Weg, W., Clow, A., &
   Glover, V. (1993) Changes in plasma cortisol and catecholamine concentrations in
   response to massage in preterm infants. *Archive of Disease in Childhood* 68: 29–31.
Bion, W.R. (1962) *Learning from Experience*. London: Heinemann.
Bion, W.R. (1970) *Attention and Interpretation*. London: Tavistock.
Bowlby, J. (1961) Processes of mourning. *The International Journal of Psychoanalysis* 42
   (3): 17–40.
Bowlby, J. (1981) *Attachment and Loss*. Harmondsworth: Penguin.
Brierley, M. (1937) Affects in theory and practice. *The International Journal of Psycho-
   analysis* 18: 256–263.
Candito, M., Albertini, M., Politano, S., Deville, A., Mariani, R., & Chambon, P.
   (1993) Plasma catecholamine levels in children. *Journal of Chromatography* 617:
   304–307.
Cannon, W.B. & de la Paz, D. (1911) Emotional stimulation of adrenal secretion.
   American Journal of Physiology 28: 64.
Danieli, Y. (1981) Countertransference in the treatment and study of Nazi Holocaust
   survivors and their children. *Victimology: An International Journal* 5(2–4): 355–367.
De Casper, A.J. & Fifer, W.P. (1980) Of human bonding: new-borns prefer their
   mothers' voices. *Science* 205: 1174–1176.
Fairbairn, W.R.D. (1943) The war neuroses: their nature and significance. In *Psycho-
   analytic Studies of the Personality*. New York: Routledge, 1994.
Freud, S. (1920) *Beyond the Pleasure Principle*. S.E. 18: 34.
Freud, S. (1937) Letter to Marie Bonaparte, 27 May 1937, Appendix A, letter no. 33.
   In *The Life and Work of Sigmund Freud* (Ed. E. Jones), vol. 3. New York: Basic
   Books, 1957.
Gaddini, E. (1992) *A Psychoanalytic Theory of Infantile Experience*. London: Tavistock/
   Routledge.
Garland, C. (1991) External disaster and the internal world: an approach to psycho-
   therapeutic understanding of survivors. In *Textbook of Psychotherapy in Psychiatric Prac-
   tice* (Ed. J. Holmes), pp. 507–532. London: Churchill Livingstone.
Garwood, A. (1996a) *The Long-Term Effects of Traumatic Stress: Holocaust and the Power
   of Powerlessness – The Unsolved Enigma*. Presented at the Second World Conference
   of the International Society for Traumatic Stress Studies, Jerusalem.
Garwood, A. (1996b) The Holocaust and the power of powerlessness: survivor guilt,
   an unhealed wound. *British Journal of Psychotherapy* 13(2): 243–258.
Hamilton, W.J. Boyd, J.D., & Mossman, H.W. (1957) *Human Embryology*. Cambridge:
   Heffer.
Hopper, E. (1991) Encapsulation as a defence against the fear of annihilation. *The Inter-
   national Journal of Psychoanalysis* 72: 607.
Illingworth, R.S. (1987) *The Normal Child*. London: Churchill Livingstone.

Jones, E. (1927) Early development of female sexuality. In *Papers on Psychoanalysis*. London: Bailliere, Tindall & Cox, 1950.

Jones, E. (1957) *Sigmund Freud, Life and Works, Vol. 3: The Last Phase, 1919–1939*. London: Hogarth Press.

Kelly, D.D. (1982) The role of endorphins in stress-induced analgesia. *Annals of the New York Academy of Sciences* 398: 260–271.

Khan, M.M.R. (1974) *The Privacy of Self*. London: Hogarth Press.

Kubler-Ross, E. (1970) *On Death and Dying*. London: Tavistock.

Lindemann, F. (1944) The symptomatology and management of acute grief. *American Journal of Psychiatry* 101: 141–148.

MacFarlane, J. (1975) Olfaction in the development of social preferences in the human neonate. In *Parent–Infant Interaction* (Ed. M. Hofer), Amsterdam: Elsevier.

Parkes, C.M. (1986) *Bereavement: Studies of Grief in Adult Life*. Harmondsworth: Penguin.

Pincus, L. (1974) *Death and the Family*. London: Faber & Faber.

Salk, L. (1973) The role of heartbeat in the relation between mother and infant. *Scientific American* 228: 24–29.

Segal, H. (1981) *The Work of Hannah Segal*. London: Aronson.

Stern, D.N. (1985) *The Interpersonal World of the Infant*. New York: Basic Books.

Stern, D.N. (1988) Affects in the context of the infant's lived experience: some considerations. *The International Journal of Psychoanalysis* 69: 233–238.

Sullivan, H.S. (1953) *The Interpersonal Theory of Psychiatry*. New York: Norton.

Winnicott, D.W. (1974) Fear of breakdown. *The International Review of Psycho-Analysis* 1: 10–17.

Chapter 10

Inaccessible memories
Recovered traumatic memories, true and false

Introduction

In my work with the youngest of the Holocaust survivors who suffered their massive psychic trauma during the period of infantile amnesia, the issue of accessibility of memory was always central. My return to Bergen-Belsen concentration camp and the physical experience of memory I recovered has made the accessibility of early memory of personal importance. Over the years at Holocaust gatherings, a number of individuals have claimed to be survivors of early Holocaust trauma. This has proved to be false, which has drawn me into this controversy.

In this chapter I will initially discuss infantile amnesia and then present a representative selection of recent research and opinion regarding the continuing controversy over false memory (FM) and recovered memory (RM).

I will then present some clinical examples taken from my clinical and personal experience, which illustrate FM and authentic RM, including an example of memories recovered from the period of infantile amnesia. I will then focus on traumatic memory inaccessibility (IM) and its recovery. It seems worthwhile reminding the reader of the limitations of the research methods available and how, in many cases, they fail to reliably measure what is examined or gain answers to questions they pose. Research is steadily improving, but still lags far behind the highly developed body of theory of psychic function used to understand psychic processes by group analysts, psychoanalysts, and psychotherapists, which stands up to repeated examination and which clinical experience repeatedly tests and supports.

Infantile amnesia

Clinicians will be familiar with amnesias such as normative infantile amnesia and traumatic amnesia, seen with head injuries as well as patients who profess to have no accessible memories of their childhoods. The period of childhood approximately before the 3rd birthday is known as the period of infantile amnesia (Bauer, 2002). Freud (1905) initially suggested infantile amnesia was solely due to repression. White and Pillemer (1979) suggest Freud had two formulations for infantile amnesia, the first being due to repression and the second described as selective reconstruction, in which he suggests young children are unable to form narrative memories due to an inability to organise early fragmentary images. Observation and object relations theory suggests that infants are object-seeking and thus have a narrow focus of attention on the primary carer. Nachman and Stern (1983) and Stern (1985) have found evidence that very early memory exists but is not language-based. Stern (1985) offers evidence of the capacity to recognise the smell of mother's milk. Infant observation supports this, and shows that with increasing psychic security comes increasing capacity to separate from mother and explore further from mother's presence. This might be described as secure detachment. I wish to posit that the converse may apply such that insecurity makes detachment less possible, and thus what is observed is proximity-seeking, commonly known as clinging. Trauma causing regression and clinging is established and widely recognised. I wish to suggest that the outward psychic direction of focus will parallel the strength of psychic security, and the capacity to detach and focus externally away from the primary object relations increases with increasing security. I wish to further suggest that for a more mature memory to be formed, a process of psychic detachment must develop through the development of the observing ego function. This would appear to be a function of the proposed developing psychic guardian function discussed in the next chapter (i.e. the capacity to be self- and other-observing).

In immaturity, the primary psychic focus is secure attachment within the primary object relations, this being the primary psychic priority until psychic detachment is developed due to a secure base being formed (Bowlby, 1981). Earliest memory seems to be sensory and somatic and lacks the detached observer quality of later narrative memory. Thus, this exploration supports the existing view (Mollon, 2002) that infantile amnesia reflects psychic immaturity, which I propose is due to the necessity for development of, and thus focuses on, the primary object relations. It might be suggested that physical development might force the psyche beyond the phase of infantile amnesia in its instinctual drive for independence or autonomy. To obtain autonomy, focus must be directed to the external world.

Recovered memory current research

Dalenberg and Paulsen (2010), in their rigorous and comprehensive review of the specialist literature on both sides of the controversy, suggest that there is now largely a professional consensus on this subject. They quote the International Society for Traumatic Stress Studies (ISTSS, 1998), who suggest scientists in North America, Europe, Australia, and New Zealand state that "(1) traumatic events are usually remembered in part or in whole; (2) traumatic memories may be forgotten, then remembered at some later time; and (3) illusory memories can also occur" (p. 15).

Trauma and memory disruption

There is now a substantial body of research demonstrating an association between traumatic experience and explicit memory deficits. Research has shown that combat veterans and other sufferers of what we would now describe as complex post-traumatic stress disorder (Herman, 1997; ICD11, 2018), such as acute or prolonged child sexual abuse, perform worse on explicit memory tests (Bremner et al., 1995, 2003; Combs & DePrince, 2010; El-Hage et al., 2006; Yehuda et al., 1995). Further research (Golier et al., 2003) has shown that "PTSD is associated with both general deficits in explicit memory performance and heightened memory for trauma-related stimuli" (Combs & DePrince, 2010, pp. 217–218).

Dissociation and memory disfunction

Dissociation is described in the psychodynamic literature as the psychic escape where there is no escape (Putnum, 1992) and in the psychiatric litera-ture as "a lack of integration in typically connected aspects of information processing" (APA, 1994), and is suggested as a method whereby individuals may keep threatening information from awareness (Freyd, 1996). Brewin (2007) suggests that memory of trauma as compared to memory of non-traumatic events differs, is more vivid and associated with greater emotional or sensory experience, and is experienced as occurring in the present, not the past. Brewin suggests this subject remains a controversial issue and requires further research. Brenner's (2015) work on dissociation is an important contribution to this debate.

False memory research

The work of Loftus and Pickrell (1995) is frequently cited. They found that in their study, in which attempts were made to implant a false memory by relating a suggested shopping mall event, approximately 25 per cent of parti-cipants claimed to remember the event. This study involved a *plausible* event. Hyman et al. (1995) confirmed these findings with a plausible but more unusual event. However, Pedzec et al. (1997) found that no partici-pant accepted the false memory of an *implausible* traumatic event.

"This amendment to the 'ease' of implanting a False Memory has been largely accepted in later work, so that most cognitive researchers now state that it is difficult but not impossible to implant an implausible memory" (Dalenberg & Paulsen, 2010, p. 227). Questions remain as to how authentic-ally the experimental circumstances relate to real traumatic events, and their psychic processes causing actual memory to become inaccessible preventing their recall. I will endeavour to address some of these issues later in this chapter.

Case reports

Infantile amnesia

I will use the vignette presented in a previous chapter to illustrate this. This vignette may be bypassed if you have already encountered it.

I was born in a Nazi ghetto in Poland, and at 8 months of age was taken with my parents and older sibling to Bergen-Belsen concentration camp, where we survived from its first day as a concentration camp to our liberation, almost two years later. Throughout my adult years, I had seen photographs and heard horrific details of the Holocaust and Bergen-Belsen without conscious anxiety in response, even though death and annihilation threat had been ever-present from my birth and throughout my first two and a half years of life.

Some 45 years after our liberation, my entire nuclear family of four survivors returned to Bergen-Belsen to commemorate our survival. On arriving at Belsen, we visited the site and the museum, with its horrific photographs of our past. I was told many details of our time there but did not experience any emotional response.

I awoke very early the following morning and decided to return to Belsen alone, ostensibly to shoot some video footage. The drive from my hotel took 30 minutes. A few minutes after starting to drive towards Belsen, I found myself overcome by feelings that I could only describe as "intense dreadfulness." I was forced to stop until I regained some equanimity. This was my first conscious emotional response to the return to Belsen. After recovering sufficiently to continue the journey, I constantly took wrong turnings even though I was familiar with the simple route. On arriving at the car park at Belsen, I was unable to leave my car. I became aware of how alert, sharp-eyed, and acute of hearing I had become. I was hypervigilant, conscious of slight movements of birds in the trees and the sound of voices. I reflected on my sense of relief that at last, I had some emotional reaction to my childhood in this terrible place.

Eventually I left my car and walked into the camp itself. On reaching the approximate site of the entrance to my part of the camp, I began to notice something strange. My stride shortened and slowed. My shoulders and head started to drop, and my legs weakened until I had to stop. I found myself rooted to the spot, unable to lift my head or move. I felt so weak as to be barely able to support my weight. My eyes kept scanning the ground in front of me in repeated arcs. I was conscious of people walking past but could not move or look up at them, and felt a sense of menace from those that moved quickly. These feelings lasted for many minutes, eventually dissipating.

Reflecting on this strange occurrence, I believed I recognised it as a memory. An age-appropriate, preverbal, somatic memory, remembering feeling how I had felt as a weak and starving child in Belsen, scavenging for food, suffering from rickets, barely able to stand or move, constantly terrified.

My parents and older sister had wanted to believe that I had been spared the terrible suffering their memories would not let them forget. All my life, they had told me that I had been too young to remember or understand what was going on. Anyone who has observed infants of this age will know they have a good grasp of what is going on in their immediate world, including the emotional state of mind of their parents.

On returning to the UK, I noticed a change in my reaction to photographs of Belsen. At their sight, I would tremble uncontrollably and those terrible feelings, for which I had no name, returned. I concluded that my memories and their associated dreadful affects had been, in my words, encapsulated. Later I recalled having had these feelings of dreadfulness during an earlier psychoanalysis, which went unrecognised for what they were at the time.

The above vignette illustrates the evocation of memory from the period of infantile amnesia evoked by being at the site of the original trauma, which was previously inaccessible through psychic defences, most likely encapsulation (Hopper, 1991).

Inaccessible memory

Memory inaccessibility is an everyday phenomenon with which we are all familiar. Memories such as the name of a place or a person may be temporarily inaccessible for many reasons. It is well recognised that women forget the severity of the pain of childbirth, or that during a grief reaction it is common that the memory of the face of the loved one is temporarily forgotten. When searching for a memory fragment, we often use cues or linked memories to make the memory accessible. However, some memories may be inaccessible because they have been deeply, defensibly buried. This is a colloquialism for making them unconscious in such a way that they remain inaccessible except in special circumstances. For a memory to be inaccessible, it must by definition have existed and had been accessible before becoming inaccessible.

The question of why some memories become more inaccessible than simply temporarily forgotten is central to this exploration. It is important to state that memories are inseparably associated with their emotional content, which may vary from the pleasurable to the severely noxious. As therapists, we deal with the formative and in many cases the deformative past experiences of our patients. This is often inaccessible at the beginning of therapy and becomes increasingly accessible during the progress of the therapy.

The following vignette illustrates one example of inaccessible memory:

When in his late twenties, soon after the birth of his first child and without warning, M began to have nightmares. These were repetitive, frightening, and involved images of being sexually abused. He had no conscious or accessible memories of being abused. He feared for his sanity. His nightly nightmares were unremitting. Slowly, he began to recognise these as memories, eventually recognising the Scoutmaster as his abuser. His initial response was a severe depression in which he used excess alcohol to try to sleep and quieten his mind. This continued for six months, during which he was disabled and unable to function, spending every day drunk in his bedroom.

When he improved through medical treatment, he considered his options. He seriously considered taking violent revenge. However, the recent birth of his son precluded taking the risk of imprisonment and forced separation from this precious child.

He decided to go to the police. Fortunately, they took him seriously. An experienced child abuse investigator interviewed the alleged perpetrator. He was an unmarried man. His home was found to contain almost all of the special items commonly used by paedophiles with which to groom children. He was remarkably self-confident. He had groomed the parents of the abused boys with such success that he was repeatedly invited to family meals such as at Christmas. He denied the allegations and suggested they all go together to see M's parents. After he was investigated and charged, a large number of other men came forward with further allegations. He was found guilty and sentenced to a long term of imprisonment.

M was referred for long-term psychotherapy because his nightmares changed from traumatic memories to fantasies and continued unabated. In these, he had the ability to fly. He flew only at head height and at walking speed. He would fly along the familiar streets to collect his son from school. However, his ability to fly was treated by his dream neighbours and those who acknowledged him in the street as a normal activity.

The most frightening dream event described was being chased along a corridor in an apartment where there was no escape. He would then wake in terror. His parenting of his son was noteworthy for its thoughtfulness, commitment, and underlying protectiveness. He was highly protective, but with an awareness that his son needs to have sufficient freedom to become streetwise and unafraid of normal risks.

M's abuse took place during a period from 4 to 11 years old, which would normally be accessible to memory recall. Why this was inaccessible will be explored below.

Vignette discussion

Analysing the material, certain features seem significant. First, the memory of the traumatogenic sexual abuse became inaccessible. The psychic processes available for this to occur are limited. It would seem most likely that a form of encapsulation (Hopper, 1991) of the memory of the traumatogenic experiences took place. Hinshelwood (1989) suggests that Kleinian theory proposes noxious or malign experiences are split off and projected away from the representation of the good object in order to preserve it. Thus, it could be suggested that they were projected into an encapsulation. The purpose of the encapsulation was to isolate the noxious experiences and thus allow the remaining psyche to progress along a less disturbed developmental path. It also preserved the parents as good objects.

This man's function demonstrates some aspects of the psychic damage that paedophiles frequently cause. It was particularly toxic as he seemed powerfully psychically controlling, being highly seductive to the parents, thus removing any escape path or safe haven for his victim. It is regularly reported that paedophiles entrap children and make them feel responsible and guilty, causing self-blame (Hinshelwood, 1989), which may suggest that the psychic entrapment was designed to cause absolute powerlessness. It is likely that M dissociated during the abuse experiences, and thus removed himself from the emotional toxicity of the abuse, and his abused self inhabited the dissociation. However, when the memories needed to become completely inaccessible or psychically destroyed and buried, new psychic processes were necessary to change the dissociation into a toxicity-isolating encapsulation that was not to be inhabited.

Inaccessibility overwhelmed

In the case of M and his memories emerging in his dreams, the man's partner had just given birth to his son. It could be argued that the reason for the memory evocation in his dreams was due to a conflict of psychic needs. It might be further suggested that his psychic representation of himself as a child relating to adults would have been of an abuse victim. He was not able to turn to his parents for psychic protection as they had been duped by the paedophile. Thus, they failed to protect him. He now needed to psychically change his representation of himself as a vulnerable and powerless victim into a secure, dependency-providing parent. These fundamental needs can be seen to be instinctually driven, demonstrated by the need to protect his progeny and thus preserve the species. This was brought into conflict with his instinctual need to avoid psychic annihilation. This was achieved by making the memory inaccessible, by dissociation and encapsulation. Once the encapsulation was disrupted, the contents were released still possessing the capacity to overwhelm the psyche. The effect was to create an acute stress reaction, defined in DSM-IV as F43.0 (APA, 2004). This threw him into survival mode functioning. I have suggested that the psychic responses to trauma are psychic fight/flight/freeze. Fight was unsupported by his parents, whom he could not turn to. Flight was obstructed as the paedophile had been invited to his home, thus removing this safe haven. Thus, freeze, in the form of encapsulation or dissociation or both, was the only psychic option remaining.

The psychic conflict created by the birth of the son was the conflict between the need to protect his son or to protect himself, the victim, who must maintain silence and secrecy to protect himself, his family, and his parents. The conflict of powerful needs made continued encapsulation of his trauma impossible. It should be said at this point that paedophiles are known to control victims by threats to harm or kill parents and other precious family members, thus achieving a terrified silence in the victim. He describes his first response to the memories as thoughts of killing the paedophile and, only after this was rejected, of going to the police. These were both fight reactions that were possible now he was an adult and should and could protect his son. Thus, it might be suggested that psychically the need to develop a protective father–son object relations disrupted the encapsulation, releasing the traumatic memories of his abuse.

A salient observation was that in his group therapy, all the mothers in the group learned from his deep understanding of parenting. He had acquired great wisdom through careful thought and analysis of various parenting responsibilities and the optional courses of action. His parenting skills impressed and gained the respect of all the group members. He was not going to let his son down in the way his parents and all the authorities had let him down, nor was he disablingly overprotective.

Dissociative regression

I will now present a vignette of another example of recovery of an inaccessible memory:

> David, aged 29 years, brought his 7-year-old son to his general practitioner suffering with anal discomfort. When the GP tried to take a history, David cried loudly, rocking backwards and forwards. He acted and spoke like a young child involved in a conversation with his father. He begged him not to hurt him. He wanted his mummy. He seemed to be suggesting he had been abused, but did not state this clearly, and it was left uncertain. He could not engage in a normal consultation conversation. His child would not submit to any form of examination.

David had a history of adolescent psychosis and had been treated with potent antipsychotics and antidepressants for many years. The need to explore this situation was clear, but doing so was fraught with difficulties.

My first consultation was with them both. My child protection duty made it essential that I obtained a sense of the child's mental state. I was looking for any degree of caution with an adult such as silent watchfulness, a red flag sign for abuse. These were absent. There was a degree of concern shown by the child for the distress displayed by father, whom I thought indicated signs of parentification. He was happy to play with one of the older maternal female staff. What was noticeable was that his play consisted of carefully tidying and ordering the magazines in the waiting room. This suggested a degree of obsessionality and thus deep insecurity.

Having read father's extensive records as well as his family's medical records, when I saw David alone I asked him about his disclosure of his alleged abuse in childhood to a psychiatrist. This confused him. He did not recall making this disclosure to the psychiatrist. This quickly changed to distress, but he did not cry. He behaved like a young child, moaning very loudly. He stared at me with his mouth wide open, as though this spoke for itself. He struggled to gain self-control, making grunting and whining noises. Eventually, he was able to gain control and was concerned he did not distress his son when he collected him after the sessions. It became clear that with an effort of will, he could recover from the childlike state. After discussion with a senior colleague, it was decided to see him with a mature female member of staff.

The succeeding consultations were short and were deliberately arranged fortnightly because of his perceived fragile ego strength and the as yet unknown risk of breakdown. He usually brought his son, who would play in the waiting area, continuing to carefully tidy up. My approach was to show interest and concern, to be carefully supportive, and to avoid disapproval. In the face of his history of psychosis, it seemed important to listen and simply receive his communications, to be real and accessible rather than psychoanalytically opaque or reflective. His initial transference to me seemed to be to that of a good parental figure.

The presence of male and female parental figures in the room seemed enough to evoke childlike re-enactments. These childlike enactments were of recent onset. He reported he had confronted his father and questioned him. His father had become angry and called him insane. His recounting of these events was fragmented, disjointed, and had the quality of his internal dialogue about his past. He frequently complained he felt confused and unclear. He stated the initial therapeutic objective was not wanting to have these distressing episodes in front of his son, who also found them distressing. Thus, one objective was to assist him to gain his equanimity at the end of the consultation when he took his son home. Another was to gather information that would allow the assessment of the risk to the 7-year-old, thus fulfilling my duty of child safeguarding.

During the consultation, he would become distressed, crying out very loudly in his childlike way as though he wanted his distress to be heard. He continued to cry out and stare at me for some time with his mouth wide open. It seemed as though he was saying, "Look what is in my mouth." I was careful to say nothing, nor to ask leading questions regarding abuse.

Over the following year, he slowly became more coherent. He recounted a traumatic holiday when he witnessed his father with his hands around his mother's throat. He recounted this as though he was reliving it. He was warned by his father to tell no one or something terrible would happen. He also recalled watching his brother drowning while his parents were arguing when he was too terrified to call out. Eventually, his older brother rescued his sibling. He recalled how he and his siblings were made by their father to stand in a line and call their mother a "nutter" [mad]. He later explained his mother was admitted to a psychiatric hospital with schizophrenia after this holiday. He cried when explaining this, frequently saying, "I want my mummy," which now had greater meaning. His mother was admitted to a psychiatric hospital for many months.

After some time, his mother, who had become estranged from his father, helped him attend consultations on time by looking after the 7-year-old. Eventually, she accompanied him during the consultations. Mother slowly allowed herself to believe that what her son was experiencing or expressing were memories, although these were not always lucid and were sometimes confused with what may have been fantasies about family members.

In this latter period, he began to write his thoughts down. Initially, they were a few words to a page, scribbled in large block capitals. The sentences slowly increased in length and number. Eventually, the lined page was dated and each line was written in neat, coherent writing. These pages described his abuse in increasing detail. There was a period when he psychically deteriorated. He became more concrete in his thinking, trying to shake the confusion out of his head with sudden jerking movements. This episode required antipsychotic medication to reduce the symptoms. I believe the regressive process described may be thought of as a dissociative regression.

Dissociative regression discussion

I suggested that David's psychic functioning demonstrated what I have called dissociative regression. David did not just function at the age at which the trauma had occurred, but seemed to inhabit his psyche at 7 years old, which had been preserved and then re-emerged to overwhelm and dominate the adult psyche. Not only dissociation was displayed, but psychic fission and fragmentation too (Hopper, 1991). Decompensation occurred to the point of psychosis, delusions with concrete thinking and acting on the delusion. This resulted in a period of hospital admission. Apart from trying to shake the confusion from his head, he had described filing his front teeth with a rasp when a teenager because of teasing by his older sibling. The psychic processes of fight/flight/freeze described in Chapter 11 would seem to enable this dissociative regression by utilising the suggested psychic pathways or superhighways that offer a means whereby the preserved regressed state can force its way into the conscious psyche.

Inaccessible memory and survival

Memory can be seen as having survival benefits. In our hunter-gatherer past, the capacity to memorise the detail of the surroundings and thus recognise any changes, which may have been caused by predators and thus may imply danger, has clear survival value. I suggested in Chapter 8 that there can be excessive psychic insecurity, which reduces survival capacity. This could suggest that there is an optimal level of psychic security. In order that the psyche is not overwhelmed and exhausted by the need to deal with perceived or imagined danger, the capacity to contain the psychic representation of traumatogenic experience necessitated the development of some psychic processes to separate these psychic representations. This protects the psyche and allows it to continue developing and functioning. This is likely to be to facilitate survival. Perhaps one memory function is to remember, and thus recognise and warn of, or signal, danger? What monitors external and also internal danger is discussed in the next chapter.

Memory evocation

The question of why and how memories of traumatic experiences are reawakened or evoked is challenging. In the three clinical examples described, there are three apparently different modes of memory evocation. Closer examination of the similarities and differences may be helpful to our understanding of the process.

In the return to Bergen-Belsen concentration camp, there were a number of relevant factors. First, there was a powerful response to the impending loss of my wife, through illness, causing a creative response to loss and a drive to address and possibly master this through preparatory mourning, which would inevitably re-evoke the Holocaust losses. This may have been one reason for the return to Belsen. The powerful need of the rest of the family to believe I had escaped the traumatic experiences untouched had obstructed the memories on the first day. Returning alone to the camp, which was surrounded by dense forest as it was during the Holocaust, and without the obstructing presence of other family members, had enabled the rupturing of the memory encapsulation from the period of infantile amnesia.

David's accessing of his traumatic memory was in the form of re-enactment of his speech and behaviour when approximately 7 years old, the age of his abuse. However, unlike the return to Belsen, these were not age-appropriate somatic memories, but appeared to be the enactment of the self-created dissociated memories during the abuse. Thus, it was named dissociative regression. For much of the time during which this behaviour was exhibited, it was not known whether he was conscious of what he was saying and enacting. His surprise regarding the divulgence of the abuse to the psychiatrist recorded in the notes suggests he dissociated at that time and the incident was inaccessible to the current functioning self, and that the dissociative regression during the consultation was inaccessible when not in this dissociative regressed state.

Why was it evoked at this time? He believed it was due to a change of medication. However, it is more likely that his son having reached the age when he suffered his own abuse, and also the suspicion that his son was being abused by grandfather, his alleged abuser, provoked it. The soreness of the son's anus may have evoked memories of his own abuse.

Thus, the psychic conflict of needing to protect his son by becoming a protective father rather than a victim forced him to psychically oppose his defensive escape by dissociation. During his attempts to psychically approach his traumatic memories, the fight response, directed towards the construction of a coherent psychic narrative, caused him to become repeatedly overwhelmed, oscillating between his adult state, his dissociated child self, and the self, trying to be a protective, coherent parent. During this struggle, he was observed to suffer psychotic delusional ideation, believing there was something wrong in his head, and he believed he could literally shake it out, which he attempted to do.

During this time, he continued to have contact with his mother, who was reasonably well controlled on antipsychotic medication but was pathologically attached to her abusive husband. Mother initially denied any abuse took place, perhaps to protect her marriage or avoid the risk of prosecution.

His mother supported him in his care of his son, and thus was needed. During the attempts at support and the holding phase, I took advice from the child protection specialist. The advice was that David was to ensure his son was not left alone with his grandfather. Apparently, this had already occurred, and worryingly descriptions of how grandfather had played with and amused his grandson were related. The difficulty in connecting this with the possibility that this was grooming, as had been carried out on David, was apparent, precipitating further episodes of dissociation.

Eventually, David and his mother made a formal complaint to the police and his father was arrested. Photos were found of his naked grandson and items were found described in the alleged abuse activity.

Discussion

The subject matter of this article occurred as a consequence of my traumatic childhood and my work as a clinician. I have never sought to enter the debate regarding recovered memory, but due to my many years of work with child Holocaust survivors who were traumatised during the period of infantile amnesia (Garwood, 1996), I have observed the recurrent effects of these traumata on the psyche of the survivors. I have also met a number of those falsely claiming to have suffered Holocaust trauma in their childhood. Their mode of behaviour in the cases I have dealt with clinically betrayed them. This led me to the belief that the formative influence of the traumata required further exploration and delineation, which was attempted (Garwood, 2003).

The literature of early memory tells me I am unlikely to have autobiographical memories before the age of approximately 4 years. However, I have clear, detailed memories of traumatic experiences from 3 years 6 months of age. These are verifiable. I have also described somatic memories from the earlier infantile amnesia period, approximately at the age of 2{1/2} years. These are not verifiable. I published them in the service of furthering understanding of trauma and its effects. I have heard many others offer memory fragments from their traumatic experiences from the infantile amnesia period. It is self-evident, and supported by attachment research and my observations, that these experiences had formative effects, thus influencing the survivors throughout their lives.

I am not suggesting that early memory or recall is likely to be complete, full, or accurate in every detail. I have my experiences and the reports of many others, which challenge the views of some experts. Scientific research is based on accurate observation and the consequential search for valid and reliable explanation. It seems that in some cases, scientists have become expert in the field and are dictating to the courts what should or should not be believed depending on how early these memories originate. Either the research is flawed, which is common, or I am delusional or being dishonest or both, and thus putting my professional reputation at risk.

In the recovered memory controversy, indefensible practice has been seen and described. I in no way would defend this re-traumatisation of patients and the damaging of others. However, it seems there is still much to be understood regarding inaccessible memories.

Note

Since writing this chapter, I have proposed the concept of the psychic guardian (see Chapter 12). This would seem to offer an explanation as to how the psychic guardian of the patients I have described is forced to regress into amnesia, preventing the psychic guardian from protecting their children or to go into fight mode and confront the challenges of their new situation, attempting to face rather than avoid their childhood abusive trauma.

References

American Psychiatric Association (APA). (1994) *Diagnostic and Statistical Manual of Mental Disorders*, 4th edition. Washington, DC: APA.

Bauer, P. (2002) Early memory development. In *Handbook of Cognitive Development* (Ed. H. Goswami), pp. 127–145. Oxford: Blackwell.

Bowlby, J. (1981) *Attachment and Loss*. London: Penguin.

Bremner, J.D., Randall, P., Scott, T.M., Capelli, S., Delaney, R., McCarthy, G., & Charney, D.S. (1995) Deficits in short-term memory in adult survivors of childhood abuse. *Psychiatric Research* 59: 97–107.

Bremner, J.D., Vermetten, E., Afzal, N., & Vythilingam, M. (2003) Deficits in verbal declarative memory function in women with childhood sexual abuse-related post traumatic stress disorder. *Journal of Nervous and Mental Disease* 192: 643–649.

Brenner, I. (2015) *Dark Matters: Exploring the Realm of Psychic Devastation*. London: Routledge.

Brewin, C.R. (2007) Autobiographical memory for trauma: update on four controversies. *Memory* 15: 227–248.

Combs, M.D. & DePrince, A.P. (2010) Memory and trauma: examining disruptions in implicit, explicit and autobiographical memory. In *The Impact of Early Life Trauma on Health and Disease: The Hidden Epidemic* (Eds. R.A. Lanius, E. Vermetten, & C. Pain), pp. 217–224. Cambridge: Cambridge University Press.

Dalenberg, C.J. & Paulsen, K.L. (2010) Historical themes in the study of recovered and false memories of trauma. In *The Impact of Early Life Trauma on Health and Disease: The Hidden Epidemic* (Eds. R.A. Lanius, E. Vermetten, & C. Pain), pp. 25–32. Cambridge: Cambridge University Press.

El-Hage, W., Gaillard, P., Isingrini, M., & Belzung, C. (2006) Trauma-related deficits in working memory. *Cognitive Neuropsychiatry* 11: 33–46.

Freud, S. (1905) *Three Essays on the Theory of Infant Sexuality/Standard Edition* 7. London: Hogarth Press.

Freyd, J.J. (1996) *Betrayal Trauma: The Logic of Forgetting Childhood Abuse*. Cambridge, MA: Harvard University Press.

Garwood, A. (1996) The holocaust and the power of powerlessness: survivor guilt, an unhealed wound. *British Journal of Psychotherapy* 13(2): 243–258.

Garwood, A. (2003) *A Child Survivor's Search for Healing*. Conference presentation, "Beyond Concentration Camps and Forced Labour," Imperial War Museum, London.

Golier, J.A., Yehuda, R., Lupien, S.J., & Harvey, P.D. (2003) Memory for trauma-related information in Holocaust survivors with PTSD. *Psychiatry Research* 121: 133–143.

Herman, J. (1997) *Trauma and Recovery*. New York: Basic Books.

Hinshelwood, R.D. (1989) *A Dictionary of Kleinian Thought*. London: Free Association Books.

Hopper, E. (1991) Encapsulation as a defence against the fear of annihilation. *The International Journal of Psychoanalysis* 72(4): 607–624.

Hyman, I., Husband, T., & Billings, F. (1995) False memories of childhood experiences. *Applied Cognitive Psychology* 9: 181–187.

International Society for Traumatic Stress Studies (ISTSS). (1998) *Childhood Trauma Remembered: A Report on the Current Scientific Knowledge Base and Its Applications*. Deerfield, IL: ISTSS.

Loftus, E. & Pickrell, J. (1995) The formation of false memories. *Psychiatric Annals* 25: 720–725.

Mollon, P. (2002) *Remembering Trauma*. London: Whurr.

Nachman, P. & Stern, D. (1983) *Recall Memory for Emotional Experience in Prelinguistic Infants*. Paper presented at the National Clinical Infancy Fellows Conference, Yale University.

Pedzec, K., Finger, K., & Hodge, D. (1997) Planting false childhood memories: the role of event plausibility. *Psychological Science* 8: 437–441.

Putnum, F. (1992) Discussion: are alter personalities fragments of figments? *Psychoanalytic Inquiry* 12: 95–111.

Stern, D. (1985) *The Interpersonal World of the Child*. New York: Basic Books.

White, S.H. & Pillemer, D.B. (1979) Childhood amnesia and the development of socially accessible memory systems. In *Functional Disorders of Memory* (Eds. J.F. Kilstrom & F.J. Evans), pp. 29–49. Hillsdale, NJ: Erlbaum.

Yehuda, R., Keefe, S.E., Harvey, P., & Levengood, R.A. (1995) Learning and memory in combat veterans with posttraumatic stress disorder. *Journal of Nervous and Mental Disease* 192: 137–139.

Chapter 11

Psychic survival management

The psychic guardian and compartmentalisation

Introduction

When beginning to explore psychic dangers, traumatogenic stimuli, and survival, the systematic approach would suggest beginning with the neonate. I have previously attempted this in Chapter 9 on the power of powerlessness, focusing on survival instincts. The individual's survival instincts, together with the instinct for survival of the species in the carers, will drive the dependant neonate to seek to progress towards independent existence. This is seen in the infant when striving for increased mobility, and thus the capacity for exploration and escape. Observation shows that carers will repeatedly teach the infant what dangers must be avoided until it is safely learned. The infant's drive to explore and improve their mobility results in increasing exploration such as climbing. Exploring beyond the carer's sight means that the infant must be restrained until it learns to safely assess risk and only attempt them when its capacities are adequate to manage them. This occurs repeatedly, and thus poses a risk of injury for infants, and is a challenge to their carers in this development phase. The acquisition of this understanding by the neonate of its limitations and these dangers of exploration away from its carers may be seen as the nascent development of the danger assessment and management skills.

The importance of pattern recognition (Stern, 1985) in the assessment of danger is an essential part of this process and is now established. Clinical observation shows the internalisation of the carer's teaching regarding dangers and survival. This would seem to be the developmental process by which a primary survival function of the ego is developed, which I wish to describe as the *psychic guardianship function* or the *psychic guardian*.

The developing psychic guardian

Physiologists (Cannon & de la Paz, 1911) have established the instinctual development of the existential fight/flight/freeze response, which is the primary response to danger. Clearly, the psychic guardian (PG) must acquire the capacity through carer teaching, as well as through experience and learning to assess and recognise dangers that require the physical fight/flight response. This will be learned early on in the development of the PG. An essential aspect of survival learning must be that the fight/flight response, with its great energy costs, should not be wasted when dangers are not survival threats (Garwood, 1998). Thus, danger assessment, or triage, and psychic management must be an essential survival skill of the PG.

The protective shield

The concept of a protective or guardian capacity in the infant's development was an early part of Freud's theorisation. Freud (1894), in his model of the mind, initially proposed the psychic existence of a contact barrier. Later he suggested this acted as a precursor to the ego. He developed this further into the concept of the protective shield provided by the mother (Freud, 1920). Freud suggested it is internalised and becomes a part of the child's developing psychic apparatus. The concept implies an observing aspect of the ego, both internally and externally observing. It seems self-evident that an observing aspect of the ego is an essential component of the nascent psyche, which is essential for survival.

The maternal container

Bion (1962, 1970) developed the new paradigm of the containing function. He proposed that primitive stimuli named beta elements, which were unmanageable by the infant's mind, must be detoxified by the mother by her alpha function (i.e. her capacity for reverie), making these beta elements into alpha elements. If this containment process fails, the infant experiences "nameless dread," which has been suggested may be a combination of annihilation anxiety and primal powerlessness (Bion, 1962), which is traumatogenic. The maternal container is introjected and becomes part of the trauma defensive psychic apparatus, which may be overwhelmed, allowing damage to the psychic apparatus (Garland, 1991), and is experienced as failed dependency.

Psychic defences

Rycroft (1967) reminds us that:

> The function of defence is to protect the EGO, and defences may be instigated by (a) anxiety due to increased instinctual tension (b) anxiety due to a bad conscience (super-ego threat) (c) realistic dangers. The concept of defence is usually stated in terms which imply that the human ego is beset by threats to its survival emanating from the ID, the superego and the outside world and it is, therefore, perpetually on the defensive. But the

concept is better regarded less negatively and taken to include all techniques used by the ego to master, control, canalize and use forces which may lead to a "NEUROSIS."

(p. 28)

Survival threat: the initial responses

The FFF hypothesis

The cliché that "the only certainty in life is our death" reminds us of the fundamental truth of our mortality. We are at constant risk of annihilation from disease or injury. This painful reality tends to be denied and/or repressed. Our complex immune systems and our physiological capacity for bodily repair testify to the constant presence of this risk and the evolution of complex physiological systems to protect us from these threats.

Psychic fight/flight/freeze (FFF)

The instinct for self-preservation (i.e. the instinct for survival of the individual) has generated the development of the autonomic nervous system (ANS) (Green, 1992). It exists in the wider animal kingdom and has a distinct anatomical structure that demonstrates its presence and evolution over millions of years. Thus, it was present and active in humankind when we were evolving from our primitive ancestors. It has widespread effects throughout the body and brain. In situations of potential danger, it produces the fight/flight/freeze response (Cannon & de la Paz, 1911; Selye, 1956).

If the instinct for survival of the individual has generated the evolution of the autonomic nervous system, then its influence was present during the development of the human psyche.

I wish to suggest that the physiological flight/fight/freeze response produces equivalent effects on the psyche and in traumatogenic situations psychic fight/flight/freeze (FFF) is precipitated as the initial response.

Incoordination between the physical and the psychic survival response would reduce survival efficiency. Coordination would enhance the survival response. Psychic FFF may thus be seen as instinctually driven.

The initial psychic response to a potentially traumatogenic stressor is to attempt to internalise and process its representation using the available, established, psychic mechanisms. These include attempts to incorporate it into existing object relations(hips) (Howell & Iskowitz, 2016). If these are successful, the representation of the traumatic experience is largely contained within the unconscious. If this fails, the psychic representation of the trauma remains intrusively conscious and continues to possess the power to overwhelm the psyche. The psyche having failed to provide a container (Bion, 1962) within the internal world, what is observed is a turning to the external world for strategies in the form of vehicles or containers to reduce the trau-matogenic stressor's noxious power. Examples of such external relief providing containers are seeking comfort from those who may take the role of carer and container, such as partners, relatives, friends, and allies, and/or turning to seda-tive medication, alcohol, tobacco, food, and narcotic drugs for comfort. At a fundamental psychic level, the trauma is experienced as dependency failure and abandonment.

Psychic fight/flight/freeze

What, then, are the psychic equivalents of somatic fight/flight/freeze?

Fight

Psychic fight is more than aggression or rage directed at the perceived threat or traumatogenic stressor. It may be understood as the opposite of flight or avoidance. Fight is psychically moving towards the perceived threat or trauma to defeat or master it. Rycroft (1967) reminds us that the etymology of aggression is "ad-gradior, I move towards" (p. 5). This may be adaptive and/or maladaptive. Van de Kolk (1987) indicates that physically abused children may repeatedly expose themselves to constant danger (Green, 1983). This was named traumatophilia by Abraham (1907) and developed by Rangell (1976), Horowitz (1986), and Hopper (1995). Freud (1920) suggested this was in the service of attempts to gain mastery. Some Vietnam veterans became mercenaries and sexual assault victims may become prostitutes (Sharfman, 1967). These responses may be considered perversely defensive and failed attempted reparation. Here, the seeking of mastery and avoiding powerlessness via the fight response generates destructive self-victimisation and endanger-ment, which seem to be due to repetition compulsion. A less severe form may commonly be seen when analysands miss the last session before a break, now described as an enactment, thus making the therapist experience the powerlessness they wish to avoid. Fortunately, the severe forms would seem to be the less common response. The fight response may bring patients into therapy and often generates activity that offers a greater opportunity for repar-ation than flight or freeze.

A Polish Holocaust survivor was the only surviving member of his large extended family. He was a man of action constantly, covertly resisting the Nazis in any way he could. After the Holocaust one of his responses to his multiple losses of family, social group, community and country was to repeatedly go to Israel to look for survivors he might have known in his past life. He would perpetually approach people and ask them where they came from. If they were Polish survivors they were questioned for knowledge of other survivors. This way he found a scattered few childhood friends. This reduced his sense of loss and isolation.

None of his murdered family had known graves. This prompted him to place a memorial plaque with the names of his mother, brothers and sisters and his wife's parents and siblings in a Yeshiva, a rabbinical college in Jerusalem's first Holocaust Museum, the Chamber of The Holocaust, some years before Yad Vashem was built.

He visited almost every year reciting Kuddish, the Jewish prayer for mourners. The Yeshiva walls were covered with gravestone like plaques placed there by Landsmannschaften survivors, those who survived from a shared community forming an alumni association and producing a written record of the community, a book of Yiskor (Memory). They held annual services of commemoration on the anniversary of the liquidation of the community, usually the date of the murder of their family.

These life strategies may be understood as reparative attempted empowerment and mastery over powerlessness and loss. However, fight may also generate self-destructive consequences. His fear of dependency prevented him from ever seeking therapeutic help. Fight may generate adaptive creative use of aggression as well as the established destructive ones. Fromm (1974) suggests there is a benign form of aggression in addition to the established malign forms.

Flight

Psychic flight implies a moving away to avoid the stressor. Flight may be wholly unconscious as in freeze, which is discussed below. It may evoke both unconscious psychic defences such as repression, denial, splitting, and projection as well as conscious behaviour such as phobic avoidance.

> Most commonly, Holocaust survivors respond with habitual panic when exposed to triggers that in some way symbolise the Holocaust. Such Holocaust associated triggers may include … crowded trains, medical examination, the yellow colour, gas … In addition, happy occasions such as weddings, Jewish holidays and family celebrations may also evoke sudden grief reactions … As a consequence there is frequently a contradictory effort both to remember and to forget, *both to approach and to avoid the traumatic event.*
>
> (Kellermann, 2001, p. 202, my emphasis)

Flight is self-explanatory, and is what is described as avoidant behaviour in section C of the description of post-traumatic stress disorder (DSM-IV

F43.1) (APA, 1992). However, what is frequently observed is attempted fight by approaching the traumatic stressor, which alters to flight when the conscious or unconscious fear of being overwhelmed becomes dominant. Thus, an oscillation is frequently observed that turns to freeze if fight and flight fail.

Freeze

Although for clarity this is presented as a separate response, freeze may be thought of as a special form of intrapsychic avoidance or detoxification response.

> A 13-year-old was sitting in a windowsill, apparently detached from the outside world after a pogrom in which her father was taken away and beaten at the police station. He was later shot and thrown into a mass grave and she never saw him again. As if encapsulated from all affect, she was reading from a book, keeping her overwhelming emotions locked in. But the emotional development of her life had stopped at that moment. She never created a family of her own and now in her late 60s, it is as if she is still waiting for her father to return.
>
> (Kellermann, 2001, p. 209)

> One has to include in one's theory of development of human beings the idea that it is normal and healthy for the individual to be able to defend the self against specific environmental failure by a freezing of the failure situation.
>
> (Winnicott, 1958, p. 281)

Scharff and Scharff (1994) suggest Fairbairn (1958) believed that patients maintain their inner world as a closed system frozen in an unchanging state. Casement (1985) discusses the original freezing of the traumatic situation and the post-trauma personality organisation to freeze the trauma so as to preserve an area of unencumbered self-function. This has been described as the "frozen tableau" by Fairbairn (1958). Davies and Frawley (1994) suggest the trauma representation is "frozen in time" (p. 21).

Psychic freezing involves neither moving towards nor away from the threat. It is wholly unconscious, implying the psychic processes of compartmentalisation discussed below are mobilised – that is, encapsulation (Hopper, 1991) or dissociation (Rycroft, 1967) are mobilised to reduce or nullify the psychic stressor.

Dozier et al. (1999) suggest dissociation is adaptive, avoiding trauma overwhelming the psyche.

Encapsulation as a freeze response

Hopper (1991) defines encapsulation as "a defence against annihilation anxiety through which a person attempts to enclose, encase and to seal-off the sensations, affects and representations associated with it (Tustin, 1972)" (p. 607). Hopper (1991) further suggests that "the first defence against it is an attempt to fuse and confuse the nascent, incipient representation of self with the nascent, incipient representation of the lost and abandoning object" (p. 609) This relates to the neonate and implies internalisation of the experience of the caregiver has begun. Scharff and Scharff (1994), citing Hopper, suggest that traumatised children try to freeze and encapsulate their traumata.

An elderly man arranged a holiday to the USA with his wife. When he arrived he found the travel agent had failed to arrange accommodation. He was moved to three different hotels before he was settled in secure accommodation. He then became confused and psychotic. He held the delusional belief he had bankrupted himself and his wife leaving them both penniless. He returned to the UK and was admitted to a psychiatric hospital.

His history then emerged. He was born in Germany. He was put on a Kindertransport to England as a teenager. This involved a sudden decision by his parents to pack a small suitcase of his belongings, to take him to the station and put him on a train for Great Britain. He was too shy to kiss his mother goodbye and he never saw his parents again. They were murdered in the Holocaust. When he arrived in Britain he was sent to three different families before he was settled. Adjusting to his exile and fostering was likely to have dominated his psychic activity at that time preventing the process of mourning.

It would seem that his traumatic Holocaust experiences were encapsulated and never psychically processed. The triple relocations on holiday resonated with the earlier trauma, rupturing what may be described as the isolating encapsulation. The situation forced him to reinhabit the encapsulation and thus re-experience the traumatic separation and abandonment. This may be seen as evoking and re-experiencing the psychotic anxieties he had encapsulated. This is suggested by the retained capacity of the memories to overwhelm his psychic cohesion, precipitating a psychotic state.

Dissociation as a freeze response

Dissociation, first formulated by Briquet (1857) and developed by Janet (1886), has in recent years generated great interest. Psychobiologists (Hamilton, 1989; Harvey & Pauwels, 2000) associate the freeze response with what is termed "general inhibition syndrome." They suggest that when stress is prolonged, functional exhaustion should replace the heightened ANS activity. This hypothesis does not explore or address the psychodynamics of the traumatised psyche.

Van de Kolk (1987) suggests that Freud (1920) links "the defense mechanism of dissociation to the issue of fixation on the trauma. He proposed that the repetition compulsion originated in the repression of the trauma" (p. 7). Repression and dissociation can be understood as distinct processes. Davies and Frawley (1994) suggest that repression is an active process in which the ego gains mastery over conflictual material, while dissociation is the last-ditch effort of an overwhelmed ego to salvage some semblance of adequate mental functioning. They also suggest that repression is a response that adds a sense of mastery as it allows for ongoing psychic work, whereas dissociation "is experienced as an inadequate response, a submission and resignation to the inevitability of overwhelming, even psychically deadening danger" (p. 65). Bromberg (1998) states that "psychoanalysis must continue to study the nature of dissociation both as a process and a mental organisation" (p. 204).

Putnum (1992) called dissociation "the escape when there is no escape" (p. 104). Bromberg (1998) suggests:

> it is a defense against trauma, which, unlike defenses against internal conflict, does not simply deny the self access to potentially threatening feelings, thoughts and memories: it effectively obliterates, at least temporarily, the *existence* of that self to whom the trauma could occur, and it is in that sense a *quasi-death*.
>
> (p. 173, original emphasis)

In his constant searching, the survivor previously mentioned had discovered that there might be a surviving *Landsmann*, a fellow exile from his home community who was a pre-war friend and a ghetto policeman by the name of Myer Dormbusch, living in Paris. Forty-five years after their liberation, they found him. On meeting, the conversation was entirely between the men, with the survivor's wife a silent onlooker sitting close by. Their conversation was confined to the confirmation of who had died and how they had died. Eventually, they came to the death of his wife's parents. Although the ghetto policeman reported having seen her father's body in the square, she was unable to retain this. After they parted, she became confused, and on questioning said that she could not remember what he had said. Her husband was most careful to protect her from this affirmation of her losses, being uncharacteristically gentle and sensitive, allowing her this defensive amnesia.

This vignette illustrates the survivor's wife creating an escape where there was no escape.

A form of what Bromberg (1998) describes is frequently seen in normative grief when the bereaved complain that they cannot recall the face of their loved one. This suggests the creation of a psychic barrier to accessibility of a key internal object representation, a significant part of the psyche, the recall of which will evoke associated overwhelming affects. Separation through dissociation would seem to be the most effective defence.

When the dissociative defence becomes established as a repeated pattern in situations of anxiety precipitated by potential or perceived trauma, and as anxiety is a constant presence in life (Garwood, 1998), it becomes incorporated into the psychic structure and becomes the predominant psychic response, and thus a dominant part of the psychic apparatus, the personality, forming a character trait or disorder. This suggests a mechanism for the formation of dissociative personality disorder. Dissociation may be the escape method, but the destination offering release and relief will be discussed below. Brenner (2015) suggests that dissociation is ubiquitous but goes unrecognised by clinicians.

Psychic trauma

The important concept of post-traumatic stress disorder (PTSD), which was developed in the late 1970s and early 1980s (DSM-IV F43.1) described the symptoms of psychological trauma accurately, but not its causation. The psychological explanation offered by researchers for the cause of psychic trauma was due to a failure of the psychological processing of the traumatogenic stressor. No explanation of normative or successful psychological processing of trauma was offered. In this chapter, I wish to offer a hypothesis for the psychic processing of traumatogenic stimuli. Failure leads to trauma of the psychic apparatus and organisation, which generates the symptoms described in the DSM-IV as PTSD and complex PTSD.

However, before I do so, I wish to offer a working definition of psychic trauma. Observation suggests that Psychic Trauma results from an interaction between traumatogenic stimuli and the psychic trauma protective capacities in which the stimuli overwhelm the protective capacities, causing psychic injury and pathological change (Howell & Iskowitz, 2016).

I wish to suggest there are three categories of psychic injuries. The first is an acute stress reaction (DSM-IV 43.0) or *minor trauma*. This is a temporary psychic injury in which the psyche is symptomatic for less than one month and recovers to its pre-trauma state. This may often be diagnosed as an adjustment disorder.

When the traumatic symptoms continue for one month or more, I suggest this is *major psychic trauma*, and it is classed as PTSD (DSM-IV F43.1), causing longer-term persistent psychic injury and trauma symptoms.

This may persist and not resolve, or may develop into a long-term anxious depression.

The third form that we are seeing increasingly frequently due to the many conflicts currently taking place in the Middle East and Africa may be described as *massive psychic trauma*, and is now described as complex PTSD (Herman, 1989). This causes long-term, often permanent changes to or deformation of the psyche.

Psychic compartmentalisation

Clinical observation suggests the PG may possess a range of strategies and capacities with which to detoxify or diffuse the traumatogenic power of stressors.

In this exploration, I have taken a number of established and frequently used concepts regarding psychic structures and processes, then related and integrated them so that they may offer a more coherent psychic organisation. These processes may be readily observed within ourselves as well as our patients, thus offering empirical verifiability. This follows the fundamental processes of empirical science in which an observed phenomenon is described and, when repeatedly independently corroborated, becomes established. Then follows the search for explanation.

Recent genome studies have shown nature's great economy with physiological processes, including psychic processes, which are frugally used and reused. It has shown that some genes are shared by all life forms, including single-celled animals. Basic evolved processes may be seen to be developed into systems within the psyche. I have previously privileged the instinct for survival over the instinct for preservation of the species in the pre-puberty period for the obvious reason that without survival to puberty, procreation will not take place. As survival is a fundamental instinctually protected necessity, a great number of survival-dedicated psychic and physical process have evolved. These physical and psychic processes may often be seen to be linked (e.g. fight/flight). Humankind is mammal and primate (Morris, 1967). The risks of predation, trauma, and annihilation in the animal kingdom are well established. However, humankind's dominance as a species and the dominance of our intellectual function over our animal functioning seems to obscure the fact that these risks applied equally to humankind in our Neolithic and hunter-gatherer periods when our psyches were evolving. We are irrefutably reminded of this reality by the existence of our autonomic nervous system (ANS).

The psychoanalytic literature has been deeply concerned with annihilation anxiety (Bion, 1962; Hopper, 1991; Hurvich, 1989; Winnicott, 1958). The non-psychoanalytic trauma literature has followed the medical model in developing some diagnoses in the manuals categorising diseases and disorders of the mind.

Physiologists began studying survival function defining the fight/flight reaction in 1911 (Cannon & de la Paz, 1911). Klein developed the concept of splitting of good and bad stimuli into good and bad objects (Hinshelwood, 1989). The stated priority was to preserve the good object. Bowlby (1981) and his successors developed the linked concepts of secure attachment being essential for healthy survival (Ainsworth et al., 1978).

When considering hunter-gatherer times, death of mothers with dependent children was a relatively common event. For the child, maternal loss is psychically equivalent to abandonment and dependence failure. This leaves the infant with a psychic survival threat to manage. The dependant infant must detach from this lost object relations/attachment and reattach to a security-providing maternal surrogate. This example describes the capacity for and survival benefits of replacement of object relations/attachments. This capacity to replace an object relations by development of a new object relations or attachment would seem to be fundamental to physical and psychic survival and development. It would seem to be a ubiquitous psychic process used for many psychic purposes and in many ways throughout life. The Kleinian concept and process of splitting off the bad parts of the object could thus be seen to be survival-related, and the object into which the bad or noxious experience is projected may be thought of as the nascent superego as well as a bad object relations within the psyche. This isolating and detoxifying suggested process would seem to be a fundamental one.

Encapsulations and psychic compartmentalisation

Remembering the economical use and reuse of psychic processes, the process of isolating and detoxifying stimuli would seem to be an essential one. The process of developing and separating an object relation or attachment from others such that it can be interacted with separately in the psyche is likely to be achieved by using the same psychic processes as the creation of encapsulations. Kadish (2010) suggests the processes of inhabiting an encapsulation when her anorexic analysand was functioning as an anorexic. If this concept is applied more widely, it would appear to have widespread implications for psychic organisation. Observation would support Kadish's hypothesis and suggest there are a number of psychic structures that are forms of encapsulation which we may inhabit and which perform various psychic functions. Hopper (2011) has suggested there are positive and negative encapsulations.

Negative encapsulation

Negative encapsulations may be thought to be associated with the isolation and detoxification of psychic representations of traumatogenic or potentially traumatogenic stimuli. Negative encapsulations may be seen to serve the purpose of detoxification by isolating their contents. This process is predated and perhaps has its physical antecedence in tissue cells where intracellular vesicles are found, known as vacuoles, which are encapsulations of the toxic substances contained and thus isolated until they can be excreted. This may be an example of the evolutionary economy of functional usage by creating a psychic process analogous to the physical one.

Positive encapsulation

Positive encapsulations may be considered to be protective and comforting forms, containing without isolating the encapsulation. An example of such a positive encapsulation may be seen when we carry out professional roles such as when practising psychotherapy or medicine. We may be seen to inhabit an object relation in which the self predominates but functions within very clear functional boundaries. When we are in role, it may be seen to dominate our conscious functioning and is separated from intrusion of other roles and functions by maintaining psychic boundaries, which may be seen to be those required to maintain encapsulations. The processes of encapsulation, positive and negative, may be described by the generic term *psychic compartmentalisation*.

Thus, this encapsulation, or a created O/R for the purpose of carrying out a role or professional task, may be thought of as a healthy form of encapsulation. These functional roles, which will be familiar to us all, may be derived from the survival necessities of single-minded and intense concentration when in Neolithic times, when we were hunting or being hunted. Stalking or being stalked by a predator were the possible origins of the capacity to create intense task concentration and single-minded, disciplined functioning. Intense concentration can be seen in these circumstances to have clear survival benefits. It also excludes distracting emotions, and thus may be used as an escape or a form of psychic haven, which may in part explain the intense devotion shown to sporting activities and sports heroes such as footballers and their teams, as well as leaders in competitive and combative sports. Morris (1967) suggested that sporting contests were substitutes for primitive tribal battles and conflicts.

This exploration leads us to suggest there is a psychic system of encapsulations that vary according to the purpose of their psychic formation and function. These psychic organisations may be considered to be possible due to the capacity for psychic compartmentalisation. They would have evolved due to their psychic survival benefits.

Sublimation, which Anna Freud regarded as a psychic defence (Rycroft, 1967), but was normative rather than neurotic, would seem to be consistent with the occupation of a role or professional compartmentalisation/encapsulation.

Compartmentalisation, psychic development, organisation, and structure

For the suggested psychic compartmentalisation processes to be accessible, a form of psychic mobility and an appropriate psychic organisation and structure is required.

Intrapsychic mobility

Symbolisation and resonance

To make possible the psychic movement to and from inhabitation of different compartmentalisation, the existence of psychic pathways, which must be two-way pathways, and because of their speed may be described as superhighways, is required. I wish to offer a hypothesis regarding the creation of psychic pathways that enable the psychic mobility suggested to take place.

It would seem helpful here to revisit the subject of symbolisation from the point of view of a psychic mechanism. Within the process of symbolisation is the finding or creation of links between one psychic experience, usually an affective one, and the psychic representation of another.

A simple example might be the psychic experience of powerlessness and the reaction formation of turning to images of power as represented by the phallus. Then objects with phallic qualities will resonate with the phallic symbol. Thus, guns, skyscrapers, and rolled diplomas of qualification, which are common phallic symbols, may become symbols of psychic power. The psychic creation of the link is the process of symbolisation. The experience of perceiving a phallic object and it stimulating an unconscious process related to power and/or powerlessness may be thought of as resonance. The term "resonance" used in this way suggests the process of symbolisation in the reverse direction using the psychic pathway created through the initial process of symbolisation. Foulkes' (1990) use of the term "resonance" describes processes as described above, taking place simultaneously in several members of a group.

The pathways of symbolisation and resonance may be seen to be a system of superhighways of the unconscious, allowing movement to and fro along them, creating a psychic Internet available to the conscious as well as the unconscious. Paralleling these will be the creation of neuronal links that correlate with the suggested psychic Internet. This description of the processes of symbolisation and resonance allows us to understand how regression may be seen as backwards movement along the developmental pathway, as well as the oscillations suggested between psychic roles and relations.

Psychic comforts and havens

Further study suggests that it may be possible to develop the concept of encapsulation types further. The question arises as to what the psychic processes are that are used to separate and keep separate individual encapsulations and object relations from one another. Bearing in mind the frugality of the psyche in its development of functional systems, the same psychic processes are likely to be used as for the creation of encapsulations.

Dissociation, the escape where there is no escape, may be thought of as the psychic escape to a psychic haven from a noxious experience. Thus, for a haven to exist, a separation must be maintained between the noxious experience and the psychic place of safety, which then becomes the psychic inhabitation. This is likely to use the same psychic processes as when moving from one encapsulation to another. These same psychic mobility processes would seem to be ubiquitous, and thus will be utilised when dissociating.

How, then, does the PG separate traumatogenic stimuli from psychic safe havens? Repression, splitting, and projection may well be the psychic means of moving entities around the psyche. These defences as well as the psychic processes utilised by the denial defence may be used by the PG to obstruct leakage from an encapsulation. If this is achieved, then dissociation may be seen to have two parts: first, the initial moving away from and the escape from a noxious psychic experience; and second, the process of moving within the psyche to find a safe encapsulation or haven. If a psychic haven is not immediately available, a new encapsulation must be created to provide an escape.

Psychic havens may be considered to be encapsulations which contain object relations that soothe through providing anxiety containment or pleasure or comfort through providing the memory of past comforting experiences. These theorisations may encompass what Steiner (1993) described as psychic retreats.

A simple example could be the experience of a child who falls and scrapes its knee. Usually, the child is picked up and held and comforted by an adult carer. This does not take away the pain of the injury, but I would suggest psychically transports the child to an encapsulated, comforting part of the maternal object relations or attachment representation. Thus, this experience may reinforce and intensify the strength of the comforting capacity of the psychic haven and the PG.

It would seem normative to seek and possess comforting processes. These are usually pleasurable experiences that are encapsulated within a relationship, and thus an object relation, such as with comfort eating. Included will be the well-known comfort foods such as chocolate and warm drinks such as tea, coffee, and alcohol, which are likely to unconsciously mimic being breastfed. The symbolic meaning of feeding oneself and its relationship to possessing the maternal capacity to feed, nurture, and comfort is well established. Other comforts that may become encapsulated havens may take the form of hobbies such as listening to and making music, leisure reading and writing, hobbies, and roles or professional occupations. These may become psychic retreats and havens as in the case of artists and practitioners of various professions. These forms of encapsulations may be thought of as occupational possessions available for use and comfort. These may relate to the primitive phantasy of maternal object possession. The postulated psychic processes would appear to be the equivalent of a psychic toolkit with which to manage traumatogenic stimuli.

Summary

In this chapter, I have proposed that the initial response to a traumatogenic stressor is psychic fight/flight/freeze. It is suggested that this function is instinctively driven by the instinct for individual survival and relates to the ANS. Its development and maturation is embodied in the PG in which it is the normative developmental goal to achieve independence. Adequate learning and skill in the management of traumatogenic stimuli is essential to attaining independence and autonomy for the individual. The psychic processing of traumatogenic stressors by the PG is described, and the processes of psychic mobility between inhabitations of different forms of psychic encapsulations, such as object relations, psychic havens, psychic retreats, psychic comforts, and psychic roles, have been suggested.

References

Abraham, K. (1907) The experiencing of sexual traumas as a form sexual activity. In *Selected Papers*, pp. 47–63. London: Hogarth Press, 1927.

Ainsworth, M.S., Blehar, M.C., Waters, E., & Wall, S.N. (1978) *Patterns of Attachment: A Psychological Study of the Stranger Situation*. London: Routledge.

Bion, W.R. (1962) *Learning from Experience*. London: Heinemann.

Bion, W.R. (1970) *Attention and Interpretation*. London: Tavistock.

Bowlby, J. (1981) *Attachment and Loss*. Harmondsworth: Penguin.

Brenner, I. (2015) *Dark Matters: Exploring the Realm of Psychic Devastation*. London: Routledge.

Briquet, P. (1857) *Traite clinique et therapeutique de L'hysterie*. Paris: Bailliere.

Bromberg, P.M. (1998) *Standing in the Spaces: Essays on Clinical Process, Trauma, and Dissociation*. Hillsdale, NJ: Analytic Press.

Cannon, W. & de la Paz, D. (1911) Emotional stimulation of the adrenal secretion. *American Journal of Physiology* 28: 64.

Casement, P. (1985) *On Learning from Patients*. London: Tavistock.

Davies, J. & Frawley, M. (1994) *Treating the Adult Survivors of Childhood Sexual Abuse: A Psychoanalytic Perspective*. New York: Basic Books.

Dozier, M., Chase Stovall, K.,, & Albus, K.E. (1999) Attachment and psychopathology in adulthood. In *Handbook of Attachment: Theory, Research and Clinical Application* (Eds. J. Cassidy & P.R. Shaver), New York: Guildford Press.

Fairbairn, W.R.D. (1958) On the nature and aims of psychoanalytic treatment. *The International Journal of Psychoanalysis* 38: 374–385.

Foulkes, S.H. (1990) *Selected Papers of S.H. Foulkes*. London: Karnac.

Freud, S. (1894) *The Neuro-Psychosis of Defence*. S.E. 3: 43–61.

Freud, S. (1920) *Beyond the Pleasure Principle*. S.E. 18: 3–44.

Fromm, E. (1974) *The Anatomy of Destruction*. London: Macmillan.

Garland, C. (1991) External disasters and the internal world: an approach to the psychotherapeutic understanding of the survivors. In *Textbook of Psychotherapy in Psychiatric Practice* (Ed. J. Holmes). London: Churchill Livingstone.

Garwood, A. (1998) Psychic security, its origins, development and disruption. *British Journal of Psychotherapy* 15(3): 358–367.

Green, A.H. (1983) Dimensions of psychological trauma in abused children. *Journal of the American Association of Child Psychiatry* 22: 231–237.

Green, J.H. (1992) *An Introduction to Human Physiology*. Oxford: Oxford University Press.

Hamilton, L. (1989) Fight, flight, freeze: implications of the passive fear response for anxiety and depression. *Phobia Practice and Research Journal* 2(1): 17–27.

Harvey, J.H. & Pauwels, B.G. (2000) *Post-Traumatic Stress Theory: Research and Application*. Philadelphia, PA: Bruner/Mazel.

Herman, J. (1989) *Trauma and Recovery: The Aftermath of Violence from Domestic Abuse to Political Terror*. New York: Basic Books.

Hinshelwood, R.D. (1989) *A Dictionary of Kleinian Thought*. London: Free Association Books.

Hopper, E. (1991) Encapsulation as a defence against the fear of annihilation. *The International Journal of Psychoanalysis* 72(4): 607–624.

Hopper, E. (1995) A psychoanalytic theory of "drug addiction": unconscious fantasies of homosexuality, compulsion and masturbation within the context of traumatogenic processes. *International Journal of Psychoanalysis* 76: 1121–1142.

Hopper, E. (2011) Personal communication.

Horowitz, M.J. (1986) *Stress Response Syndrome* (2nd ed.). New York: Jason Aronson.

Howell, E.F. & Iskowitz, S. (2016) *The Dissociative Mind in Psychoanalys: Understanding and Working with Trauma*. London: Routledge.

Hurvich, M.S. (1989) Traumatic moment, basic dangers and annihilation anxiety. *Psychoanalytic Psychology* 6(3): 309–323.

Janet, P. (1886) Les actes unconscients et la memoire et le doublement de la personnalité pendant la somnambulisme provoqué. *Revue Philosophique* 22: 577–592.

Kellermann, N.P.F. (2001) The long term psychological effects and treatment of Holocaust trauma. *Journal of Loss and Trauma* 6: 197–218.

Morris, D. (1967) *The Naked Ape: A Zoologist's Study of the Human Animal*. London: Vintage Books.

Putnum, F. (1992) Discussion: are alter personalities fragments of figments? *Psychoanalytic Inqiry* 12: 95–111.

Rangell, L. (1976) Discussion of the Buffalo Creek Disaster: the course of psychic trauma. *American Journal of Psychiatry* 133(313): 316.

Rycroft, C. (1967) *A Critical Dictionary of Psychoanalysis*. London: Penguin.

Scharff, J.S. & Scharff, D.E. (1994) *Object Relations Therapy of Physical and Sexual Trauma*. Lanham, MD: Jason Aronson.

Selye, H. (1956) *The Stress of Life*. New York: McGraw-Hill.

Sharfman, M.A. (1967) Delinquent adolescent girls: residential treatment in a municipal hospital setting. *Archives of General Psychiatry* 17: 441–447.

Steiner, J. (1993) *Psychic Retreats: Pathological Organisation in Psychotics, Neurotics and Borderline Patients*. London: Karnac.

Stern, D. (1985) *The Interpersonal World of the Infant*. London: Routledge.

Tustin, F. (1972) *Autism and Childhood Psychosis*. London: Hogarth Press.

Van de Kolk, B. (1987) *Psychological Trauma*. Cambridge, MA: Harvard University Press.

Winnicott, D.W. (1958) *From Paediatrics to Psychoanalysis*. London: Hogarth Press.

Chapter 12

Functional disorders of the psychic guardian and pathology

Clinical implications

Introduction

In recent years in my capacity as a physician, I have been asked to assist in the diagnosis of acute delirium states in patients known to me and to share in the care of others diagnosed with acute delirium. These states involve dramatic changes in psychological function and include severe dysfunction such as confusion, paranoid ideation, and severe anxiety states. These had been precipitated by severe physical illness. They had usually resolved with the treatment and resolution of the illness. Further, acute alcoholic intoxication has precipitated psychological dysfunction. This behaviour may be seen in the non-intoxicated psychological dysfunction. Unpredictable changes in the psyche are known to be caused by the use of narcotic drugs and have brought a number of patients to seek help with psychotic and paranoid symptoms. With the increased incidence of violent crime and conflagrations and political upheaval worldwide, this has caused much clinical pathology. I have diagnosed and treated a large number of those suffering with acute and chronic post-traumatic stress disorder (PTSD) and complex PTSD (ICD11, 2018) from such conflagrations. The symptoms of the above conditions may be postulated to be due to weakness, dysfunction, or disorders of the psychic guardian (PG). In addition, there is now the established group of conditions that come under the term "developmental disorders" (van der Kolk, 2014). The concept of disorders of the PG function would appear to allow for further theorisation and linkages with a number of concepts, clinical processes, and disorders.

Attachment and the psychic guardian

Clinical observation of infants shows variability of security, from fearlessness and determination to explore and master the external world to the other extreme of constant insecurity and clinging to carers. It can be suggested that the secure, adventurous child has what Bowlby and the attachment theorists would describe as a secure base within their psyche. Using the concept of the PG, it can be suggested the carer has taught the child adequate skill with which to feel secure in exploring the external world and to be secure in the PG's capacity to manage unexpected challenges or dangers.

Attachment theorists describe insecure attachment of three kinds: anxious/ambivalent, anxious/avoidant, and disorganised/disorientated attachment. These arise from various forms of attachment-rejecting and failing behaviour by the caregiver, which prevents the child from incorporating into the PG reliable and reassuring attachment behaviour from the caregiver. The learning of how to achieve and obtain adequate attachment needs is described as the acquisition of an internal working model. This can be seen to be learned by the PG as part of its capacities to manage the external and internal world and its vicissitudes.

Transference

The psychoanalytic concept of transference is now established and used widely. I wish to suggest that it is possible to relate attachment internal working models and transference phenomena as related psychic organisations. It is suggested that the PG introjects the attachment pattern of the main caregivers within object relations psychic compartments or encapsulation and is accessed when needed. Thus, when a contact is made that resonates with a childhood caregiving situation, the PG will turn to the internalised representation of the primary object relations and project on to the potential caregiver the expected qualities of the primary object. This is consistent with transference, as described by psychoanalytic theory (Rycroft, 1968).

Bereavement or object loss

Although bereavement and object loss are considered normative unless they become pathological, it would seem to be a helpful exercise to explore the function of the PG during this period of psychic change and adjustment.

> During the later stages of writing this book, my mother died. This came at a time in my life when I endured a number of losses, including the loss of the self-delusion of a degree of immortality that my Holocaust survival, together with my knowledge as a medical practitioner, created. This was an omnipotent belief that I was capable of avoiding and surviving mortal illness.
>
> I did not experience the first stage of bereavement (i.e. shock) as my mother was in her nineties and had become increasingly frail. She suffered a sudden change and quickly entered a coma from which she did not recover. I stayed with her throughout the three

days it took for her to die. I tried to ensure she did not endure any avoidable discomfort. This allowed me to feel I had fulfilled my life-long obligation, my parentification, to care for and support her in all her difficulties and illnesses. My parentification remained undiminished to the last.

I did not feel any sense of shock. Also, I did not feel a sense of denial or protest. I had ensured she was well cared for, and because of her sweet nature, which became more predominant as she developed more advanced dementia, she was loved by all around her, especially those who cared for her.

However, what I did notice was that I developed an increasing sensitivity to those around me and their capacity to be carers. It was as though I needed to take stock of those around me and assess if they could replace my mother as a carer if I were in need. I found I turned to my older sister more than previously. My sister had acted as a surrogate mother when we were sent to the children's home. I seemed constantly aware, albeit unconsciously, of the loss of my mother as a caring good object and constantly searched for a potential surrogate or replacement.

It would seem that my PG was searching for replacement good objects to rebuild the strength of the group of good objects I relied on to make me feel secure. With the added traumatic effect of a number of catastrophic life events, I found myself overwhelmed, and without the protective shield of my key good objects, I found myself thrown back into my childhood. I felt alone and abandoned, struggling with intense fear and isolation. My PG and its capacities had been weakened by object loss and my own illness, and I found myself overwhelmed, terrified, and desperate to escape from my feelings of abandonment and helplessness. Fortunately, I obtained good medical care and this terrifying episode was short-lived.

My observed object-seeking would seem to be a reparative PG activity to replace the lost object. The hasty and ill-judged replacement of a lost object is a frequently observed phenomenon by clinicians caring for those that are bereaved.

However, I did not experience shock, nor protest or denial. Shock may be seen if the PG reduces psychic activity as a protective measure while it assesses its psychic capacities. All psychic activity may be seen to be diminished or stopped and inactivity is induced. Protest and denial, as well as confusion, may be seen as protective strategies by the PG to protect the psyche from further being overwhelmed and injured. With time, the internal representation of the lost object may be transformed into a more accessible and transmutable attachment object.

Psychosis

It would seem that one essential function and capacity of the PG is to maintain separation between distinct object relations. This is so that objects with distinct needed qualities such as good objects may be protected. These may be seen as potential allies and comforts in situations of danger. Hopper (1991) reminds us that psychic annihilation threat may come from fusion and confusion. The PG has the capacity to encapsulate and separate psychic entities. The ability to maintain boundaries between psychic entities would seem to be essential for sanity and psychic security. If absent or weak, it would seem to be a sign of the PG's incapacity to differentiate between real and fantasy, internal and external, conscious and unconscious.

A young female patient was severely sexually and psychically abused by her father, who dressed as a woman and wore a devil's mask, preventing her from developing a sense of reality or the capacity to function adequately. A crisis brought her into treatment, and she began to struggle to clarify her constant confusion and to identify her memories of sexual and psychic abuse for what they were. As her memories became clearer, her psychotic symptoms of persecutory auditory hallucinations dissipated and resolved. The clearer her memories became, the stronger she became. She eventually became the strongest of her siblings, all of whom had been abused, and they became progressively dysfunctional.

Her therapy was focused on her PG, more usually described as her ego being strengthened, and her tendency to dissociate almost instantly being resisted by her PG. As this took place, her memory of her abuse and psychic function became clearer and she coped with increasing competence in her life. Her dissociations stopped and her ability to reject the lies and dysfunction of her family strengthened as she showed greater ego strength, which I wish to suggest would seem to be in part her incorporation into her PG of the experience with her therapist of repeated reality confirmation and guidance regarding healthy mental function.

My clinical experience has repeatedly shown abusive trauma causes a weakness of the PG such that abusive object representation become potent, malign objects residing in the psyche. They would often seem to be stronger than the PG, dominating psychic function. These are commonly clinically observed and described by clinicians as intrusive and persecutory, auditory hallucinations. These clinical experiences as well as many others lead me to suggest that sexual and psychological abuse by a parent cause developmental and deformative trauma such that the PG does not develop adequate strength and capacities. The parental abuse becomes introjected and preserved as a malign dominating object relations. This overwhelms the PG and frequently induces self-harm as well as suicide attempts, both as instructions from the malign object but also as an attempt by the PG to escape from this constant malign domination.

Anxiety disorders

Anxiety disorders may be understood as developmental, traumatic, or both. If a child has a primary caregiver who suffers with an anxiety disorder, they will transmit this to the child by the constant communication that the world is full of danger, and thus a constant guard must be kept by the PG to ward off and survive these imagined but rarely materialised dangers. If a traumatic illness or life-threatening accident occurs, the PG will of necessity be extra alert to danger. Using the hypothesis of the PG, the anxious mother is unable to teach the child how to manage anxiety, and thus the PG is less likely to learn to deal with anxiety unless this is learned from another caregiver. When anxiety is uncontained, it can increase in intensity such that the individual feels it is annihilation anxiety and they will die. These crescendos of anxiety are commonly called panic attacks. It has been my clinical observation that anxious patients monitor their pulse rate and the sound of their heartbeat. This increases anxiety and the release of catecholamines (adrenaline or epinephrine), thus setting up a toxic cycle of increasing anxiety. The PG would seem to be unable to find the psychic resources to contain or dissipate the anxiety. Psychologists treat this with cognitive behavioural therapy and relaxation techniques based on breathing control and somatic relaxation, the physical manifestation of raised autonomic nervous system activity.

Obsessive-compulsive disorder

In my clinical experience, although obsessive-compulsive disorder (OCD) is described as being characterised by obsessions and compulsive rituals, the predominant symptom is severe, often psychotic, anxiety until the obsessive behaviour or ritual has been completed satisfactorily. My observations of several generations of families suggest undue stress or dysfunction may cause OCD in children. Insecurity with obsession over the placing of food, crockery, and cutlery is a common observation in anxious children.

It could be suggested that the PG having discovered that keeping an aspect of life unchanged reduces the risk of unexpected change. This may not be managed and thus the anxiety becomes locked into an invariable and increasingly repeated ritualised process.

A young woman who suffered kidney failure and needed renal transplant as a teenager recovered well. Some years later, she became increasingly obsessed with handwashing and the avoidance of contamination. This obsession was accompanied by the anxiety that she would die if she failed to clean and wash until she felt she had eradicated the risk of contamination until it returned the next day. It could be suggested that her PG had absorbed the necessity of infection avoidance following the post-transplant treatment to prevent rejection. The life-threatening process of renal failure and transplant is likely to have increased the annihilation anxiety level that the PG was attempting to manage. With the constant attendance to hospital for renal checks, the PG was unable to recover to its former level of security and it was functioning under constant threat of mortal illness.

Confidence loss in the elderly

It is a common clinical observation that a number of elderly patients who observe their health, faculties, and vigour diminish with time suffer an anxiety disorder that presents as a crisis of confidence and the fear of the change from independence to encroaching dependency. This would seem to be the reverse of the development of independence at the beginning of the life cycle. It is seen more frequently these days as medicines and lifestyle improvement prolong healthy life expectancy. It could be suggested that this is due to the self-monitoring PG observing reduced physical capacity for fight/flight and reduced mental capacity and speed in assessing and responding to threats. Those who have secure, caring relationships with partners and children may progress into secure existential dependence. However, for those who suffered childhood dependency failure, permitting oneself to become dependent is more difficult and generates increasing anxiety. In my experience, this may be managed by lifestyle changes, exercise, and anxiolytic medicines until reducing faculties cause sufficient debility that dependency, usually residential care, must be accepted.

Borderline personality disorder

The diagnosis of borderline personality disorder (BPD) has increased in recent years such that a large proportion of the work of mental health services is taken up by the treatment of patients suffering with this condition.

The two main disease categorisation systems, the Diagnostic and Statistical Manual of Mental Disorders (DSM) and the International Classification of

Diseases (ICD), vary slightly in their grouping of BPD types. However, the symptoms are similar, and I am discussing these here as they would seem to relate directly to disorders of the function of the PG.

Researchers (Bateman & Fonagy, 2004; van der Kolk, 2014) have agreed that a high proportion of sufferers of BPD have experienced significant and psychically deformative childhood trauma. The symptoms for the diagnosis of BPD by the ICD are:

Borderline subtype

1   fear of abandonment;
2   self-harm;
3   emptiness; and
4   impulsiveness.

Impulsiveness subtype

1   impulsiveness (no thought of consequences);
2   quarrelsomeness;
3   anger outbursts; and
4   unstable and capricious mood.

A young woman from West Africa was brought to the UK by people smugglers. Her father had been politically active, and when the regime was unable to find him they arrested her instead. She spent a year in captivity being tortured.

When she was given asylum in the UK, she impulsively changed her name, without discussion with her carers, to that of the tribe from which she came, which had been persecuted in her country. This caused dreadful problems with her documents, which needed the name change. She heard from a fellow refugee that some family members had survived persecution and she believed they must be in a refugee camp in Europe. She decided to travel to Europe to look for them, but her documents were needed for her to travel. These were caught up in backlogs at the Home Office, even though she had paid the money they demanded. She was helped to move to what was a safer neighbourhood but she ran out of medicine. She repeatedly phoned her new GP, getting angry with the staff when they did not supply the help requested. She continued to make impulsive decisions and get angry with all of her helpers such that she had to be warned they would wash their hands of her if she did not stop.

This young woman's behaviour typifies the impulsive BPD.

BPD also causes an increased mortality risk. Death from suicide is reported at between 6 and 10 per cent. This may be higher in those with severe substance abuse.

BPD symptoms can be readily related to disorders or weakness of the PG following attachment trauma and/or developmental trauma, as seen in young people who have been trafficked and abused, or those traumatised by violence and war (Melzak, 2015).

Extreme fear of abandonment, together with self-harm, substance abuse, and eating disorders, have all been strongly associated with childhood abuse and failed dependency. The traumatic and deformative impact on the development of the PG of abandonment, abuse, failed dependency, and annihilation threat would seem to be self-evident.

Depression

Depression is probably the most common mental health disorder, affecting more than 20 per cent of the population at some stage in their life. Clinicians will be familiar with the DSM and ICD categorisations. These focus on chronicity, precipitation, symptoms, and severity. However, despite their usefulness, I find clinical experience and the challenge of healing the patient and relieving their distressing symptoms suggests there are generally two forms of depression I commonly face. The first is anxious or agitated depressions. These generate anxiety, often with panic attacks that prevent obtaining sleep and/or remaining asleep. They also cause anxiety in an unpredictable pattern. Taking a detailed history often elicits a childhood pattern of failed dependency and neglect. Observation often elicits a frantic struggle by the PG to find relief through sedation-inducing drinks such as alcohol or other forms of soothing self-remedies. This repeated pattern would suggest that the object relations/attachment available to the PG do not provide adequate containment or soothing memories.

The second most common form, but less commonly observed, is the form of depression dominated by an overwhelming desire to escape into bed and containing, womb-seeking behaviour. This regressive behaviour may dominate to the extent that all other behaviour is largely obstructed. This form tends to conform with the descriptions of melancholy.

The question now arises as to whether these forms of depression can be related to PG function or dysfunction. Observation suggests anxious depression commonly arises from life events such as a loss or a negative event, often categorised as an adjustment disorder. This could be understood as the exposure of the inadequacy of the capacity of the PG to process and respond to the event. Many of the symptoms observed are similar to those of the acute stress reaction. Clinical experience suggests that containment of the escalating anxiety and distressing symptoms is achieved through quietening of the unquiet mind. The experience of sedative medication may be seen to be used by the PG as a reassurance that care and containment is available from the medical profession, which becomes a strengthened psychic ally to be used and called on when necessary. Achieving regular sleep has been shown to give speedy relief to those suffering anxious depression. It also facilitates the use of the PG to find further strategies with which to overcome the traumatic life events. The converse (i.e. failure of the PG and/or the clinician to provide relief) often causes increasing desperation and psychic exhaustion, which may cause the despairing response described above.

Despair with regression to womb-seeking behaviour is always a disturbing observation. The turning to bed and foetal positions indicates extreme despair and reliance on intrapsychic reparative resources such as endorphin release. This deterioration in psychic function is likely to reduce the psychic security of the PG. This may deteriorate, spiralling downwards, increasing the risk of successful suicide.

Therapies

Treatment and healing

The proposed psychic organisation and structures of PG, security-providing attachments or good objects/object relations, psychic havens, and comforts allow for a more systematic approach for thinking about treatment. The history of medicines abounds with treatments that have been found empirically to offer some relief to sufferers before the underlying disease process has been understood. A recent book on the treatment of PTSD listed 23 different treatments (Shapiro, 2010). This is a clear indication that no particular treatment has been established as the most effective.

It can be seen that psychotherapy, particularly group and psychoanalytic psychotherapy, should strengthen the PG by improving ego strength by increasing insight, as well as adding to the benign internal objects that should support and strengthen the capacity to re-experience traumatic memories.

However, a recent development would seem to offer insight into the functioning of the PG: psychic organisation and the management of psychic trauma.

Narrative exposure therapy (Schauer et al., 2011) is a form of therapy that is designed to overcome the initial fight/flight reaction of the PG. It has been used in refugee camps in Africa and has shown it can help healing and improve function in those that have been recently severely traumatised.

The therapist uses a long rope, coloured paper flowers, and stones and sticks. The therapist leads the trauma survivor through their life story from childhood. The rope represents their whole life and they begin at one end.

Flowers are placed at points in which good or happy events occurred, stones are placed where traumatic events occurred, and sticks are used for events in which the survivor played an active part as would have occurred with child soldiers. The task of the therapist is to assist by support and guidance in slowly managing difficult emotions evoked by the therapy and to prevent avoidance. Successive sessions review the work so that the survivor can correct or alter the narrative so far. The therapist's skill is required in assisting the survivor with the difficult emotions which accompany the memories that are re-experienced. The explanation offered by the authors is that hot or emotionally loaded memories are, with guidance, converted to cool (i.e. non-emotionally loaded) memories. This process would seem to use and strengthen the observing function of the ego (i.e. strengthening the PG and its capacity to move memories and emotions). This initially overwhelms the psyche and the traumata remain active as though they are still in the present. The technique moves them into the past rather than the present such that they can be seen from a more distant perspective by the PG.

In practice, this is a slow and meticulous therapeutic process. Memory avoidance is not allowed, and returning to past traumas must be repeated and re-explored in order that effective treatment is achieved.

It can be seen from this description that the capacity of the PG to move traumatic memory representations to different parts of the psyche is used and guided until the PG has gained mastery of the traumatic memories by processing them by repeatedly examining them, thus gaining a perspective by putting them into that part of the psyche where past events (i.e. memories) are stored.

Having proposed the concept of the PG as the psychic manager of survival and potential psychic traumatogenic stressors, the question now remains as to how this psychic system works when dealing with overwhelming traumatogenic stressors. Further, if this proposed psychic structure and organisation has validity, it should guide our thinking regarding the focus and direction of treatment to heal the psychic injuries. Thus, the PG concept should direct our understanding and thinking regarding treatment. Here, to follow the psychic processes, I will use the description of the symptoms found in an acute stress reaction which if they persist for more than four weeks and is defined as PTSD. I shall annotate the sections as a method of clarifying the psychic processes, thus linking them to other sections of this volume such as the traumatic triad of annihilation threat, powerlessness, object loss, primal agony and the PG and compartmentalisation.

Following the process when a traumatogenic stressor overwhelms the PG, the psychic representation of the stressor remains active and undiminished in the psyche. It will generate anxiety, which resonates with annihilation anxiety and neonatal or primal powerlessness, and create a sense of dependency failure, which resonates with and is experienced as psychic abandonment. These will cause psychic regression, with a desperate seeking of protection and safety, and reduction of anxiety and the quieting of the mind such that sleep and psychic escape are possible. The symptoms are systematically described below.

If these symptoms persist, they may cause psychic exhaustion and despair, causing anxious depression, and if persistent they may cause psychosis and active suicidal behaviour.

The fight response may generate the seeking of relief from clinicians. However, in many conflict situations and with childhood abuse, care and healing may not be available. Many forms of healing have been tried. Some are discussed below and what part of the proposed psychic organisation they influence, and thus how they may be effective.

Psychoanalysis

Psychoanalysis can be understood as creating a safe physical and psychic space, which then allows for safe regression to where the PG is malleable and can be strengthened. That is, the primary object relations and the protective shield can be strengthened and repaired, as well as introjecting the psychoanalyst as a benign and protective good object, to support and strengthen the PG.

Group analysis

Group analysis may be considered to work at level of the PG in a similar way to psychoanalysis but in addition to add the group as a whole. The individual members of the group are added to the existing attachments or object relations increasing the strength and numbers of the psychic allies. This effect may be increased by the cumulative and multiplied psychic effects of the dynamic forces.

Basic assumption groups

Bion's (1961) basic assumptions functioning of fight/flight, pairing, and idealisation can be seen to be due to excessive anxiety. Thus, they can be related to defensive behaviour to support or strengthen the PG. Hopper's (2003) fourth basic assumption of aggregation and massification may be understood as a PG function in defence against abandonment, isolation, and danger exposure by seeking proximity.

Cognitive behavioural therapy

Cognitive behavioural therapy (CBT) attempts to guide the PG to tolerate and not be overwhelmed by the fear generated by the memories of the traumatic events. It attempts to add to the psychic tools available to the PG by strengthening the capacity to think positively and reduce negativity. Usually, the restraints of costs within the health service reduce the number of sessions such that the benefits are limited and may not be maintained.

Meditation, yoga, and exercise

These physical activities have value in adding to the range of comforts available to the PG. Researchers have shown that these activities increase the release of endogenous opiates, thus calming and soothing the PG.

Medication

As a practising physician with a large psychiatric practice, I have at my disposal a large range of medications. This has been of great value to my patients, who I often see at an early stage of their illness. By careful and prompt use of anxiolytics, hypnotics, and antidepressants, I have been able to reverse overwhelming symptoms in a short time. This has a strengthening effect on the PG due to the short time before symptom relief, thus reducing the damage to the strength of the PG. In addition, the power of the medical profession and services is added as a symbolic psychic ally of the PG.

Careful selection of medication frequently brings improved sleep and waking with a sense of calm, which is a potent healer even before psychotherapy is available. If symptoms are too severe or active, they will prevent psychotherapy from being used or from being effective. Often I have found that medication quickly reduces symptoms to a level that will allow psychotherapy to be initiated and benefited from. It can be seen that psychotherapies and medications work to increase the psychic tools available to and the strength of the PG. This exploration of the dysfunction of the PG and its relation to psychopathology is at an early stage. Further exploration should bring greater understanding of a number of common conditions, in particular those generated by adjustment disorders and failed dependency, disorders that are known to generate long-term depressions.

Summary

In this chapter, I have examined the link between some recognised psychic processes such as transference and attachment with the function and the dysfunction of the PG and of psychic compartmentalisation. The link between PG dysfunction included common pathological processes and states, which included object loss, psychosis, anxiety disorders, obsessive-compulsive disorder, age-related confidence loss, and BPD. Further, I have examined the links between treatments and the PG and compartmentalisation, including psychoanalysis, group analysis, basic assumption groups, meditation, and CBT.

This exploration of psychopathology linked to dysfunction of the PG and compartmentalisation is at its beginning. I believe that with further exploration, many more types of psychic dysfunction will become apparent.

References

Bateman, A. & Fonagy, P. (2004) *Psychotherapy for Borderline Personality Disorder: Mentalisation Based Treatment*. Oxford: Oxford University Press.

Bion, W.R. (1961) *Experiences in Groups*. London: Heinemann.

Hopper, E. (1991) Encapsulation as a defence against the fear of annihilation. *The International Journal of Psychoanalysis* 72(4): 607–624.

Hopper, E. (2003) *Traumatic Experiences in the Unconscious Life of Groups*. London: Jessica Kingsley.

Melzak, S. (2015) Personal communication.

Rycroft, C. (1968) *A Critical Dictionary of Psychoanalysis*. London: Penguin.

Schauer, M., Neuner, F., & Elbert, T. (2011) *Narrative Exposure Therapy: A Short-Term Treatment for Traumatic Stress Disorder*. Boston, MA: Hogrefe.

Shapiro, R. (2010) *The Trauma Treatment Handbook: Protocols across the Spectrum*. New York: W.W. Norton & Company.

van der Kolk, B. (2014) *The Body Keeps the Score: Mind, Brain and Body in the Transformation of Trauma*. London: Penguin.

Index